INSIDE

INSIDE

BORIS BECKER

WITH TOM FORDYCE

INSIDE

WINNING

LOSING

STARTING AGAIN

HarperCollins*Publishers*

HarperCollins*Publishers*
1 London Bridge Street
London SE1 9GF

www.harpercollins.co.uk

HarperCollins*Publishers*
Macken House, 39/40 Mayor Street Upper
Dublin 1, D01 C9W8, Ireland

First published by HarperCollins*Publishers* 2025

10 9 8 7 6 5 4 3 2 1

© Boris Becker 2025

Boris Becker asserts the moral right to be identified as the author of this work

A catalogue record of this book is available from the British Library

HB ISBN 978-0-00-873779-5
PB ISBN 978-0-00-876902-4

Printed and bound in the UK using 100% renewable electricity at CPI Group (UK) Ltd

All rights reserved. No part of this publication may be reproduced, stored in a retrieval system, or transmitted, in any form or by any means, electronic, mechanical, photocopying, recording or otherwise, without the prior written permission of the publishers.

Without limiting the exclusive rights of any author, contributor or the publisher of this publication, any unauthorised use of this publication to train generative artificial intelligence (AI) technologies is expressly prohibited. HarperCollins also exercise their rights under Article 4(3) of the Digital Single Market Directive 2019/790 and expressly reserve this publication from the text and data mining exception.

MIX
Paper | Supporting responsible forestry
FSC
www.fsc.org FSC™ C007454

This book contains FSC™ certified paper and other controlled sources to ensure responsible forest management.

For more information visit: www.harpercollins.co.uk/green

This book is dedicated to my late mother, Elvira, and the woman who saved me, my wife Lilian. They are the reason I am here today.
I love you both.

CHAPTER 1

It's the screaming that cuts you deepest, on your first night in prison.

Screaming like someone is hurt. Like they need help. Like someone is dying.

You don't know where it's coming from, it's just out there somewhere. Out there in the gaps between the bright fluorescent lights of the halls and the darkness of the cells. Out there beyond the locked metal doors and suicide nets. Bouncing off thick brick walls, high vaulted Victorian ceilings, metal bars. Coming through the cold night. Coming for you.

My life was always about noise. About pin-drop silences and explosions of applause. The elastic pop of a volley and the snap of a net cord. White shoes sliding on green grass and camera shutters flickering and camera lenses tightening.

You stand on the baseline of Centre Court and you're the conductor of it all. You control it.

Signal to the ball boy. Catch the ball he bounces to you in your left hand. There are shouts of encouragement and hope from the stands. Your first name ringing out all around. Always your first name.

You wipe your hand across your face. Purse your lips and blow cool air onto your clammy fingertips.

Now there is silence. Sixteen thousand people here on this late Sunday afternoon in a south-west London summer, and every single one of them waiting on you. They're close enough to see the dark sweat patches on your white shirt and the pale grass stains on your hips. To hop the low walls and run across and swamp you.

Instead they barely breathe, as you throw the ball high, bend your knees and back and hurl yourself forward. Barely breathe, as the white Slazenger ball bends the tight strings of your racket. Barely breathe, as the ball fizzes through the warm summer air.

It's only when it lands across the net that you hear them once more. As it ricochets from the edge of your opponent's racket frame and spins away beyond the tramlines. As your arms go up again and your feet do a little stuttering dance and you tip your head back to the blue skies above.

Then it's chaos. It's noise so loud you can feel it in your chest and inside your head. It hurts. It almost scares you. But it doesn't, because you know.

I did this. I created it. I control it.

The bedlam never lasts at Wimbledon. It escapes up past the old wooden rafters and the dark green painted roof. It settles gradually from wild cheering to thundering waves of applause pouring down the gangways and tiers.

It's familiar too, when you return in other summers. The corridors and practice courts begin to feel like home, as you settle into the rhythm of the fortnight and the routine of waking late and walking down Church Road to stares and smiles and policemen waving you through. The locker rooms and the

INSIDE

members' lounge, the honours board of champions you've watched and played and now beaten. The lines from Kipling's 'If –' inscribed above the players' entrance to Centre Court: 'If you can meet with Triumph and Disaster/And treat those two impostors just the same'. A challenge, a rallying cry.

It's your soundtrack and your world. You know the difference, as a player, between the oohs for a frantic forehand return deep in the rally and those when you slip and scramble to your feet, the gasps when you fling yourself full length to reach a backhand half-volley and the disbelief when you flick it back across the net at some impossible angle, and the backspin bites and the ball dies where it lands.

I never thought prison would be my world, but here I am at HMP Wandsworth. HMP – that strange and cruel British abbreviation for Her Majesty's Prison. I'm here for the foreseeable future, and all my control is gone.

I can't walk away. I can't stop the noise. And none of it makes sense, because I'm lost, and none of the old rules matter, not here.

Wandsworth prison is just over two miles from Centre Court at Wimbledon, depending which way you go. SW19 to SW18 – a single number in it but an impossible distance in between.

Perhaps worse than the screaming itself, as it echoes round this cold cell, with its mould and dirty toilet bowl and broken hatch on the door, is the not knowing why it's happening. Are these men asleep with nightmares, or awake and raging? Are these wounds real or imagined, assaults from enemies or assaults on themselves?

Out of control, out of reach. There are multiple layers to these screams. Some are a relentless wail, others go up and down with peaks and troughs. Some are sobbing and self-pitying, others wild and ranting. Sometimes it all drops away, and you have a minute of quiet and wondering why before it starts up again. Sometimes you get ten minutes, and you go back to your bunk and thin blanket and try to fit your body into the strange contours and confines of a mattress shaped by a hundred strangers.

But it always begins again, and always triggers more. Shouts from other cells.

– Shut the fuck up!

Bangs on other doors. Hip-hop beats coming from far away. Moans and threats and revenge being promised.

The more they scream at them the more they scream back. An endless rally between opponents who can't see each other but want to destroy each other just the same.

So I panic. I call out myself.

– Is there anyone there? Can't you hear this? Can you help?

You hit the alarm button on your wall. The Listeners take their time, but they come to your door, eventually. Pull back the metal panel over the security grille and stare in at you. Let me tell you about the Listeners. They save you sometimes, when you're first locked away, and they help you understand parts of this new world, this new way of compressed living. But they don't save you now. They can't. This is me. This is now. This is my baptism and accelerated education.

You shout at them, almost screaming yourself. A few deep breaths away from it all.

– Someone's killing themselves. Someone's dying!

And they look back at you, not surprised, because they've seen it all before, and not moving, because they hear it every night. And they tell you.

INSIDE

– Get used to it. It's gonna carry on.

– But what's happening? Can't someone check?

– There's crazies in here, and there's others doing it for attention. Doesn't matter, mate. And don't get your hopes up if they stop. They'll start again.

You ask them how you sleep. You still think, at this point, that someone's going to fix all of this.

That's when they tell you. You're not going to sleep on your first night. You're not going to sleep tomorrow. Three days' time? You'll sleep a little bit. Four days? You'll be so tired you might get through to midnight. By the fifth night you won't hear them any more.

So you sit there, on your bunk, and it all goes round your head. If I tell this story, no one will believe me. This is torture. Surviving it all is an impossibility.

I'm in a cage with a bunch of psychopaths. I'm alone and I'm lost. I am a number that nobody knows.

This story begins for me a long time before. It begins on 7 July 1985, on that grass court in south-west London, with that serve out wide to Kevin Curren's backhand. All that it meant and all that it brought upon me.

So why was I standing in the dock at Southwark Crown Court on 29 April 2022? Because of mistakes I made, and misjudgements; some of these I understood and others I didn't, until it was too late. But none of it happens without me winning Wimbledon at seventeen years old. That was the moment everything changed. The moment my path was set.

I sensed it then, in the hours that followed serve and celebration. The way people I knew well looked at me – my mother and father, my coach, my manager – like they no longer knew me at all.

Now it was happening again. Early on the morning of 29 April, the day I was due to be sentenced. Standing in the small bedroom of a tiny rented flat in central London, packing a bag for what might be a chance to start again but might also be seven years inside. Pulling open the wardrobe door and trying to find something to wear that made sense.

Grey suit, white shirt, black sneakers. Easy. Your lawyers tell you not to wear a smart tie for your trial. Nothing ostentatious. Maybe even a little down-at-heel.

I had been charged with twenty-nine counts under the Insolvency Act. Five of those were dropped before the trial and I was then acquitted of twenty of them but, on 8 April, convicted of four. On this strangest of days I wanted to get back in touch with a version of me I could feel good about again. So I reached for my Wimbledon tie and put it on.

Had I not twice broken Joakim Nyström's serve when he was serving for the match in the fifth set of our third-round meeting in 1985, I don't think this day at Southwark Crown Court would ever have happened. And if Tim Mayotte had been at the net and not the baseline when my ankle went in our fourth-round match? Same deal. I shake his hand and quit the match. I didn't know my trainer was going to strap my injured ankle up. I didn't know it would take my trainer quite so long to get out to Court 14, so the pain stabilised and I could carry on. And if I hadn't won the gentlemen's singles title until I was twenty-two years old? None of this would be happening.

And so the Wimbledon tie. A statement to the court, to the watching world. To the hundreds of journalists and camera crews in the street outside. Here is your wunderkind. Here is your old champion. I knew the boy I was. But who was I now, and what had happened to the man in between?

It's a long wait, between verdict and sentencing. Almost three weeks for me, a life in limbo, an endless loop of questions and recriminations and guessing games.

My lawyers had talked me through the scenarios. At one end of the scale I could get a suspended sentence; I'd be broke and exhausted, but I'd be free. I could start figuring out a better way forward. If the judge went the other way, it could be seven years in jail. Broke, exhausted and broken.

You play the match in your head, every morning and every night, just as I used to as a player. I'm free: how do I live my life better now? How do I move forward, and with whom, and where? I get a year: where will I be, and what will I be doing there? I get three: now who am I? I get the full seven: I try not to think about this one. Obsessing about a bad defeat just makes it more likely.

When we are back in court, my lawyer spells it out. Jonathan Laidlaw QC is a barrister who operates within the system and its arcane language and games, setting the scene for what is to follow.

'The defendant has literally nothing, and there is also nothing to show for what was the most glittering of sporting careers.

'His fall is not simply a fall from grace but amounts to the most public of humiliations for the defendant. The degree of his suffering – and it will continue – is punishment at a level that no other bankrupt in this county is likely to experience.

'In terms of the defendant's future, there is not one. These proceedings have destroyed his career and entirely removed any future prospect of him earning an income. His reputation – an essential part of the brand which gave him work – is in tatters. He will not be able to find any work, and he will have to rely upon the charity of others if he is to survive.'

I had been told to pack a bag for that day of sentencing, because this could be the day I didn't go home again. It becomes the first of many tasks that mix the practical with the farcical. No one really gives you an official list of what you might be allowed to take in, should you be sent down, so you find yourself making decisions based on prison movies you've seen in the last few weeks. I watched what happened in the showers. I watched the bullying. I watched the fights where men got hurt and nobody came to help them. Didn't matter that most of the films were American. You see those things and they stay with you.

I've always been a good packer. Even as a player I liked to do my own packing. The reassurance of knowing you had everything you needed for the battle ahead, the comfort of the process. But this bag – a Puma one, my old sponsors, but not a free one this time, a cheap holdall picked up from Sports Direct just a few days before – took much longer than any other packing ever did.

Asking yourself questions but not knowing the answers. How much do I need? How much will they let me take in? How often can I do laundry? Let's think – take thick socks (maybe they last longer), put in boxer shorts. I have trouble with my feet from all the wear and tear of a hard career and the multiple surgeries that followed, so I need the right sports shoes to keep the pain away. Am I allowed spare pairs? Will I need them inside and out? Shorts. Okay, I like shorts, but this is England. Even in

INSIDE

summer it's cold, and I'm not going to be out in the sun. So shorts no, but tracksuits, yes. Three black ones, a dark blue one with white stripes. I might be wearing this stuff for a long time. It can't rip easily or get worn out. The autobiography of Barack Obama, another book about Karl Lagerfeld. Both thick, both with plenty of reading in them. Toothpaste, how much toothpaste should I take? Hey, this is a small bag, but I don't want to fill it up completely, because this is ridiculous, I mean I'm not going on holiday ...

You pack your bag, and you say your goodbyes. You don't know how long you're going to be gone, or where you might be going to, or even if it might be just for that day. You don't know what words are most appropriate, and you're a former tennis champion who grew up in a different world, so you're still working out how much real deep emotion you can reveal and how much all of this should be a show, looking calm and confident and in control even as inside it's all a churning mess.

The first goodbye is to Lilian, my partner. I'll tell you all about Lilian, because this is her story as much as mine, her survival and strength, her patience and fortitude. It's her birthday too, on 29 April. (I told you about the practical and the farcical.) The second goodbye is to my eldest son, Noah. My new family and my old. The roots and branches of my family tree.

And then I am in the dock, behind glass, in my Wimbledon tie. The Puma bag at my feet, my family over there in the public gallery. In front of me is the power: Her Honour Judge Deborah Taylor.

You want to listen to every word she says, but it's difficult. The glass in front of you is thick. The speakers relaying her words to the dock are small and feeble, so you lean closer.

'Boris Becker, you were found guilty after trial of four offences under the Insolvency Act 1986. All of these offences arise from your actions after a Bankruptcy Order was made on 21 June 2018 following a creditors bankruptcy petition presented to the High Court by Arbuthnot Latham & Co, a private bank. You were acquitted of twenty other offences, including all charges relating to your conduct prior to the Bankruptcy Order being made.'

Sometimes the sound crackles. You ask if she could possibly speak a little louder or the microphones could be turned up, and then it's the legal language that tangles you up and leaves you always one phrase or sentence in arrears.

'In relation to Count 10, irrespective of the lack of disclosure in the PIQB, you were told at the 13 September 2017 meeting that if you had a property, say in France, that the Trustee had not asked about, it was incumbent upon you to say, either, that you own the property, or it is owned in trust for these reasons. The fact that in relation to Im Schilling you had doubts about your mother's interests did not prevent you from raising this with the Trustee.'

Your brain offers strange thoughts. Comments on her delivery, because you've worked in TV, so you understand how to make clear, concise points. Your own rolling verdict – that line sounded more positive, this one less so. Analysis too – why is she saying this, was that accurate, is that fair?

The emotions build with every sentence and every clause squeezed in next to clause. I could no longer pretend I was handling it all okay. One moment wanting to believe she's moving towards a suspended sentence, the next a punch of panic in the guts – she's going to give me seven years, she's going to give me ten …

I just tried to look at her. Hold her gaze to hold myself in check. Eyes on hers, and my fingers around the rosary in my jacket pocket. The rosary I've had for years, as a young man sprinting from baseline to net, as an older man trying to find a new path. Moving my fingertips over the beads, one to ten.

Brain trying to keep up, to differentiate between critical terms. Concurrently, consecutively. Consecutively, concurrently.

Talking to myself. Okay, Boris, once you know the damage you know you can deal with it somehow. But I don't know how bad the damage is. Okay, Boris, listen, keep listening.

And praying. A Hail Mary for each bead, an Our Father, *Vater Unser*, on the bigger bead in between the sets of ten.

You lose track of how long the judge has been speaking for. Ladies and gentlemen, time is suspended. Is this ten minutes now, or thirty? Mentions of legal precedent, even though there's no real precedent for the specifics of what I'm here for, and there's an incongruity in even thinking about this having happened before when it's all so strange and disturbing to me.

'In the absence of specific guidelines, the starting point is the Sentencing Council's General Guideline Overarching Principles. In this respect I take into account the statutory maximum sentencing judgements of the Court of Appeal Criminal Division for the offence, and definitive sentencing guidelines for analogous offences. In this case some assistance can be gained from the Bribery, Fraud and Money Laundering Guideline, although care must be taken as the offences are different in significant respects …'

Hopes fall, hopes rise.

'In terms of aggravating features, I do not consider there was significant planning. I accept that you were in chaos – having learned of the bankruptcy order, you did what you could to pay those closest to you, which was not a decision which was sophisticated or planned. The effect on others is taken into account in the offending.'

Holding the rosary, fingers moving along the beads.

'I also take into account the previous conviction for tax evasion, which I consider to be a similar offence. Although some time ago, it is of significance in this case in that you did not heed the warning you were given and the suspended sentence which was imposed. That is a significant aggravating feature.'

You are drowning in stormy seas, and this formal, emotionless woman in her sixties is both your only hope of rescue and the freezing current dragging you down.

'In mitigation I take into account what has been described as your fall from grace. You have lost your career, reputation and all of your property as a result of your bankruptcy. I have taken into account the letters from your family and your reference for charitable works. However, you have shown no remorse or acceptance of your guilt, and have sought to distance yourself from the offending in your bankruptcy. Whilst I accept the humiliation you have felt as a result of these proceedings, there has been no humility.'

I don't understand this mix of moral and legal assessment, this strange remorse code I'm meant to have sent out. How could I show remorse for something I didn't realise was wrong? I made maintenance payments to my ex-wife, to my children, for knee surgery and for rent. It's not something I tried to hide, not least because I thought I was doing what I should. It confuses me, that I was supposed to stop paying child support to my own kids.

But I do feel regret, of course. So much of it. For things I did, for other paths I could have taken. I don't know yet how much I'll learn about myself in the next year, how I'm going to be pushed to breaking point, how much I'm going to change. For now I'm still lost in the fine print. I think the problem is that I've failed to reveal enough of my inner emotions in the dock. My legal team had told me not to explain myself too much. Just say yes and no. And in yes and no you can't show anything except the black and white and the binary.

Suddenly the judge is on to the numbers. Now I am listening more intently than to anything else in my life. Silence like a serve on Centre Court, but the judge is now the one conducting it all. The one moving to the advantage court.

'In relation to Count 4, the sentence will be one of two years and six months.'

Two years, six months. So thirty months in total. Okay, it's not seven years. But I'm in jail. I'm in jail for a long time.

'I impose concurrent sentences of eighteen months in relation to Counts 10, 13 and 14.'

Concurrently, consecutively. Consecutively, concurrently.

Does this mean thirty months plus eighteen, plus another eighteen, plus eighteen more? Then we have exactly seven years. Or does it mean the thirty months and those three counts of eighteen months somehow sit inside that? Maybe some do and some don't …

Now time has really slowed. Match point, ball fizzing through the south London air, waiting for it to land.

I look at Lilian, sitting there over to my right. I look at Noah, twenty-eight years old, my son but also now a grown man. I can see Lilian is crying. I can see the sadness on my son's face.

I try one last time to hold on to my emotions. We don't know how bad this is. Eyes back on the judge. Wait for the ball to bounce.

'The total sentence is therefore one of two years and six months.'

And so this is how the goodbye happened, when it came. There is no last embrace, no physical contact. No final kiss. Lilian and Noah walking down from the gallery and to the dock; me putting my palm up on the glass.

Lilian mirroring me and matching her palm to mine. Noah doing the same. The hardest part of all.

Then I turned, and I stepped from one world to the next.

To the judge, Southwark Crown Court

My name is Noah Becker.

I have spent the last week of my father's trial in court with him as it was important for me to support him the best way I could – just like he has always done for me. These past five years haven't been easy on me and my family. Especially when he is portrayed as someone that he really is not.

Although I'm very proud of my father and his accomplishments, the way people have been portraying and slandering his name has been weighing heavy on me for a long time, which has affected my mental health. To be honest, a majority of the time that I spend talking to my therapist is dedicated to this topic in order to assess my mental state.

INSIDE

As the eldest of four children: if my father was to go to prison, I feel like I would have such an immense amount of responsibility which I am not ready to carry without him around. The way my father has been leading this family through love, while all my siblings live in different countries, has been keeping everything together.

We all stand for him and if he was to be imprisoned, I believe we would all be imprisoned as a family and a collective.

My biggest wish is for my father to be free, so our family can be free.

Sincerely,

Noah

CHAPTER 2

Die Rheinpfalz

By Jörg Allmeroth, tennis writer
29 April 2022

When Boris Becker was first spotted by the cameras on the morning of 29 April 2022, he had a sports bag on his shoulder and was wearing a Wimbledon tie with his suit. One would have thought the six-time Grand Slam champion was on his way to an appointment at the All England Club, the place in the south-west of the British capital where he won his first major career title almost thirty-seven years ago.

But Becker had completely different, rather bitter obligations in London. He was appearing in court to find out what the verdict would be after serious misconduct in his bankruptcy proceedings. After hours of waiting, it was clear by the afternoon that Becker would not be leaving the courtroom as a free man – Judge Deborah Taylor gave him two and a half years in prison for money laundering and evasion of assets as a debtor.

This court day in London is as drastic for Becker as 7 July 1985, when he became the youngest Wimbledon winner of all

INSIDE

time – and has remained so to this day. Because for Becker, the self-inflicted turbulence, which reliably accompanied him more than two decades after his great tennis career, ended yesterday with a crash. Becker got so hopelessly tangled up in financial troubles that at some point he crossed the famous red line.

His lawyer argued in court that Becker's situation was due to naivety and excessive demands, that he put his trust in incompetent advisors who should have been taking care of the money. Judge Deborah Taylor didn't believe it and ruled that Becker knew very well what he was doing. Which, by the way, is to be expected in a grown man over fifty.

Becker's drama began when he was still active, when he rejected key figures from his entourage if they became uncomfortable or annoying. Becker preferred to trust himself during his professional tennis days – and also afterwards. Last but not least, he genuinely believed that after doing the touring circuit, he would make it in the world of business. He wasn't worried about failure as an entrepreneur – it's about taking risks. But these risks were no longer offset by sufficient income. Instead there were a series of unexpected expenses – maintenance payments for wives, children.

Becker's first manager, Ion Tiriac, recently shook his head when he looked at Becker's considerable difficulties and the tiresome court process. In the humble opinion of the Romanian businessman, who has meanwhile become a billionaire in his home country, Becker should have become one of the richest athletes ever. But as much as Becker was clairvoyant on the tennis court, following the rules and being able to assess his options coldly, he lost control after leaving Centre Court, and lived beyond his new circumstances. After all, the claims of his creditors eventually accumulated to almost 60 million euros.

The court case in Germany in 2003, in which he barely escaped imprisonment with a two-year suspended sentence for tax evasion, should have been a warning shot for him. But nothing got better for him afterwards, in any respect. Now he is faced with the hardest time of his life.

There was a guard on duty at the back of the dock, an English politeness about him even in this moment. He asked me to pick up my bag and walk down the steps.

The rooms below were all bright strip lighting and shiny yellow walls. A small office at the end of a corridor, with a desk and an open window. Two officials inside, courteous almost to the point of appearing embarrassed at the formal dance.

– Good afternoon, Mr Becker, how are you? Sorry about what's just happened ...

– Don't worry, you just do what you have to do.

– Please remove your suit and tie.

You can't ignore the crunching of gears in that moment. Stripping off my Ralph Lauren suit, unknotting my Wimbledon tie. Folding both neatly, as if I were going to be putting them back on in the morning. Swapping them for the black Puma hoodie and tracksuit bottoms from my bag, stepping aside so they could search through the rest of my gear.

The two shaving razors I had packed were taken away. So were the nail scissors. The bottle of aftershave – well, who tries to take aftershave to prison but a man who has no idea about prison? I'd packed a cheap Casio wristwatch, because even with my aftershave delusions I guessed that wandering around prison with a big expensive ex-tennis player watch on my arm wasn't a smart move. What I didn't understand yet was that time doesn't matter at all in prison. You make it not matter, because it's your enemy. Time is what eats you up inside and cooks your head.

My lawyers Giles and Peter came down to explain what might happen next, to decode what had just taken place upstairs. They still wore expressions of shock. More emotion on the surface than I was trying to show in that moment.

– We're sorry. We didn't think it was going to be this bad ...

I had always liked Giles. A kind man, a good man. Peter too. But I wanted facts, in that moment. I wanted their insight, and I needed context.

– Okay Boris, this could have been better, but it could have been a lot worse.

– Tell me about concurrently.

– Concurrently? It means at the same time. So the maximum you can serve is thirty months. But listen, thirty months will in effect mean fifteen inside.

– It will?

– You'll probably be sent first to Wandsworth, or Wormwood Scrubs. They're not great places, but you'll survive. And you'll only be there for four to six weeks, and then you'll go to an open prison. Then you can go home at weekends, and you'll only have to sleep there at night.

I felt marginally better, as they shook my hand and walked away back down the corridor. I just wanted a little certainty to hold on to. Didn't matter how good or bad the facts might be; it was more that they were solid and incontestable, in a world of strangeness and flux. The relief lasted for the sixty seconds it took to be led to a cell and hear the heavy door locked behind me.

There were benches against two of the walls with a prisoner sitting on each. More shiny yellow paint on the walls, and you have a good look at that, because you definitely don't want to be looking the other men in the eye. You don't feel safe. You don't know what they've done, just that they're a prisoner. It's easy to forget you are too, now.

There's no conversation. Just staring at the wall, as if you've always loved shiny yellow paint and this is the dream scenario, the best example of it you've ever seen, and you really want to commit it to memory for all time. When you're close to overdoing it and need to look somewhere else for a brief interlude, you begin a comprehensive examination of the floor just in front of your feet. Not in front of the other men's feet, and certainly not their actual feet. Just beyond yours, and no further.

I still wasn't emotional, not yet. I wasn't feeling sorry for myself or crying. I was thinking hard, and forming tactics, and working multiple scenarios through my head. This is what a life on the tennis court teaches you. Okay, if one of these men comes for me, it's going to take thirty seconds for a guard to come. Probably more. A lot can happen in thirty seconds in a small, locked cell housing three scared men. Three convicted criminals. So where do I move? Where is there to go?

You get a bottle of water, at some point. Time is already beginning to stretch and bend. The water gets thrown in through a hatch in the door. You need to pee? You drink the water and use the bottle.

INSIDE

Maybe I was there forty minutes, maybe an hour; I had no way of knowing. My Casio watch was still in my washbag. Then the door opened again, and a guard called me out.

– Mr Becker, the transport's here to take you to Wandsworth.

I didn't know then why they keep it from you until the moment of your departure. I didn't know that prisoners can get things organised inside. A welcoming committee, a softer landing.

I thought instead about Lilian. How strong I knew she was. I also feared she would be in the most desperate mood. I hoped she was with Noah, even though he would be feeling the same. I hoped it would be like two nights before, when he had come over to our small flat and we'd all sat squeezed on the one little sofa and eaten pizza and drunk bottles of beer. How we'd called up my second son Elias on Zoom and all seen each other and felt slightly braver as a result.

I hoped for all of that, but I didn't know. I wanted to be alert. I wanted it all to soak in. I wanted to feel everything that was happening to me and not to lose control.

Because I'm not sure I was ever as in control again after 7 July 1985. And it's easy to say you feel misunderstood and you're a victim. I wasn't a victim. I also wasn't the guy some people wanted me to be, the one some newspapers wrote about. Maybe I was a better person. Maybe I was worse. I just wasn't the man they thought I was.

It started that Sunday night in south-west London and it never stopped. My father organising an open-air parade for when I got back to my home town of Leimen in southern Germany. I didn't want a parade and I couldn't work out how in a town of 10 thousand people there could be 50 thousand on the streets. On display in the back of an open-top jeep, a friend of my father's driving, standing there with my coach Günther Bosch feeling too much like Pope John Paul II, and all of it uncomfortable, because it wasn't my style and it wasn't who I am. I hadn't asked for any of it. I wanted to be a good tennis player but I didn't want to be celebrated like this.

When that sort of fame hits you at seventeen years old, you can feel like someone else owns you. The German media told me how I should live, what I should do. Yes to military service, no to living abroad. Yes to this girlfriend, no to this one. Too tall, too skinny, too black, too white. Is her family background suitable? Let's get the chequebook out and find out.

The first time a friend of yours sells a story about you to the papers you think it must be a mistake. The second time you think maybe you're unlucky. When it keeps happening, and it happens when you're struggling with your tennis or trying to plot your way through life as a 19-year-old or a 21-year-old or a young father, you start cutting friends out of your life. You lose a little faith and hope in people.

I am not a victim. I made mistakes. I made some big ones. Sometimes I was naive, and sometimes I was childish. Sometimes I was too public with my private life. None of it was done because I wanted to be more famous. It was more out of pride and joy and honour. I wanted to show my fellow Germans I was doing well, that I was in love, I was happy.

The most read German newspaper is *Bild*. If you don't know it, it's better than the *Sun* and worse than the *Daily Mail*. Somewhere in between – the *Daily Sun*. It's read by CEOs, it's read by leaders, it's read by wives and husbands and plumbers and delivery boys. Over the past forty years, I have met most of its editors. And one said to me once: 'Since the Second World

War, we have three topics that we know are going to sell us most copies: Adolf Hitler, the reunification of Germany and Boris Becker. So keep doing what you do because it sells. It's good for our business.'

But I couldn't win every time. And when I did lose – when I lost Wimbledon finals that they expected me to win – I was terrible. I was a national disgrace.

It shouldn't have mattered to me. But I felt it, even when I tried not to. When I was playing, my internal response would be: 'Okay, I have to win another Grand Slam.' Or: 'I have to become number one.' Or: 'I shouldn't lose a Davis Cup match.' And that would be my escape then. If I won Wimbledon again, what could they say that was negative?

It became harder after my career ended because I didn't have the next Wimbledon. I didn't have an opportunity to silence everybody with a good weekend on a big court. Right when I stopped, my first marriage also faltered, ending in divorce and a huge scandal. That was on me.

The bankruptcy, the court case, the prison sentence two decades later? I was still nowhere near to working out my life, how to process it, how to find a place that wasn't blaming other people but wasn't breaking down, either. I wanted to stop caring what other people thought of me, but it was hard. I knew what the subtext would be, in *Bild* and the other dark corners of the media world: 'We told you so. It's been a long time coming. We're not surprised.'

I still wanted to show these strangers that they'd got me wrong. Never a victim, but not the man they thought I was, either.

* * *

The van waiting outside was white, with a door at the rear. The word 'Serco' in lower-case black letters. Inside it was divided into six tight, separate cells. A small square of window in each, the glass dark. A bench, no seatbelts.

They don't linger once you're on your way to prison. Accelerating through the black metal gates at the back of the courthouse, leaning and listing round the corner, revving again out towards Tooley Street.

It's tourist London, round Southwark way. HMS *Belfast* moored on the brown swirling Thames a few hundred yards in one direction, the steep shiny metal and glass of The Shard the other way. The arches and lines of London Bridge station up ahead.

I knew all this from the last month of making my daily journey to the trial by black cab. I could see none of it now, because the same guard who had told me our destination had also warned me about the photographers waiting in the street beyond the gate. The windows are dark, but that's why they hold their cameras up tight to them and fire off the flash. I kept my head down and held on to my bottle of water. I tried asking the guard, as we lurched around another steep turn. How long is the journey? A shouted response, with typically British attention to traffic detail: usually forty-five minutes or so, but it's Friday early evening, so it's getting busy, could be an hour and a half …

You know you're not the only one on the same journey. You saw a few being led into the van ahead of you. Most of them younger. There are shouts from the other cells: questions and swearing and insults. One voice demanding to know where we were going. The guard telling him to be quiet. The voice getting louder, the language angrier.

INSIDE

No one tells you not to look weak or vulnerable, but an instinct kicks in. Control the fear. Put your shoulders out, show presence, just like you do when you walk out on Centre Court as a teenager, like you do when you're a kid in the locker room surrounded by men who want to intimidate you before you get out there.

An hour of yelling and screaming from the angry guy, then silence as the van slowed and he began to realise where we were. He seemed happier, then. He was the one the wardens recognised, when they led us inside. Oh, it's you again, is it?

More flashes from cameras as the van went through the main gate at Wandsworth. The paparazzi had got there ahead of us. A great wooden door under a stone arch, two towers either side with thin windows like the arrow slits in the keep of a medieval castle. The doors thrown open by guards with guns on their belts. Okay, this is real now.

There must have been forty prisoners in the first holding cell inside. You could feel the attitude all around you, a toughness in demeanour and dress. A couple of guards standing well back. Watching, but leaving this mass of men alone.

Now I was intimidated for the first time. Now the fear started crawling towards the surface. I didn't have to work out where to sit, because I wasn't going to be sitting. There was no room. I worked out where to stand by looking where everyone else was standing and doing the opposite.

I still didn't make eye contact with anyone. But I could feel it all the same, the looks and the judgements. I could sense them gauging my weakness. Whether I knew the rules – the big official ones, and the dangerous unspoken ones. I heard the deals and I heard old enmities and alliances straining and reforming.

– You getting a double cell?

– I'm with you. Yeah?

Pairing up, forming groups. Recruiting and filtering.

They talked among themselves but not to me. I stood in my dark hoodie and black trainers, trying to blend in, to hold a little circle of space in the corner of the cell. Trying to do it without making it clear I was doing it.

Maybe the guards spotted something. I don't know. Maybe word gets around about the new intake, and which ones know their way around and which might get swallowed up. When they called me from that cell and put me in a much smaller one with only four others, I didn't care about the reasons. I was just glad it had happened.

There are clichés in prison, and there is a dark humour, if you want to find it. Having your mugshot taken is exactly as you might imagine: a little booth, a bright light in your face, a row of letters and numbers in front of you.

A2923EV. That was who I was now. And then you look at the photo they have taken on the screen of their computer, and you think: actually, that's not bad. That's quite flattering, given the circumstances.

You are given your prison badge. A rectangle of plastic on a thin lanyard. You don't know it yet, but you'll wear that round your neck everywhere you go, whatever the hour. When you're with others, when you're on your own. When you're on the toilet, at night when you're trying to sleep.

I was inside the factory now. Being processed through the machine. A man goes in; a number comes out.

They told me about my top and tracksuit bottoms next. You can't keep those. Wrong colours – you can't wear black in prison. Too close to the colours worn by the wardens. So I went through my bag, and there was only the blue one with white stripes I could keep. They gave me two light grey tracksuits and sweats and a couple of white T-shirts.

It bothered me that I didn't have my clothes. I felt too open, like I lacked armour. I wanted to tell them that the stuff they had given me was too small, and that it itched my skin. Then it creeps up on you, like so much else does: this is not my choice any more. I wear what I'm given, or I wear nothing.

More black humour. A full body search. Those washed-out borrowed clothes piled on the floor next to you, the guards snapping on rubber gloves.

They told me to spread my legs. Then they touched everything. Balls, penis, rectum. You almost laugh. Not quite, but almost.

– What exactly are you looking for?

– Oh, it's your first time here, is it? You'd be surprised what we can find ...

They gave us food, after that. You should be hungry when you haven't eaten since breakfast and it's now the evening. But I wasn't hungry. I looked at this thin white bread sandwich in its clear plastic packet, and I put it back on the table in this reception area and left it there. I was thirsty, though. My mouth was dry. My throat hurt when I swallowed.

Another shouted instruction. A set of stairs, and into an office. One of the senior prison officials there to tell you how it will be, from now on.

The atmosphere of the holding cell had stayed with me. I kept thinking about the conversations and clandestine deals being made. Who would be sharing with who. Codes and illicit alliances, all excluding me. Please give me a good cellmate. Please give me my own cell. Somewhere I can be safe.

– Mr Becker, we define you as high risk. Others here may try to take advantage of you. So, for your own protection, you will be in a single cell.

A surge of relief. Actual happiness, for a moment. Like I'd just hit a forehand winner down the line. Like I'm at the net and clenching my fist.

Then a swift return to reality. Questions you want answered.

– How do I go to the toilet? What is the shower situation?

– You have a small toilet and small sink.

– Great, thank you.

– But. Be careful in the showers. We don't go in there. So don't stay too long and just make sure you're taking showers with guys that you're accustomed to. Find a group you can go with every time.

The officer explained I would have a health check. I told him about my medical history, about the pills I needed for my bad knees. Next lesson: it didn't matter what my doctor in Munich had prescribed me; you don't get to choose your medication in prison, and you don't get to keep it in your cell. They'll bring you something, and they'll decide what it is.

Then the warning.

– I know it's your first time. This is a dangerous place. Watch your back.

– What do you mean?

– We'll try to look out for you. You're one of the most famous guys in here. But there are only seventy or so of us, and there are almost two thousand prisoners. We'll do what we can, but make sure you don't do anything stupid. Don't accept anything – no drugs, no invitation, nothing – because they will take advantage of you.

The attitude in the holding cell, the way they could smell the doubt and fear on me? That couldn't happen again. I was on my own now.

Maybe I'm glad I didn't know then how far I would fall. I hoped I was strong enough. But I had no idea, really. This was how little I knew: I didn't even know enough to understand how scared I should really be.

I was being processed through the machine. Except sometimes, quite unexpectedly, you meet the warmth of another human, and the surprise and the relief light you up from the inside.

They took me through into the main prison building itself. That's where I was introduced to two men called Charlie and Jake. Both late twenties, early thirties. Tattoos on their arms.

– Hey. We're Listeners.

Here's what the Listeners do. They're prisoners, just like you, but they're the link between the inmates and the wardens. They're there when you first arrive and you're lost. They're trained by the Samaritans, and they're your local guides. They're not snitches, definitely not. They're respected. They're experienced prisoners, and they're considered trustworthy by the wardens. They're your guardian angel in tattoo sleeves, some of the time.

Charlie explained it to me. We will answer any question you have. We'll show you the ropes. If you have a problem, any time of the day or night, we're the ones to call. You're in your cell and you hit the emergency button? We'll be the first ones outside, because we have privileges, and we're not always locked up like the others. We will talk to you.

And you have so many questions. Where do we go next? What time do they lock the doors? Where do we get food? How can I phone home?

They listen, and they answer. You'll be taken to your cell. Lockdown is at 5.30pm, usually. We'll show you the canteen, tomorrow. There's a phone in your cell, and you'll get an allowance for a few calls, but you can't get any coming in.

It wasn't any form of special treatment. They did it with every new prisoner who came onto their wing at Wandsworth. And although they're not wardens, and they're definitely not snitches, they are closer to the power than any other inmate. There is trust between them.

They would be the ones who introduced me to the head warden on our wing, a big strong guy in his early fifties. An extendable baton, cutdown knife, handcuffs and a radio to go with the black uniform and cap. Not someone to fuck with. But when I met him, and we talked, he wasn't hostile towards me. Not so much a tennis fan, but a Black man who seemed to know about my first wife and my eldest two boys. Someone who would look out for me in those first few weeks, and sometimes give me a tour of other wings, to show me how things worked and tell me where to avoid going when he was no longer close.

Because you are lost and you are ignorant, at the start. I didn't know about the five wings of the prison, how badly overcrowded each one was. I didn't know about the notable and notorious who had previously stared at these ancient Victorian

INSIDE

stone walls: Ronnie Biggs, the Krays and Gary Glitter, Pete Doherty and Oscar Wilde.

It drips through in conversations and comes to you in overheard stories and conjecture-turned-truth through constant repetition. Think of it like a dark Tripadvisor entry in oral form, where no one can post photos or write their review down and no manager ever replies.

– One wing is for older guys, surprised you're not in there mate.

– There's one for paedophiles; they can't be in with the rest of us. Then there's one for gang members.

– They put mainly Muslims in the other one.

I had no idea of the reality of it. Only how my wing looked as I was walked towards my cell: a separate building from the rest, four floors high, maybe 400 men squeezed in. White painted walls, more of that sickly sheen again. You'll never find a matte finish in a British institution. An open atrium, great wide nets under every overhang. It took another week for me to work out what those nets were for; I hadn't realised yet that falling might be something you chose to let happen.

Everything metal and harsh and cold. Everything clanging and echoing and reverberating on for ever.

They took me first to a cell on the ground floor. I looked in and thought: this can't be right, it's too small. Still the old me judging the new me. I could smell the damp and I could see it in the corners and on the ceiling – green smudges of mould, darker blooms of fungus along the floor and the bottom of the walls.

Two minutes of self-evident explanation from Charlie and Jake. That's your sink, there's your sheets. Boxes there for your stuff, no hangers or wardrobe, yeah? Little TV for you there, BBC One, ITV, Channel 4, a couple of movies on a loop.

It didn't take long. Then they said goodbye, and the door shut, and the key turned, and that's when it really hit me, for the first time.

What do I do all day?

When do I next see someone?

If I want a drink, there's no place to get a drink. If I want to smoke, it's the same.

There's no food. Where do I get food?

How do I sleep on this tiny bed?

When can I speak to Lilian?

How can I be in here how can I be in here how can I be in here …

I have a breathing technique, for when I'm under stress. I always fell back on it, sometimes in the locker room before big matches, sometimes in the chair by the side of the court. Definitely whenever I got anxious, when I could feel the nerves coming for me and tugging at my serving arm and turning my Pumas into concrete boots. I breathe in through my nose and pull the air in really deep and hold it and then let it out long and slow. Ten times in, ten times out.

I stood by the side of this narrow sagging bed, not even as long as I was, and I did it right away. Boris, you need to calm the fuck down. You can't lose your nerve, not now. You need to focus on what's going on here.

And I scanned the room, to slow my breathing more. Eyes resting on each object, on every angle and detail.

A grey steel door, a hatch set within it. The single bed and its blue plastic mattress. Folded white sheets in clear plastic shrink-wrap. It's been a long time since I made my own bed, and then thinking, this is ludicrous, but it can be my first easy win. Okay, let's stretch the sheets out, let's get the elasticated corners on over the mattress. One pillow, one blanket. The cold already settling in the cell along with the damp. You will sleep in your tracksuit, always your tracksuit at the very least.

Back to scanning the room. A little metal sink, a small toothbrush. You can't bring your own; a sharpened plastic toothbrush is a very useful weapon. So they give you a short feeble one that could snap in your hand if you brushed too hard.

The toilet, small and metal and without a seat or lid. I looked at it and decided to be a stander or squatter from now on. One metal chair, against the wall, and a basic wooden wall unit, for when you were ready to unpack.

A window, dark outside now, metal bars across it. Nothing to open except a small sliding metal grille with holes drilled in it. The only way for air to get in and try to circulate and push a little of the heavy dampness aside for a moment or two.

I didn't walk around too much. Not ready to play the caged animal just yet. In the strangest way, I almost felt relieved. The worst part had been the unknown – yes, you're going to be released, no, you're getting seven years. The constant tension of an existence without certainty. Now it was all real, these walls and this dented furniture and smell. This is it now. So relieved is the wrong word, but I was okay, once I'd made the bed, once I'd brushed my teeth. The comfort of familiar gestures, a new version of an old routine. I even turned on the TV, the smallest screen I'd ever watched. This will be my entertainment. *Channel 4 News*, you have a new regular viewer.

Except nothing is ever truly certain in prison. I was there an hour before the wardens knocked on my door.

– You have to change to a different cell.

– But I'm just here …

– We have an older guy in a wheelchair coming in. He needs the ground floor.

– I've made the bed, I've unpacked.

– Please pack your clothes and move.

This time I was taken to the first floor. Right in the middle of a long row. A dank mouldy cell becomes a noisier dank mouldy cell. A solid cell door between you and the chaos out there becomes a solid cell door with a broken hatch so the light and the shouts and all the madness just pour straight in.

Same routine all over again. Still alone. Clothes into the storage unit. Sheets over the mattress, a bunk bed this time. Mould in the corners, mildew on the ceiling.

This time I could see the sky. Two small windows, still barred, but looking to the west, to the sun going down. To the last fading trace of natural light in a world of fluorescent tubes and flashlights. No rooftops or chimney pots or trees, the sort of things you'd expect to see from most windows in this part of south-west London. No way of looking down into the courtyard just below, where I would end up walking and walking, or the football pitch, or even the walls between us and the world outside. But that was all right. I had the sky, and the light, and that would be enough for now.

I lay down on the bottom bunk for the first time. I draped a few clothes over the edge of the top bunk to create a little curtain of privacy, for some protection from those who might stare in. Felt the depression in the middle of the mattress, the imprint of those who had slept here before. Stared at the walls and the scribbles and messages upon them. Names and phone numbers, stories and conversations with the long gone.

That's when the screaming began. And after pressing the emergency button, and the Listeners coming and going, and after feeling intently the impossibility of ever falling asleep in this place, I asked myself again: why is this happening to me?

Once I was the best tennis player in the world. I had all the money I ever needed. I could take it all for granted, and nothing really changed.

Who was I now?

And I didn't find an answer, not then. I still felt as if I were watching a movie about myself and living it in the same moment, but I did my best to hold the desperation at arm's length. Experienced the instability and tried asking something else.

Do I have what it takes to get through this? Can I find it, if I don't? Who will I be, whenever it all ends?

Then, a resolution: I will try. That's all I can do. I won't give up. And then I lay there, and I didn't sleep, not for a long time.

From Bark & Co

14 New Bridge Street

London EC4V 6AG

PRESS STATEMENT

From Boris Becker: I wish to make it clear that I accept the verdicts of the jury. I accept the sentence imposed upon me and that is why I have no intention of seeking any form of appeal. I will serve my sentence in accordance with the court's decisions.

From Bark & Co: Following his conviction and sentencing Mr Becker would like us to clarify some matters about his trial.

Mr Becker was acquitted of 20 of the 24 charges and the Insolvency Service lost the majority of its case against him. In particular, Mr Becker was acquitted of every single charge alleging offences by him before the making of the bankruptcy order on 21 June 2017. It was decided by the jury, followed by the Judge in sentencing, that Mr Becker did nothing wrong or illegal regarding his bankruptcy before the bankruptcy order was made. Mr Becker actively tried to avoid being declared bankrupt and to meet his debts.

Following the bankruptcy order being made on 21 June 2017, Mr Becker's assets fell within his bankruptcy estate. Payments were made from a company account to his dependents and to meet his business and personal expenses as had been done prior to the bankruptcy order. It is in these circumstances that Mr Becker was convicted of removing of monies between 22 June and 28 September 2017 from his bankruptcy estate (Count 4). This was the main conviction against him. Mr Becker accepts that these payments should not have been made after the bankruptcy order without the permission of the trustee in bankruptcy. These payments were primarily to meet Mr Becker's commitments to his children and other dependents, medical and professional fees, and other expenses.

Mr Becker was also convicted of matters relating to non-disclosure of a property in Leimen, Germany where his mother lives (Count 10), a mortgage on that property (Count 13), and some shares (Count 14). Mr Becker accepts that the trustee

INSIDE

in bankruptcy should have been provided with information regarding these assets at an earlier time. Details of this property were provided to the trustee in bankruptcy soon after meeting on 13 September 2017.

CHAPTER 3

Guten Tag, Mr Boris Becker

I found an interesting book called *The Leopard* by Giuseppe Tomasi di Lampedusa. He is famous for saying, 'If we want things to stay as they are, things will have to change!'

    Hemingway told a story of meeting a friend who went bankrupt. How did it happen? It was gradual and then it came very quick.

How are you finding life if I may ask?

    Regards

You wake up before you want to wake up. Of course you do.

    I didn't remember falling asleep, that first night. I remembered the screaming still going on at one in the morning, maybe it settling to just a couple of wild voices at 2am. Then it was flashlights shining in my face, sometime before dawn. You learn to organise, after a few days. You drape more clothes over the top bunk so that the light doesn't hit you straight in the eyes. But the first night, when the wardens come to do their rounds, you have no idea what is happening. You don't know that for the first few weeks they'll check on you every two hours. Instead you throw your hand over your face and then stand up with your arms in the air like a crazy, scared man. And then

INSIDE

they say, *alright?* and you mumble *yes* and you either fall back asleep and you don't know any more or you're up now and that's it.

It was a Saturday, my first morning in Wandsworth. I was awake and nothing was happening, except one of my new neighbours was practising his singing. He turned a radio on when it was still dark and sang a succession of notes that were different to the ones in his backing track. I shouted, after three hits.

– Hey, you're not a singer!

– Yeah but I like to sing!

– It's six in the morning. Don't you think we want to sleep?

– Yeah, but I like to sing in the morning …

He couldn't have cared less. The more you yelled at him the more he would sing, and the more he would ignore every other voice telling him to shut the fuck up.

Then it was 6.30am, then 7am. I could hear other noises outside, shouts and whistling. I waited for someone to come and open my door. I wondered what was for breakfast and how it would come. Then I waited some more, and nothing happened and nobody came.

Doors deep inside the wing were clanging and echoing; 8am came and went, 9am. Had they forgotten me? It was now 9.30am. Yeah, they must have done. I'll ring the bell; I'll tell the Listeners.

Charlie and Jake didn't look surprised. This was normal to them.

– Boris, it's the weekend. They'll open your cell door at 11.30am.

– 11.30am? But what do I do until then?

– You stay here. At 11.30 they'll open your door, and then you get your lunch, until 12.15pm. Then they close them until 4.30pm, when you go for dinner, and then 5.15pm it's shut again.

– But this is crazy …

– It's prison. Monday's a Bank Holiday, so it's the same rules. Your bad luck you didn't start on a weekday. Nobody works on a weekend.

I read my Barack Obama book for a while, appreciating a few hours of comparative calm amid the chaos. It was a good book. I just couldn't read it all morning. Nothing against the remarkable story of the first Black man to be President of the United States, but three hours of reading is too much reading, even if you're sat in a deep armchair at home with a whisky or lying on the beach.

Everything dragged. So tired, so wired. Ready to fall asleep, twitchy and edgy and ready to run.

I wanted to wash. I smelled. I wanted aftershave. Screw that, I wanted food. I would have liked a smoke, but I'd written that one off with the cologne.

I could hear the wardens, and I could hear their keys. Great splayed bunches of silvery metal, looped together on belts and around wrists. A sound that becomes familiar every morning and every night, a sound you never forget again, no matter how far you go.

When you hear that sound coming closer you learn to stop. Whatever you are doing, you freeze. Put things down, hide them, straighten things out. You wait for the face at the hatch in your door and the eyes looking in and around. They always look in, before they push the key in and turn the lock and shove the door open.

INSIDE

It was a female warden, that first morning. Not what I expected, maybe, but someone who knew the rules and understood how it all worked. In time you figure out the big secret they don't want to tell you – that prisons, when you're inside, are run not only by the guards but sometimes by the inmates. But she knew that I didn't know and behaved that way. Not the slightest hint of any weakness. Tough as hell, with language ripe for a Centre Court code violation.

I didn't know how to behave. I put my blue tracksuit top on and I walked out into the noise and echoes and harsh lights, and I followed the others going to the canteen, and I stayed close to the wall because I was afraid. Afraid of the not knowing, afraid of what might come in the next corridor. Afraid of these other men, unsmiling, staring, looking awful in the same grey tracksuit bottoms as me.

You can feel danger like a physical force, sometimes. Radiating off other people, hanging in the air between you. I stood in the line at the canteen and it was all around me. I couldn't stop looking at the trays of plastic knives, the plastic forks. You don't want metal in there, but plastic still cuts. Plastic still pierces.

The Listeners were the ones who felt it all and understood the rules. The official stuff – the theory – and then the reality: the pull of the undertow, the currents of dark power.

I saw Jake watching me. He was in his late twenties, mixed race, quite tall, carrying himself with confidence. He came over and stood with me and spoke quietly while looking around.

– Don't stare, not now, but this guy here, he's okay. The guys behind – don't look at them. Stay with me. Come and meet Mohammed.

Mohammed was working in the kitchen. Another Listener, another insider who would be on my side. I would get to know him well, and to me he would become Mo. A Londoner, but a diehard Liverpool fan. Tattoos everywhere and a gym nut who was crazy for Jürgen Klopp and his *gegenpress*.

For now he was just looking out for me as the new signing. Leaning forward over the big stainless-steel trays of food as I reached the front of the queue.

– What you want to eat?

– I don't know.

– This one is shit so take this other one. If you want some more, come back to me in 20 minutes.

I had my tray. The classic metal one you recognise from prison movies, subdivided into sections. Some mashed potato, a bit of chicken. Not the sausage, on Mo's recommendation, but some bread. Salt on the side, no pepper, no sauces in bottles. Fine. I'd eaten no breakfast and no dinner. I was empty enough to eat anything.

I carried the tray back to my cell, eyes on the floor ahead of me, and I ate it all. In prison I would feel hunger for the first time in my life. I'd never known the feeling before. Now I would become used to going to sleep hungry, waking up in the night hungry, eating and not caring about the taste and whether it was meant to be hot but had ended up cold. Always finishing it quickly, so I could go back again if I was lucky and knew the right people in the kitchen. It's a powerful thing, hunger.

By 12.15pm I was back behind the locked door. I felt a little better now I had something in my stomach. Basic animal needs sometimes trump your deeper human desires. I put on the little TV and flicked between the channels. I tried to find a programme

INSIDE

I knew, but that didn't last long, so I watched whatever came on. A small remote control, not working at all, but I didn't want to be difficult, and I didn't want to ask too many questions, so I left it as it was. Later the Listeners would tell me: you can ask us, and we can see if we can find one. For now it was staying low key and being as easy as possible.

Everything that first day and first weekend was the beginning of new rituals. When you have so little to fill your time you'll use anything to pad out the gaps, and you soon get a pretty good sketch in your head of what programmes come on at what time. I came to like the morning shows: *BBC Breakfast*, to get a round-up of what was happening in the UK and a little bit elsewhere; *Lorraine* on ITV, and the guests she had on, some of whom I even knew. I looked forward to Kate Garraway and Ben Shephard. I even began to make time for *Loose Women*, later in the day. You make time for any distraction you can, in prison.

And I let the thoughts come at me. Strategies first, like I was back on court, like I needed to work this one out.

There was something I had begun to realise over the past couple of years. There are many disadvantages of becoming older: you can gain weight, you can lose shape. Your hair might turn grey or disappear altogether. But your mind gets better. You figure out where your qualities lie, and your talents. Your weaknesses too.

With age had come the understanding that, for good or bad, I could thrive in the middle of a fight. Maybe physically less so than in the old days, but definitely mentally. It shouldn't have been this way, but I knew it by now. The energy of a battle brought me peace and made me happy.

Maybe it was the hardship my mother experienced as a child, maybe it was the strictness of my father. The discipline, the beatings with shoes. Having a survivor as a mother and a disciplinarian as a father hardens a child.

But I always liked the simplicity of a fight, its primal nature. Tennis is complicated but straightforward at the same time. Either you win or I win. There's no before and there's no afterwards. It's all about the now. It erases all other thoughts.

Thinking my way into a fight was, weirdly, my self-protection. Because there was something else I'd gradually realised about myself. I get bored really easily. And if I'm bored, I make mistakes.

I wasn't good with too much time on my hands. I wasn't good in my comfort zone. I would get lazy, eat wrong, drink too much. I was never bothered by sleeping in a shitty hotel room or taking an early morning flight or eating junk food. But it had to take me closer to a goal, and I had to have somewhere safe to come back to after it all – a place to lick my wounds and recover and regain my energy. It was bad for me if I fought from Monday to Friday and didn't have a home on the weekend or still had to hunt for a girl or some fun.

So how could I map all this onto my new routine in prison? In here the instinct was to avoid confrontation, because confrontation had some very serious repercussions. When my cell door opened I would be going out into the wild. I knew physically I couldn't touch anyone. I would lose.

So what could I do? Maybe I could try to befriend the strong ones, to become part of their group and be protected. But do that and you have to be careful because they're much stronger than you. You cannot pick a fight, and you can't provoke and you can't be difficult.

Next problem. Of course you need them, but how can they need you? Maybe I could make myself useful. I could find a strong unit and become an important part of it. But I had seen these men and I had seen a little of how they lived. I could never really let my guard down. I could never show them any weakness, or allow them into my private world. I could never tell them about Lilian or my family or how I was.

When could I drop my guard? Maybe only when that cell door closed and I was sure nobody could come in. What felt like a trap must become my safe haven – the place I recovered and refocused so I could go again. I could see no other way through.

When my door was locked that afternoon, I tried to turn the solitude and dead hours into something else. This was how I would process things. This was when I could sort out what I'd done wrong, and what I'd done right. Sometimes to lose myself in the past, sometimes to figure it out. Sometimes to comfort myself with memories of better times, sometimes to stare into parts of myself I didn't care to examine.

I lay on my bed, and I dreamed of different things, and I took myself away.

Cell Dreams: The Nemesis #1

Some opponents I work out, and some work me out. Most I beat, when I want to. That feels good. But some of them get into my head, and when that happens I don't like what they do to me.

I am the darling prince of Wimbledon. From 1985 it is all about me, through the wins and losses and trophies and disappointments. At Wimbledon and across the whole tennis scene, nobody has the love I have from that audience.

All the way to 1992, and now Andre Agassi comes along.

The long hair, like a rock star, a lead singer. The clothes, the denim shorts, the way Nike are pushing him. A good speaker, always glamorous partners: Brooke Shields, Barbra Streisand – I mean, Barbra Streisand! One of the greatest of all time.

It's personal, now he's here. It's always personal, in tennis. I feel like shouting to all these people. Are you guys blind? Look at this clown! You can't take him seriously.

But it doesn't seem to matter. They are taking him seriously. People are falling in love with him.

Wimbledon, 1992. I'm seeded four, he's twelve. I've been a finalist in 91, in 90, in 89, in 88. In 1986 and 1985.

He can't play on grass. It's not his surface. It's mine.

Then we meet in the quarter-finals, and this kid with the long hair and the girlfriends and – wow – perfect white clothes, beats me in the fifth set. Then he's beating McEnroe in the semis, and Goran in the final.

And, just like that, it's all changed. He's flamboyant. He's the boy of summer and sunshine. He is the big superstar.

And this is hard for me to take, because I need this audience. I need their support. But when I play Andre, he has more of their love than I do.

This feels ... devastating. I haven't seen this coming. Wimbledon is about the rivalry between me and Stefan Edberg. And now, all of a sudden, it's about Andre and Pete Sampras. Almost overnight, it feels like the rivalry of Stefan and Boris is over.

How has this happened? What do I do now?

INSIDE

So. I was safe when my cell door was locked each night. But I also thought of myself as someone who was comfortable in a fight. How could I close the gap between these two contradictions?

My door would not stay locked for ever. Therefore I would have to find a way of being safe out there too. Being comfortable in a fight meant embracing doubt and fear. I would have to embrace the opening of my cell door, partly because it was going to happen whether I liked it or not, and partly because I had to make the best I could of this shit situation.

I thought about it, and I tested my ideas out in my own mind, and settled on something. I would go out there strong and I would present myself as a resilient, independent individual with the right group. I'd have to play it like a match. As if it were fun. You had to like doing it, otherwise you couldn't play it and they will notice that actually you're just bluffing. I would have to demonstrate that I was comfortable in that environment, that I could talk to anybody. Maybe I should even play with them physically a little. Like I'm at the changeover between service games and they're walking to their chair and I'm walking to my chair and they come at me and I don't deviate and our shoulders meet with a smack and I walk on and don't look back.

What was the alternative, really? Prison is about reputation. It doesn't matter if you actually are strong, only that everyone else believes you are. Once they don't, they will bully you. Everybody gets bullied if they think you're not strong enough.

So let's play. Let's be comfortable in the fight. No comfort zone, so no boredom. No getting lazy, eating wrong. No making mistakes.

Then the fight could be something else. Not a physical one, but an intelligent one. Working out what was going on here. How the system worked, how I could challenge it where necessary and duck a punch another time. Looking at my sentence and seeing if we could make it as short as possible. Maybe outsmarting your opponent, listening to every word they said. If they slip up, catch it and use it against them. Looking at the long days and lonely nights and finding something good in them too.

They would be exhausting, all these battles, but they wouldn't be impossible for me. Comfortable in the fight. There was nothing else that mattered in this moment.

Dinner came. Mo pointed out to me the bad stuff and the slightly better stuff. Afterwards a Listener called Michael took me back to his cell. He would turn out to be the most trusted Listener of all; his door was unlocked, seemingly all day. He had his own radio. He had food: snacks, fruit, breakfast cereal. The walls were a different colour to the rest of the wing. No sheen. Actual paintings hanging up. Something that looked very much like … *a coffee machine?*

It wasn't a regular room, one you'd have at home. But it wasn't my cold and bleak cell either. It was somewhere in between – a cabin on a cargo ship, or an off-season shack by the seaside. And that strange sense of almost-normal continued as Michael told me his story.

– I'm a father. I have five kids. I dealt hard drugs.

This is how it is, in prison. You make the usual type of judgement on someone's appearance. See a white guy, average build, seems calm. Ordinary. Other inmates appear to like him. Turns out he killed a man when he was eighteen, fifteen long years ago.

INSIDE

It takes weeks until you stop taking a step back when you hear the reason why someone is inside. It takes months until you begin to put some of your old judgements aside. You're in here for a reason. I'm in here for a reason. There's only one part of those phrases that matter, and that's *in here*.

You don't ask about the drug dealing, in that first moment. It takes time for it to come out, and it takes trust. It takes respect, and for you to admit some of your own accountability. Only then do you hear it.

– Drugs is how I make my money. I made a mistake. The mistake wasn't the drugs. It was being caught.

Michael and Jake had been inside for a good few years already. The things they had – the comparative freedoms – came from how they had behaved in that time, and what they could do to make a flawed system move a little more smoothly.

As the days went by I came to understand there was a reason why Jake's door was always unlocked. He was one of the other most important Listeners in there, useful to everyone. When the wardens needed someone to talk to one of the dangerous prisoners, they could ask him. If an inmate wanted books or food or a letter read or explained, he would help with that too. The door being open? This was a good and bad thing for him. Good because you could go in for a coffee and a chat. Good because he had a role, and a significance. He mattered more than a number on a plastic ID pass. Bad because everybody comes. The ones Jake wanted to talk to, the ones he was maybe less keen to see in his doorway.

And so he could float in that strange space between the two warring sides, trusted by both, feared by neither. He was a criminal but also a good man. He had the ear of authority yet was never seen as a snitch. You had to volunteer for the role, and then they were vetted and accepted or rejected, and while the role came with those privileges, there was never really any jealousy, either, in spite of what you might think, because Listeners reflected the particular mix all around them. One was mixed-race, one was Black, one was a Muslim, one was Christian. They helped us. We needed them.

It was with Jake and regular inmates he brought together that I went to the showers. Walking as a group, going into the shower room and the door shutting behind us. Now this is trust. Cubicles for each of the eight inmates, but with a swing door covering you from neck to knees, no more. Dirt all over the floor, on the tiles. I was lent a pair of flip-flops. Boris, wear them, because we don't know who was there before. The first time in my life I ever showered in flip-flops. You don't have to think about flip-flops in nice hotels.

We changed in the cubicles. Tracksuits off, hung on the door. One towel each, a bar of soap. Some of them brought shower gel. That was another quiet lesson from Jake.

– You can order this from a list.

– A list?

– Yeah. We call it the canteen. You get a £15 allowance each week. You can use that for food and phone calls. You'll want to save at least half for calls.

– £15 doesn't seem much.

– You can get a job in here. You can earn a little more. Let me see what I can do.

It's strange, feeling so lost doing something so familiar as taking a shower. A simple daily task turned complicated in an alien world. Hearing the outer door to the shower room being locked behind you by the wardens, understanding now that if you're in there with the wrong group or one person who others will turn away from then no one is coming to save you. Not knowing how long you are allowed or when the water might go off, listening to what's happening in the cubicle next to you so that when they're finishing you're finishing too. Everything to fit in, nothing to stand out.

Some days those showers would be cold. You never knew why; it would just be a shrug from a guard and a 'not working today'. Cold didn't mean tepid. It meant icy. I'd always hated cold showers. I had no interest in ice baths. They tell you it's good for you; not for me. But what are you going to do? It's just another unpleasant fact in a day you don't control. Sometimes it will be ice cold and it will have to be done.

They talked a little between them. I just listened for now, said nothing. Bits of gossip, insider information in a room without other ears. Always about the fights, because every day in Wandsworth seemed to bring conflict. Who started on who – which wing they were on, were they stabbed, where they were now. Excitement about it all, morsels to be tucked away and shared elsewhere. Remember – the inmates can run the prison, it's not always the guards. I'd been told that, and now I could see it around me.

They talked about football. You're the same man inside those walls as you were outside, at least until it gets under your skin. Manchester City versus Manchester United, always loads of Liverpool fans on every wing. Thomas Tuchel was Chelsea manager at the time, so they came to me for that. You're German, he's German, is he going to last longer than you?

Back in my cell, I felt progress. I had eaten. I had washed. I had been part of a group, if only for the fifteen minutes we had in the shower. Because of what I'd been told and what I'd seen, I had the outline of a strategy. I knew some people now, and I knew their crimes.

Now I needed a job, to get money to call Lilian and to buy some breakfast, because you only get lunch and dinner inside. I'd heard about two French prisoners who couldn't speak much English. My French is okay, because I lived for a long time in Monte Carlo, although possibly I shouldn't go on about that too much. Maybe I could be their translator. Maybe I could teach English to the foreigners who needed someone else in the strange space in between. Boris Becker, professor of English. My old teachers at Helmholtz-Gymnasium on Rohrbacher Straße in Heidelberg would be so proud.

Two other big things that day. Jake, Charlie and some of the others saw I wasn't crazy, at least on the surface. I wasn't dangerous, I wasn't falling apart. They wouldn't trust me yet, but they could start thinking about it, because when you've been inside for a while, you develop that sixth sense. Word might get around. And when I was properly part of their team, they might protect me. I could get a shower with that group every day. I could start to belong, in a place I never wanted to stay.

INSIDE

Cell Dreams: The Nemesis #2

Now Andre is in my head. When I play him, I have to unsettle him. It's raw. I have to peel back his skin and work out what makes him tick. What makes him upset and angry.

This isn't about him or me being a better tennis player. It's about me being better than him or him being better than me, in everything. In our lives, in our self-confidence. In our quiet moments when it's just us alone with our thoughts and dreams.

Tennis matches are always personal to me. If they're not personal, I'm not as good.

You think this is bad. I realised long ago that this is a useful quality to have. When I make it personal then it means more, and I will put in more effort.

Harsh to you, okay to me. At the start of every big match the question for me is always the same: 'When we finish, is your mother going to cry or is my mother going to cry?' This is the level I take it to. And obviously I don't want my mother to cry, so it becomes personal, and because it is personal, I fight harder. I play tougher.

Let's make my mother happy.

Now Andre can do this too. He's very good at it. He's able to do the mind games before matches. He can do it while we're playing. He can take the crowd with him.

I see an equal, as the clarity comes to me. I see somebody who is doing a really good job. He's inside my head and he knows it. He's inside my house and he's knocking over the furniture and banging on the doors and pulling down the curtains.

Pete Sampras? I like Pete. He's not as charismatic. He's maybe a little bit boring, to some people. The fans like him and respect him. As a player myself I love him. He does what I do – the big first serve, the volleys, the leaps at the net – and maybe he does it better. That's all okay. It's a language I understand.

Pete is maybe the best player I've ever come up against. Even better than Andre. I can see how many Wimbledons he's going to win. There is no weakness. How do I try to cope? I have to wait in the match for one slack moment and then jump on that. I jump on that like he jumps on me: with power. Take away his time with my serve and my forehand, just power through him.

With Andre, I can't do that. Look at him. He is one of the best returners of all time. My strength is coming to the net. He takes my biggest weapon and he makes it his.

Pete is about respect. It's only ever about the tennis. That's why he's not really a rival to me. For Andre it's about the lifestyle, the coolness, the love and the look.

Everything I thought I had.

To beat Andre I have to get into his personality. I have to make him think a little bit. I have to make him doubt himself.

I have to drag it out for him. Make it a longer match. If he likes these quick points, let's make the rallies longer.

That's what I do when we meet in the semi-final at Wimbledon in 1995. He wins the first set, he's two breaks up in the second. But I stretch it out, slow down the pace, throw in the backhand slice. And he doesn't like this at all, and I win in four sets, and then I meet Pete in the final and Pete is me but better, so he beats me.

INSIDE

But it's not natural for me, playing like this. That's why my record against Andre is bad. It's bad because it's against everything I did all my life. And that's why these two, Andre and Pete, in their different ways, give me the reasons to stop playing tennis. To actually walk away. Because on their good day and my good day, they are better.

Against every other player I come up against in my career – Wilander, Lendl, Edberg, Cash, Stich, Courier, Chang – I know I can beat them if I play to my best.

Andre and Pete? I have to be on my best day to win. They only have to be on their good day.

The first time I tried to phone Lilian, she didn't pick up.

How could she? She didn't know I could phone her. She wouldn't have known I was trying or recognised the number coming up on her mobile. I didn't know I could phone her, until Jake explained it.

– The phone in your cell, you can't receive calls but you can make them. You dial this number to get out, then you dial the one you want to get through to. Your first call is free, but after that it will cost you, so you don't have long. Maybe ten minutes, or it's too expensive and your allowance will be gone. After fifteen minutes they will close it off, anyway. And maybe there will be people listening, so be careful.

Lilian had printed off a sheet of the most important numbers for me to have – her, my four kids, my mother and sister, my lawyers – and tucked it into a polythene sleeve in my Puma bag. The phone was fixed to the wall of my cell. A small old-fashioned landline with a short plastic cable between the main unit and the handset.

What do you say when the person you care about more than any other in the world actually picks up, and you hear their voice? You tell them that you are okay, even if you're not. That you're in a safe place, when that clearly isn't true. You put on your most reassuring voice, the confident one from the commentary box when you're in your happy place and understand everything around you. Some practical stuff to get across – I can't make international calls, please speak to my children for me. Tell my mother I'm okay. We can do this.

That's how I survived the first weekend. Eating with the Listeners, using the Mo menu. Showering with Jake and his group. Reading, and strategising, and thinking about my next call to Lilian. Cell dreaming.

And it was pure survival, nothing more. Trying to eat, trying to sleep. Gathering as much information from the Listeners as I could in those short windows for lunch and dinner. Asking, asking, asking, absorbing everything I was told. Remembering what I could until I got back to my cell and was able to write it down in biro in my exercise books. He said this, he said that. Get it down, make a plan.

I never talked to myself. Not out loud, like I used to on court when I was young and full of fire and adrenaline and strength. There were moments when my thoughts were so loud I thought my neighbours must hear them, so potent they would make me laugh or cry or stop completely. But it was always a single voice in my head, never a debate. The right side of my brain never questioned the left.

Because I was me, I thought about tennis. Who was winning, and who was losing. April turning into May, so the clay court season, Monte Carlo and Rome and Madrid, building up for

INSIDE

the French at Roland-Garros. How Germany's men's number one Sascha Zverev was progressing. Of course I had no idea about any results. No one else had any interest in tennis. They weren't the same sort of people as me.

No one seemed to care who I had been before Wandsworth, either. The Listeners got it, but nobody came up to ask me about beating Ivan Lendl or losing to Michael Stich or whether Rafa Nadal was going to win a fourteenth French title. It was only where I was from. That was my identity, the first weekend. The German one. To the Listeners I was Boris. No nickname, no one going Boom-Boom. No shortening of it, because Mohammed can be Mo and Charles Charlie, but what do you do with Boris?

Don't like what they choose to call you? Whatever it is, it's better than the number on the pass around your neck. I was used to lanyards. That's how tennis works, whether you're a player or commentator. Sometimes you tie it to your racket bag; most of the time it's round your neck. But my tennis passes had my name. It was the real me. Not just a number.

When you left your cell, you needed your ID pass. When you lay on the bed you wore your ID pass. They don't care about three Wimbledon singles titles in here. Only where you're going and which cell they're locking you in.

I was shocked, at first. Quite soon after that I had the strangest feeling. I didn't have to explain who I was. I didn't have to talk them through my big wins and losses. I could maybe become a new me. I was inside, but somehow I could be liberated too. I was lucky, that first week. Monday was the Bank Holiday, and the same dead routine as the weekend. Twenty-two hours in my cell, all alone, but on Tuesday morning the Listeners had news for me.

– Boris, there is a job free, a new programme starting up. We need an assistant to help with maths and English. We know the warden responsible, and if you want it, we can tell him you're right for it.

Lucky? This was impossible. Usually you waited at least six weeks to get a chance of something like this. They had to see what you were like, and if you could handle the shock of the new. But this is what happens when you listen. You hear it all, what's needed from both sides of the divide. They had watched me, and realised I wasn't one of those who wanted to wreck the place from the inside out. (There are a lot of those; the ones who have been in before, who are on their third or fourth spell.)

On the Tuesday afternoon I was allowed an interview. On Wednesday morning I started.

That was the day everything changed. When you work, your door is open each morning. You are out of your cell for two hours before lunch, and another two in the afternoon. Four whole hours! You have something to do with your mind, and great chunks of time that are used up and gone without you even needing to consciously set light to them.

The classroom was small. Four rows of desks, me standing at the front with a blackboard and chalk. Not so different from the Helmholtz-Gymnasium. Ten student inmates in the morning, maybe fifteen in the afternoon.

I have coached tennis players before. I was on Centre Court when Novak Djokovic won the Wimbledon title with the tactics and mindset we planned. So this was different, but I could feel the same needs. I'm a good listener. I like tuning in to people, and I listen properly to what they have to say. I realised quite quickly that teaching is less about you telling people things and more about you taking notice of what they need and what they might be struggling with. It's about being on their side, not always at the front.

In those first few lessons I tried to show that I was not the boss but an ally. I would stand up from my desk and walk over and look at what they were writing and, even though I wasn't supposed to, I would give them a couple of hints. You know, maybe this is the word we're looking for. Hey, maybe seven and seven is fourteen and not fifteen. They saw that I was helping, and I felt a little respect in return. I had a role, even if it was a small one.

But I was still getting things wrong. The next morning in my cell I ran my hand over my chin and felt almost a week of stubble. This was no good – I had to look the part now. I couldn't let myself go. I took the stubby little razor they had given me, and the bar of soap, pulled my chair to the little sink and began to shave.

It did not go well. The razor was either blunt from previous use or had never been sharp in the first place. The soap was like cheap glue, and the mirror was just a broken piece of plastic. The blade dug in and jammed and then bit and wouldn't let go. I could see blood in the water of the bowl and I could see it on the towel when I tried to clean myself up. Nicks on my cheeks, little stabby slashes under my chin and down my neck.

I thought I looked bad, and longed for my bathroom at home with my hot water and shaving oil and brand-new razor with four stacked blades and moisturiser and aftershave. When the guard looked in an hour later he must have thought it looked worse: I was summoned to a medical with the doctor.

The questions came fast. How is your mental health? You know what you're going to expect in here, can you handle it? Are you good on your own? Did you self-harm before?

I gave my yes and no responses as required. Then the big question.

– You have so many cuts on your face, did you self-harm?

– My God, no, of course ... I was trying to shave ...

– Well everybody says that, nobody admits that they self-harm.

– Guys, I swear on my children I don't self-harm. Look at my body, I wanted to shave but I had blunt blades. I was doing it with that little mirror that we have, and I cut myself, yes, but by mistake. I stopped when I saw the blood. Okay?

I'd never thought about self-harm. Why would I? My mind was only focused on doing things to protect myself. But these men were tuned to different frequencies, which is why they confronted me. They were used to these experiences, especially with new inmates. You couldn't cope with what might happen to you, so you got there first. You felt all that fear and despair inside and you took it out on your own body. Let the blood flow and the horror slip away with it.

Bad news comes in rushes in prison. After the medical I was summoned to the head office. They asked me a simple question, which would make a mess of a whole lot of other things.

– Do you have a British passport?

– What do you mean? No, I'm German.

– You don't have a British passport?'

– No. That's why I gave you my German passport when I came in here. That's it.

– Okay. Then you have to be moved.

INSIDE

– I can go?

– No. You have to go to a different prison. One for foreign nationals.

I was confused. They were confused. Nobody had told me about this. My scenario had been clear: survive Wandsworth for five weeks, maybe six, and then the open prison. A place I could leave during the day, a place that would be the worst hotel I had ever stayed in but would be freedom and lunches out with Lilian and walks in the park and I don't know what else.

Now my plans were falling apart, my strategies and targets. They told me to leave; I asked for another meeting with the director. I didn't get one. They told me that in a couple of days somebody would come to my cell and explain my situation.

Questions were pouring into my head. What does this mean? Where will you move me? When will I go? Can you have open prisons for foreign nationals? And all they said was, we can't answer your questions. Somebody will come to see you.

Cell Dreams: The Nemesis #3

It's weird, thinking about Andre here. It's so far away, but it's so close too.

Weird how he married the German tennis queen. She grew up maybe ten miles from me. Weird how he learned his tennis at Nick Bollettieri's academy, and then Nick became my coach. It was always personal with Andre.

Weird how he talked about me in his book, even though we really had very little contact for a long time. This story about him reading the direction of my serve from where my tongue was pointing. I mean, how big is a tennis court? You cannot see an open mouth on the opposite baseline, let alone a tongue.

But that's the showman in him. Born and raised in Vegas, and it's a great story. It makes people laugh. It sells books. But realistically, you cannot see somebody's tongue unless you have binoculars. Also, the speed of it. You serve at 130mph. 'Ah, okay he puts his tongue there …' the ball's already passed you. Something else? Up until I hit the ball, I didn't know where I was hitting it. You have an idea – 'Okay, maybe the backhand …' but at the last moment you can change your mind. Regardless of whether your mouth is open or not.

You know *The Last Dance,* the Michael Jordan doc? There's a part where MJ says if there wasn't a rivalry, he'd have to invent one. A big one. Start thinking, I hate you because …

That's what I think I felt with Andre, some of the time. Other moments, in the quiet times, I could admit the other side to myself.

– Wow. he's really taken over the baton. He's the new superstar in tennis.

He has had his trials and tribulations. He seems happier now. Content. I wonder what he thinks of me in here. I wonder if he has time to look back.

I think about how it is with him now. When we've seen each other recently, we've given each other a long hug. We sit down. We are sincere with each other, because I think he felt the same about me.

We were in a strange dance as players. As rivals. As the old and the new.

I think we grew out of that. I think we probably would be friends, if he lived in Europe or close by. We would hang out.

INSIDE

We'd have a McEnroe-type relationship – not the boys of summer and sun any more, but the men those days created, for better or worse.

That's the type of relationship I would have with Andre now. An appreciation for what we did for the sport. For what we did for each other.

Cirencester, Gloucestershire

Hi Boris

My name is Mick. I am 67 years old and a huge fan of yours and of tennis especially the era you played in with the likes of Borg, McEnroe and Connors, where there were many characters in the sport.

Not being mobile means sport and telly are my life-line, and most of my time is spent lying on my bed because I also have osteoarthritis of the spine. Although I am not in prison it feels like I am stuck in a body that can't do what it should be able to do, hope that makes sense.

Over the years you and the three players I mentioned above have certainly left me with some great memories, especially seeing a young 17-year-old win Wimbledon. At times you were more like a goalkeeper with some of the diving you made to retrieve what to most people were impossible passing shots.

Hope the time goes quickly and when you get released life brings you and your family much happiness for the rest of your lives.

Stay safe, and all the very best,

Mick Ricketts

CHAPTER 4

Dear Boom-Boom

I'm sure you won't remember me – we met when you spoke at the Washington Union in 2012, I worked in the office and had photos with me from when I saw you play at Wimbledon in my youth.

    I've got nothing to say really, I just wanted to say hello and hopefully make you smile.

    I truly hope you're doing okay, I'm very sad for your situation, my thoughts and prayers are with you.

    With love,

    Melanie

I had been thinking about the passport issue incessantly since the meeting in the front office the previous week. Discussing it with Lilian in our short calls on the phone, asking her to check again with the lawyers. This was too arcane a prison issue even for Jake and the Listeners. They could help you get flip-flops and a TV remote control, but they weren't experts in the intricacies of the criminal justice process for German nationals.

    The officer in charge met me again during a lunch break from teaching. I asked him if there might have been a mistake. My lawyers had told me I should be here for six weeks, sure, but then it was definitely an open prison. A prison for foreign nationals was just Wandsworth without the British inmates. There would be murderers and paedophiles and gang leaders. That wasn't me. Whatever else I might question about the man I was, that wasn't me.

He told me the error was mine.

– You're not British, you're German.

– I agree. I've never claimed to be British. I lived in London for a long time, sure, but I'm Boris Becker, from Leimen. The accent's a bit of a giveaway …

– So you won't be going to an open prison.

– But why?

So I had no idea where I would be sent next. There is no 'why' in the prison system. They don't need to give you one. You lost that privilege when the guilty verdict came in. There's no great desire to explain anything. They could tell me I would be moved, but not when and to where, and I could try to fight it all I wanted, but it wasn't going to change any of it.

Where do you find your light in a world like this? I had my phone calls to Lilian, and I had the new teaching job that helped fund them. When I talked to Lilian I could let my guard down, for a couple of minutes every few days. The job was a different form of brief escape – an hour of English and an hour of maths in the morning, an hour of both in the afternoon. I would sometimes walk past a few familiar cells on the way to the classroom to pick up a few stragglers and ask a couple of others if they would maybe like to come along. Almost by stealth I was starting to get to know prisoners outside of the few doors around me and the Listeners beyond, and they were getting to know me too.

Prison is about ranking: where you stand in the secret pecking order, who can tell you what to do, what you have that someone else doesn't. In the classroom I found you could speak to other inmates with a lower tariff of danger. I could listen to a man's story of why he was here. The more people I got to know, the safer I felt. When you talk to your enemy, you can show them you're not the threat they might imagine. It's a conversation, not a confrontation.

For someone who still thought he was somehow apart from the others in here, I was surprised how easy it was to empathise with many of them. I enjoyed the feeling of being able to offer a little encouragement in a place that was indifferent to us at other times. No inmate questioned the wisdom of having a bankrupt man teach them mathematics, and that was a good thing too.

I was now slightly less disposable than I had been on my first weekend. Not because of my name, or for winning Wimbledon, but because of my new position. And I took it all seriously, because when your day is otherwise sterile and empty and each one is the same as all the others, anything that makes an hour feel distinctive is something you bring close and hold tight.

Sometimes my devotion to the lowest paying job I'd ever held amused Lilian, and sometimes it puzzled her. She almost found it annoying, in a comical way.

– Amore, why didn't you call when you said you would?

– I'm sorry, I was busy at work.

– You're in prison and you're busy?

Does this idea of a convicted man having a phone in his cell sound too easy and soft? Well, imagine how you would behave if you were locked up on your own for twenty-two and a half hours a day and had no one to talk to but the voices in your own head. Would your behaviour be better or worse, would you be more amenable to the wardens or more likely to blow?

Often the phone wouldn't work. Then you had to go to the public payphone on the wing, and it was you and a hundred others eavesdropping, and if some men were waiting in line more than two minutes then they would start screaming at you. When that happened you just had to cut it short and hang up. It was too dangerous to keep talking.

I was supposed to have the right to make a call abroad. This was the silver lining to my German passport issue. But it would be several months until that permission worked its way through the system. When Mother's Day came, early in that first blurry block of days, it took the intervention of the prison chaplain and the phone in his office for me to get through to my mother back in Germany. She was confused, caught between expecting a call because I always called her, and not expecting one at all because of where I was. Now in her late eighties, her mind was sometimes alive more in the past than the present, and she trusted the stories she read in her gossip magazines too much. I was still glad we could talk. Something is always better than nothing.

Some days I was desperate to call Lilian but I couldn't afford it. I didn't have enough remaining of my weekly allowance, or I had to choose between a call and tea bags, or an apple so I could have breakfast before going to work. One of the maths students told me that if I used a different number to call out from then it could save me money. So I did that for a couple of weeks and thought we were safe, but then the prison found out and blocked that service, so the old dilemmas returned. Other times you knew a third party was listening in, monitoring your conversations. The other inmates tell you: mate, they'll log the things you say; mate, don't say on the phone where you've hid your money. When you're on a call, you can hear strange crackles and clicks. Privacy is the first of the old privileges you lose.

I learned quite quickly that when you don't have your phone calls, you have no way of ever being yourself. You become the walls around you, the grey stone and damp floors and mould in the corners. They keep alive the softer parts of you that you hide at all other times. The phone calls keep you human.

And if it's hard for you, it's hard for the ones living your sentence in the outside world. If Lilian missed a call from me she would beat herself up about it. Sometimes she wanted to call me and had to remember that was no longer possible. Other times both of us had something vital to share, and we had to wait all day for a tiny window when you might forget it or rush it or just not have the time at all.

So we settled on a pattern that worked a little better than anything else. When I finished work in the morning, I would call for a couple of minutes. When I was done with teaching in the afternoon, I would do the same. You never had enough time, and you had too much to say and often nothing at all, but those short moments were always the ones I looked forward to most.

By week three we had a better routine. A few moments post-work in the morning on the practical stuff. The lawyers want this, we've had an update on that, there's a decision to be made about what we do here. Then the afternoon to think about it all, and an answer in the evening: okay, I think we should do this. In the evening, too, the gentler stuff, the lonely truths and encouraging words and quiet consolations. Even inside, love was what kept you warm from within.

Cell Dreams: The Love #1

It's April 2018. Life is not great for me; I've been in bankruptcy for almost a year, I am newly separated from my second wife, Sharlely. Germany is having a field day with my problems. I'm in the newspapers every week, and I'm not in the newspapers as a sporting hero but as a sort of uber loser. I have had my right ankle operated on, but my left knee needs doing too, so I'm not walking great. I'm limping, to tell the truth. I have lost endorsements everywhere, because my reputation is in tatters. I don't have much money. Yeah, I'm in a shithole.

But I'm in Frankfurt, and a good friend of mine is turning fifty, so he's having a house party. I'm alone, but I can be sociable if I want to, so I am talking to everybody. Then there's this girl standing there, quite tall. She doesn't look at me.

Because she doesn't know me. She's not from Germany, so she doesn't talk to me, and I don't talk to her, and nothing happens. Not even the next day, when I come back to see my friend again, and she's there too, coming back from the gym.

I'm a little bit nervous. That's not me. So I say, hi I'm Boris, and she says, hi I'm Lilian, and that's the last time I see her for a while.

This is April. My mother lives in Heidelberg, which is about forty-five minutes away, so every time I'm visiting my mother, I pop in to see my friend in Frankfurt. And when I do, I ask about this girl. Her parents are from São Tomé, an island off the west coast of Africa. She was born in Italy. She's well educated and smart and speaks five languages. She has her own career.

I ask if my friend and his wife and me and their friend can meet for lunch. And a few times we do. But when I ask my friend for the girl's phone number, and he talks to her, she says no. She has just finished with her boyfriend. She doesn't know if she wants to live in Frankfurt or London or Italy, but she does know she doesn't want to be stuck in one place because of someone else. She wants to be free to make her own decisions. She wants space.

She has done some research, too. Tried to find out who this guy is who, for almost a year now, keeps turning up in Frankfurt for lunch and dinner. She reads about divorces, and financial problems, and scandals. It's too heavy for her. And she can't ask me about it, because when we meet it's never just the two of us. It's always four people or six. And they always ask me about the tennis years, like people do, and she doesn't know anything about that world.

It's almost a year on that it happens. Same sort of dinner, same sort of people, me trying to engage her in a conversation. This time it's different. At some point she just looks at me and says, how are you? Like, how are you really? And then she asks another question that people don't usually ask me: what do you like to do? What really gives you satisfaction?

INSIDE

This stops me. I look at her in a different way. I start talking about my family. I start talking about my children. And she tells me later that this is when I become more human in her eyes. More tangible as a real person. Before I've been a person everyone seems to freak out around. Now, when I'm talking about my children, and three different mothers, it resonates with her. Because she is one of three sisters, and they have different mothers, and her father is the one who is the constant.

After this she gives me a number. Then she tells me she is going to Brazil tomorrow to see friends. But she has given me her number. After almost a year, she gives me her number.

We had the phone calls. Actual visits can take an age to come through. I was lucky that with my new job came better visiting rights. Another key area for the Listeners to guide me through.

– You get two visits a month, before you're enhanced – before you've earned some privileges and trust.

– Yeah. To get those you have to fill in a paper application form – the name of your visitor, their relationship to you, that sort of thing.

– You can ask for either Wednesday or Thursday afternoon.

But it all takes so long. You had to file the form days in advance, then wait for another form telling you your application was proceeding. One part of the system doesn't always communicate with the other, so then you have to make sure the guards who lock and unlock your door each day know what's coming.

– By the way, tomorrow, 2 o'clock, please open my cell, I have a visit …

Then you remind them again in the morning, so they don't forget. They wait until fifteen minutes before your allotted time, and then they unlock your door, and you wait in the corridor outside, and they guide you back towards reception and the big hall next to it for visits.

And that was just the bureaucracy I'd had to navigate. Lilian was doing the same on the other end, lost in a switchboard, being read standard lines from a computer screen.

– He's not appearing as available for visits in the system.
– But he's definitely in there.
– He has to get registered for visits.
– How?
– He has to do quarantine because of Covid.
– What, now? In May 2022?

When the clearance suddenly came, a week further on, there was minimal warning. A phone call she took in her gym class telling her to be there at 2pm that afternoon. She packed a new bag for me, with hoodies and T-shirts and shoes to replace the black ones I'd had confiscated, jumped in an Uber and then realised she was being followed by paparazzi. Her Uber driver saw how upset she was, stopped his car and asked the photographers to stop following them. They refused. She got to Wandsworth to find they had called ahead and alerted even more media.

Always a process, always a system. She was sent to a registration room with other wives and kids and girlfriends. Each then went through an airport-style scanner to a waiting area with plastic chairs. A nod from one of the other women.

– Don't worry, you'll get used to it.

It's a big room, the hall for visits. Three rows of small tables, each with a couple of chairs. Jake was there too, waiting for his family. I sat at one near the front, composing myself, not sure what I would be able to hold back and what would come tumbling out.

I saw her coming. Gym class clothes, Puma tracksuit and leggings. Me in my grey tracksuit and a yellow vest they made you wear for the visit. And I started crying, and she started crying, and we hugged each other, which you're not really supposed to do, and then we began to try normalising the strangest of conversations.

I could tell from the way she was looking at me that I wasn't hiding things as well as I thought. Her eyes kept scanning my face and my posture. She could see something different. Maybe the fear, definitely the cuts and scars from my shaving disaster. The way I was holding myself, the flare-up of my gout from the stress and bad food and lack of usual medication.

We started talking. Already conscious we only had one hour, the only point in the week when time would accelerate rather than turning to gloop. She asked what had happened to my face. I told her the story. I think she believed me.

Looking into each other's eyes, pushing away the distractions all around. Not looking at Jake and his wife and all their kids pulling up extra chairs to house them all, not caring about other prisoners listening in to our conversations. After the fourth or fifth visit you realise that if the guards like you they'll put you at the end of a row for extra privacy, and if they don't they'll put you right in the middle of it all. If they like you they'll allow you to hug; if they don't, they'll impose the official regulations banning physical contact, because when you hug or hold hands you can smuggle stuff in and pass it across.

It took me a few visits to understand how to use the time. I was afraid to start on a big topic in case it burned too many minutes and I'd look up with so much to say and not enough time to do it. Sometimes I would try to keep something short, but then you're worried you haven't got across what you really want to say.

Lilian asked me if I'd seen what was being written in the newspapers. I said no, already conscious of the gap between our two worlds, between inside and outside. She said: the German media are going crazy, they're saying you don't eat the food, they're saying you ring your security bell all the time. And I said, no, don't worry, this isn't true, wondering as I did why the hell they would print that when it was wrong, and if they were just making it up or if someone in here was leaking it to them.

There's stuff you've been thinking about for days that just spills out of you. From me: how is the flat, have you spoken to Noah, is there enough food in the fridge, have my friends called you? From Lilian: where did you go after I saw you last time at the court, I just saw the big van on TV, the white van, how was it?

I pointed at Jake and said I had found a couple of people who were looking after me. I told her I was enjoying the teaching and being let out of my cell more. I said I expected a visit from my lawyers to talk about the open prison mistake. I told her not to worry.

She couldn't give me the bag of clothes she had brought. They hadn't let her bring it in. Neither of us knew there was another little kink in the system where you had to book all that in and get it cleared and ticked off. I tried to hide my disappointment. The idea of my own clothes and some other shoes was a good one. It felt like it connected the old me with this reduced new version. I would have to wait. Next time, next time.

They tell you loudly. Time's up! We hugged each other, we cried again. Somebody told us to separate. Okay, it's time to go.

And I stepped back a pace and stood and watched her walking away, everyone filing out, the wives and the kids and the girlfriends, and it was like the last goodbye.

No one else was crying. Not the woman with the baby, not Jake's kids. For everyone else it all seemed quite normal. Just another day, another visit. Some were even making jokes and laughing.

Lilian was warned by the guards, as she went back through reception, that there were reporters and photographers waiting outside. Stepping out fast, some of them calling out her name, her responding instinctively.

– Yes?

– Lilian, how is Boris?

– Just let me go …

Within a few hours there were pictures of her leaving the prison in the German media and on the *Daily Mail* website. One photo where she had her hand to her face, trying to get something out of her eye, and the story being all about her crying desperately.

This had always been my life, since I was seventeen years old. Cameras everywhere you go, images of humdrum moments like shopping or walking down the street but also of small humiliations, of invented crises and captions plucked from an editor's imagination. It was not Lilian's life. It never had been, and she had never chosen it. It was hard for me but it was harder for her. I'm glad I didn't know in that moment that she went back to the flat and cried. I'm glad she didn't know that I went back to my cell and did the same.

Cell Dreams: The Love #2

April 2019. Lilian is in Rio de Janeiro. I'm in London. After two or three days, I call her. You know how it is, when you make your first one-on-one phone call to someone you like. Either it rolls, and you can talk when you're not in the same room, or it doesn't roll, and that's the end of it.

It rolls. We talk for forty-five minutes. It's long and it's relaxed and it's a deep conversation. When I put the phone down, I think: there's something here. Something I need to explore.

I know Rio a little. So I organise a drink for her at the Fasano hotel in Ipanema, one of the coolest spots. Pool and bar on the rooftop. We do a video call from there. She shows me the mountains in the distance, and the sunset. And when she comes back to Europe, we have lunch, and I think: this is when the ice breaks. This is when we kiss for the first time.

We decide to try going away together. I say, listen, we can't go anywhere in Germany, because we'll be followed, and I want to keep your privacy, and I want to keep my privacy too. I say, how about if I take you to Venice? We can do it incognito. We'll sit apart on the plane, and I have a friend who owns a hotel there, so he can keep it private.

We go on a Thursday and we come back on a Monday. I am really struggling with my knees. I actually can't walk

INSIDE

properly. We spend one night at the famous Harry's Bar, and we are sitting for two hours, the seats small and low. And when we come to leave, she's able to stand, and I am not. Like I literally can't. I don't know how to get up. The manager has to come and pull me out of my chair, and Lilian has to put my arms around her shoulders and almost carry me back to the hotel.

It's not a good sign for a man if you can't really walk. It's not a good feeling for a man who became accustomed to being the best tennis player in the world, dived full stretch at the net, chased down drop shots, ran the baseline. Who outlasted and outpowered everyone else. In a new relationship, you don't want to show your weaknesses. And yet we still manage to walk the streets of Venice, me limping and holding on to her, and apparently it doesn't matter to her. She asks me if I'm okay, and I don't want to say I'm struggling, or let's stop, I cannot walk. But I trust her, and I feel comfortable, and it's a sign of both if you let someone help you in one of the least flattering of situations.

When I was a kid growing up in Leimen, in the house at the end of the tram tracks, our television set would hold on or tune out to stations as the weather changed and the aerial moved. Sometimes you would be watching the football or tennis and the picture was clear and you could see everything you wanted. Other days there would be fuzziness and lines jumping around, bands of white and grey static making a mess and leaving you with no idea what was happening.

With time you learned where to point the aerial and how to tune in to the action. You could make the static clear and work out who that was supposed to be and what they were doing and why.

That was how it was in the first five weeks in Wandsworth. Sometimes I saw it all clearly. This man is dangerous, stay away from him. Here is a safe place, over there is not.

At other times the static raged and the signal disappeared. I could see shapes and outlines but I couldn't make sense of them. Only as the days went by did I start to tune in again and bring these new patterns into focus, to let my antennae capture the strange transmissions bouncing round this cramped echo chamber.

So it was with men who changed, at certain moments of the week or at the dark end of the day. Men who had been noisy going quiet and distant, men who had been invisible suddenly shouting and screaming and kicking up a storm. Eyes losing focus, limbs going loose, heads rolling back.

You didn't ask until you were told.

– You can get anything in here.
– What do you mean?
– Anything you want.

Alcohol was easy. People made it themselves with sugar and fruit and other things you could buy legitimately with your allowance from the canteen, the list Jake had told me about. A potent kind of schnapps was the most popular. On a Friday night you would see gatherings on every corner, water bottles being passed about and laughter and noise.

Officialdom seemed to turn a blind eye. It's Saturday the next day, so no one's getting up for work, and if you lie in bed all day until Sunday then no one's going to do anything about it. You want to keep going through Saturday? Over lunchtime the cells are open, so you can wander where you're invited and take a taste here and gather with the like-minded there. Go hard, push away all those boundaries. Sober up Sunday afternoon – Monday morning latest – before the sort-of working week begins.

That was the alcohol. One level of escape. Then there were the drugs. Weed, pills, heroin. Maybe you couldn't get needles but you could smoke it easily enough. You could get a lighter and a piece of tin foil and no one would bother you at all.

I wasn't tuned in. I just saw the changes in people I didn't know that well. Other stuff you couldn't miss. When you got told about spice, which seemed the most widespread drug, you looked around and suddenly it was everywhere. You had your sporty group – the boys in the gym, the ones who lifted big weights. They were their own gang. Then you had the spice guys. Entirely separate, away in a different place. The others told me why: it was cheap and very strong. But it was super-addictive, and it made you lose your mind. It's prison crack.

I was astonished, when these transmissions first decoded in front of me, because I was so naive. I didn't think I was, because I'd lived in a world of relentless daily competition and players who wanted to take me apart. I was one of them. Me going into every big final thinking: I want your mother to be the one crying tonight. Not mine.

It's not normal, until you live it. It doesn't make sense when you're not tuned to those signals. So when I saw wardens watching this all taking place and just looking away, I couldn't understand. This is illegal. We are in a place built by rules, and we are here because we broke them. Now these rules just disappear, every Friday night?

You got overdoses. Men dropping in the middle of the day. Sometimes you just saw the long comedown in the days before the next weekend. I didn't hang out with them, but you would notice them in the queue for the cafeteria, what they called the servery. You see they haven't showered in a week, and they really smell bad, and you innocently ask what happened to them, and you get told – they're the spice boys.

I never wanted to ask too many questions. It was just there, fizzing around in the air above my head. Tune in if you want to know the score. Turn away if you don't want to be dragged in.

It turned out they were right. When you looked around, you could get anything you wanted, if you really wanted it enough. It wasn't just that you could get a mobile phone. You could almost choose the model.

Sometimes they came in the prison version of internal mail. Up the back passage. Sometimes it was the wardens – someone taking a cut, someone with a weakness or a problem left vulnerable to a bribe or extortion. Stuff would be stashed in the cells of the weak and the compliant, the back panels of television sets opened up to hide electronics, holes gouged inside books or the soles of shoes. The power could be with those in uniform but it could be corrupted and directed by men who had always manipulated other men to their desires.

These unstructured boundaries I found disturbing. On a tennis court you understand all the parameters. The baseline doesn't move under your feet when you jump to serve; when you hit a flat forehand down your opponent's backhand side, the tramlines stay where the tramlines have been. In London or Melbourne or Paris or New York the dimensions are always the same. Certainty in straight lines and white-painted right-angles.

INSIDE

In Wandsworth the wardens were in charge until they weren't. You couldn't get breakfast but they would deliver you weed. Someone would insist you could trust them and be phoning their lawyer or friend with everything you revealed.

You had to work with the wardens. Fail there and you could lose your phone rights – and your TV and your visiting hours. Work too closely with them and you become a rat. The other prisoners develop a suspicion of you. Rumours fly in the corridors and queues, the cell parties and the shower block. You pick up your food in the servery and you don't really know what they've put in it. You watch both sides and you look for the clues and tells and you keep your true self for when the cell door is slammed shut at night.

Information is maybe the most valuable commodity of all. There was a slightly older Scottish prisoner who began approaching me in my third week. A strong guy, one you would see out in the courtyard doing push-ups and running. He was easy to talk to at first. He seemed connected, maybe sympathetic. Then it would be little nuggets handed over – I've heard they're going to move you; it's going to be seven weeks and then it'll happen.

Some of his information turned out to be true. I began to soften to him. Maybe this was someone I could use, if not a friend then a better source of insider secrets than anyone else I could find.

But there were things about him that jarred. Transmissions that came in clear and went fuzzy. I would see him exercising, and he was always loud. Shirt open, showing everyone how ripped he was, even though he was past fifty. Like he was a big figure in the prison, not intimidated by anyone else. Then

Wednesday became Thursday, and he seemed scratchy and itchy. Less chat, more stares. Friday night I'd pass him on the wing after dinner, and his limbs would be loose and his eyes out of focus. Hang on, he's one of the sport ones *and* he's one of the spice boys? Where are the boundaries with this guy?

I asked the Listeners, when the Scotsman's visits to my cell became more frequent. Who is this man? Does he really know this stuff? And Jake looked at Mo, and Mo looked at Jake, and they nodded and told me.

– Look Boris, he's in for life, so he will do anything. You're new, you don't know the rules, you don't look like you're dangerous. He will use your innocence to get things done.

Around the same time, four weeks in, I learned another thing. Most stories you hear from inmates are not true. They're bullshit. They're just trying to get under your skin, into your head. Just trying to access the little bit of heart that you have left or the little bit of empathy so they can use you for whatever it is they need. Especially when you're new.

It becomes exhausting, quickly. All this being on your guard all the time, always thinking about situations, analysing and strategising and second-guessing in a world they know intimately and you don't.

Why are they doing this to me?

What does he want?

Who can I ask?

So it leaks out, in different people. The older ones don't come out of their cells. They shrink into the background, either to hide or to run things when it looks like they're hiding. The drug abusers escape into their heads. The walls fall away, as long as it's in the lungs and bloodstream.

INSIDE

The younger ones do it another way. They can't take prison life, and they can't take the solitude. Where others wait for the cell door to slam and then at least feel safe, the kids go the other way. They're not used to being with their own heads all this time. The solitude doesn't comfort them. It begins to eat them up.

This was why the medical team asked me if I had cut myself deliberately. Self-harm happened, and it happened most to the new ones. Not necessarily to hurt themselves or end it all, but to get some attention, for a short while at least. Hey, I'm important here, I cut my wrists a little bit or I cut my face …

What they don't know, when they first do it, is that the medical care inside is terrible. A deep cut with a razor will be cleaned and bandaged but not treated so it heals nicely. The scars on your forearms, on your face? They'll be with you for life.

You felt the transmissions in the static all around, and you tuned in and tried to decode them. A kid with a cut on his wrist one week, a gouge on his thigh the next. Scabs on his chest, on his fingers.

Four weeks in, a new guy joined the Listeners group, maybe in his early thirties. Quiet, always staring around. He had a big gash on his neck, the bandages dark brown with dried blood. I didn't want to ask, but information always works its way around.

– Yeah, he's in for a long time. Couldn't handle it, tried to kill himself, or tried to make it look like he was trying to kill himself.

Maybe the Listeners were helping him. He told me about it another time, which I hoped was maybe a good thing.

– Yeah, I lost my mind, I got saved by the bell …

It was always messy and none of it made sense unless you were in there. These were not precision cuts. No clean lines or easy stitches. A knife fashioned from rough plastic or a blunt biro, jagged edges and torn skin. Scars always leaking and puckering.

You saw it each day, once you knew it was there. And when I did, it chilled me every time. It drew in my focus from the end of my stretch, whenever that might be, to the small notches in every new day, the routines and balance that might get me through. Don't be desperate. Don't be foolish. This is what you tell yourself, and you try to keep the rest of it pushed down and away.

I realised there must be eating disorders too. That desire for control in a place where you had none. For me it was just the hunger: in the morning, when I woke up; in the evening, when I lay there on the cramped bed and tried to go to sleep.

It wasn't because I didn't want to eat. It was that the food was so bad it was hard to get it in. You'd hear there was pasta and think, great, I was a tennis player in the 1980s and 90s, I've eaten a lot of pasta in a lot of places, this will be fine. And you would get a spoon of it dumped on your plate, and it would all be mashed up as if they'd boiled it overnight, and on top would be a sauce that was just cold. Maybe cooked at some point, you didn't know. Then they'd ask if you wanted rice and potatoes with it, and you would say yes because you were so hungry, and then you'd think, is this right, having mashed pasta and mashed potato and mashed rice all together?

Your answer was simple: I'm so hungry I must eat. You'd hear there were sausages, and the naive part of my brain would imagine a great Bavarian wurst, a big curling ring of something spicy. I'd push that image away and think instead of a fat British sausage, bursting with meat. Fatty but good fatty. My empty stomach sending fantasies to my brain. Then I'd see what lay in this great silver vat, and I didn't recognise it as sausage. Some burnt black, others pink and raw. Grey lumps, when you cut it open.

When Mo was there serving in the kitchen he would keep guiding me. Other times you don't want to cause a problem. You don't want to be the difficult one. So I would pick anything I was supposed to and try to remember how it had been the week before, because while Monday's menu was slightly different to Tuesday which was slightly different to Wednesday, Monday's was always Monday and Wednesday's was always Wednesday.

There was never enough to eat. In four weeks I lost seven kilograms in weight, and this as a man whose life had pretty much become sedentary. You don't burn many calories lying on your bed for fourteen hours a day. But no alcohol, no sweets, no chocolate. I could see that Lilian noticed, when she came for her second visit, and we dealt with the stress of it by trying to turn it into a joke. Boris, you look lean, maybe we should ask if you can stay in longer ...

The big treat was supposed to be Fridays. They told me we'd have pizza. Because of my old life, I imagined ... well, a pizza. Maybe 12 inches rather than 18, and obviously not a perfect crispy base like you're in Rome or San Lorenzo in London, and probably just cheese and tomato, but still a good meal. Something to look forward to each week.

And of course it was just two slices. Two cold slices, cooked in some distant period in the past, left out to go colder and solid and hard to chew. But it was pizza, and it was better than anything else, and after those two slices you really wanted two more. You weren't going to get them, so you learned the next time to eat very slowly. Partly to make the small pleasure last, partly to prepare your stomach for the reality. This is all we're having, digest it gradually for me, will you?

Something else around food. In that first month – actually, for some time afterwards – I never liked to eat with everybody else.

In those days I was only really at peace inside my cell. The one place with some privacy, with some security. While I was eating I wanted to enjoy those fifteen or twenty minutes of peacefulness. I didn't want to talk to anybody, I didn't want to be looked at, I didn't want to ask any questions. Only later do you form friendships. It took months until on weekends I might get invited to another cell where an inmate had cooked something himself. Then you would understand that eating together is a treat, and it's a sign of respect, and that's good too.

Until then I mostly ate alone. Pretty much everybody else ate in the servery. I hoped none of the others would think I was doing it for the wrong reasons – because I felt above their company, or didn't feel I belonged. I just wanted to keep it low key. I never wanted to hear the whispers: that German guy's coming to the servery, look at him, where's he going now? So I stared at the floor and only looked up to see what they were putting on my plate, and then I looked at the floor all the way back to my cell, and that was my lunch done.

You build your routine, or the routine builds you, one or the other. The Listeners showed me how the canteen menu worked. Fill in a form at the start of the week, make sure you have the funds in your allowance. I bought myself that apple for breakfast each day, and had it with an instant coffee, once I figured out the kettle.

It's hard to admit it, even now. But until Jake showed me, I didn't know how the kettle worked – an ordinary kettle, not some special issue prison one. At home I would have espresso. You don't make that yourself, you put pods in the machine, or you order it in a café, or when you're in a hotel. I never really drank tea unless I was ill, and then I would ask my partner. So when I first saw my kettle, I thought it might be for soups, or to store water. I didn't know how to make the water hot. The strangest things, the things you learn about yourself and what you can and cannot do because before you were never forced to.

Cell Dreams: The Lost Years

It's late 1999. I'm finished with playing tennis. This is okay; I'm ready for it. I'm tired. I just need something to fill the gap. And it's a big gap, so I like the answers this man I'm meeting is giving me.

We're in Dusseldorf. The man is called Hans-Dieter Cleven. Grey hair, late fifties, super successful businessman.

It's this last bit I like about him. I know about tennis. I don't know about business. But I want to learn, and he's offering me a fifty-fifty stake in his company Völkl, which makes tennis gear as well as ski gear, so this is all good, right?

And it is all good, at the start. I have no financial obligations, I think. I have no risk. The only thing I do have is my name.

I feel I can trust him, business-wise. He's made a lot of money. Track record is good. He's sort of retired, so he doesn't need my money, and this seems almost like a fun project to him. He's from Germany but lives in Switzerland, in Zug, and I can drive there from my house in Munich in three and a half hours.

For two years it's good. We're growing. I'm even testing the rackets myself. We start making tennis clothes. I enjoy his company. He's the elder statesman, twenty-five years older. He doesn't appear to need me, and I like that in people too.

In the classical business world I'm a beginner, so I need a mentor. I need somebody who is not dependent on me. When we meet, there is an agenda. We meet at nine o'clock, first point, second point. I've never worked like this. It's interesting for me. Little by little, I'm starting to feel comfortable.

Then one time, he takes me to one side. Boris, you're living in Munich, you know Switzerland is a tax haven. If you want to, I can help you move to Switzerland and we can start a company that looks after all your assets, and it can all be very good for you.

I'm divorced, at this point. I don't have a strong partner next to me. I don't have anyone else in my life who is more experienced, who is wealthier, who could lead me into this part of my second career.

My fault. I don't know yet that when money comes into play people react differently. For my age and what I've seen and done I'm an innocent. So I offer him a fifty-fifty partnership in the Boris Becker company to look after everything.

INSIDE

Here's how I'm thinking about it: I don't want to be confronted with the dull stuff – working in an office, reading every single document, going to every single meeting (in this way I'm still just a tennis player). I'm happy to make the money, and then I get to spend my money. I think I can learn from you how to make a lot of money. I got to the top in tennis, now I want to understand what it takes to do the same in business. My sign of faith is here, keep 50 per cent.

In this moment I think he likes it. We're talking millions of euros. But maybe this is already the beginning of the end. He hasn't realised how much I am making from my brand – from sponsorship deals, from commercial partnerships. Then he asks me again about moving to Zug, and I do, and very quickly I wish I hadn't, because I like places where things happen, and interesting people gather, and you can go and eat good food and see things you don't see elsewhere, and in Zug nothing ever happens except the feeling that you really want to be somewhere else.

So this is how conversations are now going.

– Cleven, I have to move.

– But the company stays in Zug.

– Then I will move to Zurich.

– But then there's a little more tax.

– Cleven, I have no life quality. In Zurich I will pay my 10 per cent more or 15 per cent more, but I'll have a life, a flat at the lake. I'll come every morning in the car to the Zug office in half an hour, and when I go home, I'll have a life.

– Okay, okay, okay.

But I think this is the start of his fear of losing control. He is controlling the money and giving me an allowance. He organises my bank accounts, my credit cards. If I need a larger payment, I call the office, and they make it happen. Okay Mr Becker, when should we transfer the money?

It changes again, after five years or so. He wants to set up a charitable arm. It's his thing, really, his idea and his baby, but he calls it the Cleven-Becker Foundation, and that's good for a while. First it's ten days a year, then it becomes twenty, and then thirty, and then I seem to be playing golf with strangers in some boring part of Switzerland every day I'm not actually working.

I'm getting older. I'm moving towards forty. Starting to meet new people, now my divorce feels a long time ago. Spending more time in London, spending more time in Miami, very little time in Switzerland. Getting married, for the second time, in 2009 (which is its own painful story), but now there are no personal strings between Cleven and me.

Which leads, as the new decade begins, to another conversation.

– Listen, no hard feelings but I can't do this, I have to let you know. The time I'm spending on this, I need to work, I have to make a living, I'm not as rich as you. I will stop with your charity and then also take my name away.

This is when it degenerates. Meeting once maybe every six or eight weeks, always cold, always frosty. Then, when he realises I have other business interests away from his, the tone changes again.

– Boris, you owe me money.

– What?

– You owe me a lot of money.

INSIDE

– You mean the money that I gave you? Which money are you talking about?

He isn't talking about £100,000. This is millions. He's claiming he's loaned me 40 million Swiss francs.

– Dieter, I mean, what are you talking about? I know you don't drink but you must be drunk …

So lawyers get involved. The story of my life. It goes to court; he makes a technical error with his documents, appeals, and so we go to court a second time. In November 2018, the Higher Court of the Canton of Zug, Switzerland dismisses his appeal. He's ordered to pay court costs of 60,000 euros and give me 60,000 euros for my legal fees.

He's tried twice; both times he has failed. I think: this is over. It's a shame it ended like this, but it's done. Now we can move on.

I don't know what's coming next. How could I know what's coming next?

Loneliness is a peculiar thing, when you're in prison. It doesn't always strike when you're on your own. Sometimes on your bed you're okay: there's a sense of relief in the locked door between you and the rest of it out there. You have your thoughts and your memory, and with time you learn to use them as a soft cushion to lie back on, a layer of insulation between you and this unreal world.

Sometimes it gets you in a crowd, because you're on intense alert, and even when you trust the person next to you, there's the person beyond them, and the ones behind you, and the ones you can't even see. Then you feel like it's just you against the majority, as if you're playing a match far from home in some hostile arena, and you know everyone there wants you to lose.

Sometimes it comes just when it shouldn't. When you've just been speaking to the people you care about most. You put the phone down or you walk away from the visitors' hall, and even as the sweet aftertaste lingers, the senses pick up on a sudden absence. Never is the contrast between love and indifference more obvious than when placed side by side.

I could recognise how hard it was for Lilian too, as each visit would come to an end, or in the reluctant goodbyes at the end of our calls. Up to the trial and throughout it we had been more of a team than ever before, the bonds between us tightened by necessity and the onslaught from the outside. Now she was in the flat on her own, and even a small place like that with one bedroom and one small living room can feel empty when it's just you and the echoes of a time now gone.

She found it difficult not being able to call if she had a question or an update from the lawyers about my possible prison transfer. It hurt her when she saw pictures of me in the German media in a Puma tracksuit with prison bars photoshopped over the image. She felt powerless, when she wanted to protect me. Maybe not physically, because we both tried not to talk about what could happen inside, but for my name and reputation. She didn't want this to be the final chapter in my story.

And it was never easy for her. They always say, when you get a prison sentence it's not just for the prisoner but for his family too. We felt that already, and we were about to feel it again.

The lease on our apartment in London was due to run until June. There hadn't seemed much point in extending it when we had no idea whether I'd be there or not. There were friends who had promised to help Lilian, if I could not. Now I was inside, we didn't hear from them so much.

Instead, Lilian got a call from the landlord.

– I want you to leave by the end of May.

– That's a month early – why?

– There's too much noise, with all these photographers outside the building each day. The neighbours have complained. It's not good for property prices. It's not good for anyone.

Paradoxically, now I was in Wandsworth, I had more certainty about where I would sleep each night than she did. We needed to find her somewhere new to live. We needed a place to store my things. And we needed to do it all in secret, so the paparazzi wouldn't just follow Lilian as she left and begin the whole dance again in a new location.

I tried to call some of the people who had promised so much. So did Lilian. We didn't hear back.

It felt like a betrayal. When someone you've known for years, who said they'd help you out when you were at your lowest ebb, instead comes out with excuses – oh, I can't do it now; actually, I'm super busy at the moment – you see them as you have not wanted to see them before. And those were the ones who replied. Others didn't. True colours on display, everywhere you looked.

It took a long time, but then one friend came through. He found Lilian a place in Canary Wharf, and he got the move done in secret, when Lilian was elsewhere and the photographers were on her tail. The friend said: this place is there for as long as it's needed. You're like my brother, it's nothing, it's no problem. Lots of people had said that to me, but he was one of the very few to act on it.

Lilian took it all on. The legal enquiries and conversations, the house move, the names and the deals. The link-ups with my children and my wider family. Organising for the immigration lawyers to come and see me in person.

Now a clearer message began to come back. You are a German citizen, correct. You will be moved.

But they couldn't tell me when, and they couldn't tell me where. They couldn't even tell me if this was the final time, or if I might be moved again and again.

This is the truth of prison. Very few people really know what's going on. As always, I would learn most from the inmates about what was happening. Not from the officials, not from my lawyers. Not from the outside world. From inside, always inside.

CHAPTER 5

Saffron Walden, Essex

Dear Boris

Ever since I saw you win your first Wimbledon as a very young man, I have admired you as a shining example to youth and a wonderful sportsman and human being.

   I am so very sorry that at this moment you are incarcerated in prison. I feel that you are mentally a very strong man and that you will cope very well in the circumstances that you find yourself.

   I am now an old man, but in my youth I spent many happy years in your country as a member of the British Army. I made some very good friends and have very happy memories of this time.

   I hope that the time passes quickly for you and that you will soon be a free man. Keep your chin up Boris and be the winner as you always have.

   Best regards

   Mike

Rumours, always rumours. You're going on this date. Then, from someone else: no, they haven't decided yet. You're being sent to HMP Maidstone. You're going to HMP Morton Hall. No you're not.

All I knew was that the big decision had been made by the system. I would be going to a prison for foreign nationals to serve out the rest of my sentence. No open prison, no day release. No ankle tag but no lunch dates with Lilian either.

So you wait, and you try not to obsess, and you wait some more. And then suddenly it happens. Monday morning, 23 May, almost a month after I had arrived. Heading back to my cell, after a meeting with my lawyers. Jake and Michael waiting outside: Boris, you've got half an hour to pack your things …

They don't bring you a case or a trolley. It's just a couple of plastic bags. The impersonality and impermanence of that cell had started to feel like home; pulling my clothes from the shelves, the old ones and the new ones Lilian had brought me, and grabbing my books and toothbrush felt profoundly unsettling. Yet I had no time for reflection, and even less to say goodbye to these men I had not known at all five weeks ago, but who but had helped and advised me, and saved me, sometimes, from things I didn't even know existed.

I heard something else on the wing telegraph. Huntercombe. Not from the officials. As I had already discovered, they don't like you to know, in case you get organised and get the insiders preparing the ground for you. I didn't know how to spell it and had no idea where it might be, but I could phone Lilian quickly and tell her.

INSIDE

— Lilian, I'm not certain this is right, but this is what I'm hearing, and I'll call you first thing when I get there.

It's your arrival reversed, when you leave. Your two plastic bags going through a scanner. Back into reception with a couple of prison officers, into the waiting hall with ten or so other prisoners. Two of them had been in Huntercombe before. I didn't ask why but they started to tell me how it was anyway. And that felt important, to put some images to the name. To downsize it from a place of unknown dangers to an institution of rules and routines, to hear about the sort of men I might meet there.

Into a white van that looked exactly like the white van that brought me to Wandsworth. Six cells inside it, all very small. Pulling out of the gates, onto Trinity Road down towards the Thames, and then it became hard to see where we were going and impossible to know where we might stop.

We drove for an hour. I guessed from the noise of the engine, the constant speed and the absence of tight bends that we were on a motorway. I tried looking out of the tiny round window with its darkened glass, and at one point thought I could make out a blue sign with 'Oxford' in white lettering.

Glancing at my cheap little Casio wristwatch. An hour and a half, two. Idle thoughts in an unsettled mind. What happens if, I don't know, a couple of people stopped a car in front of us and tried to get me out? This wouldn't be so difficult, if you were organised. Yes, there are two police officers in the front of the van, and I don't know if they're armed, probably they are, but two against five or six is going to be easy.

Your brain spins again. Okay, let's say you escape. Then what? Where are you going to go, where are you going to run to? Me with my gout and hip replacements and dodgy knee and bad ankle, how was I going to move? Me in the countryside, stumbling across fields, failing to get over hedges. Finding a village and the first person you see points at me and says, hey, aren't you that tennis player?

Thinking of all these options, in quite a rational way. And then realising: there are no options. I am not in control. They have chosen. Not me.

Cell Dreams: The Mistake

It's 2013. Things are looking ... maybe not so good. My money is ... let's just say it could be working better.

I am asset rich but cash poor. I have a house in Mallorca, a finca, but I'm not living there and it's never really been finished. I need money for my rent, for my bills, for my kids. My earnings are not keeping up with the demands of the lifestyle I've built. A house in the Mediterranean, no matter how big the pool or how beautiful the views, is bricks and red roof tiles.

So I borrow money from a private bank in the City of London called Arbuthnot Latham, borrowed against my image rights and commercial contracts. My accountants in London, Saffery, have done the introductions and the deal. Here's how it works: the bank loan me 4.5 million euros. I have five years to pay this back, plus interest.

I have a plan. If I can get the finca fixed up, it'll be worth around 10 million euros. Sell that and I can pay everyone off. I'll be free. I can start again.

INSIDE

Looking around for help, asking friends and business acquaintances, I meet a woman who owns a private equity company. The largest investor in it is a guy called John Cauldwell, a British billionaire. The woman calls him a 'business angel'. He's made his money in mobile phones, and when I meet him it's clear he likes tennis, and he likes to enjoy himself. The way it's put to me is that he'll loan me another 1.2 million euros, and there'll be interest payments, but it's good, because I'll support his charity and go to a few big nights and everyone will be happy. We can use the finca as security.

I know this is a lot of money, but this is the plan. With his loan the finca will be fixed. It'll be sold. I'll be free. Right?

Cauldwell seems okay. I know I'd better be nice to him, so we invite each other to a few places and we wine and dine each other and he's telling me about his business empire and I'm telling him a little about my world.

He invites me to his superyacht in the south of France. It's incredible. It's called Titania. *On board there's a sauna, a massage room and a beauty salon. There's a gym and there's a personal trainer. There's a swim-up bar on the main deck; there's even an inflatable waterpark with a 13-metre high waterslide. On a boat. I know. There's five times as many crew members as guests. Not just a head chef, but a sous chef too.*

This is when the sinking feeling kicks in. At first the interest rate from Arbuthnot Latham has been manageable – 5 per cent.

But there's trouble ahead. I'm losing sponsors and I'm losing endorsements. My public image is not where it was. Endless tabloid stories, one shit headline after another.

Things start falling apart, in Germany and then everywhere else. Broadcasting is okay. They still want me to talk about tennis. I still want to talk about tennis. The rest of it is terrible. I'm losing big contracts early. Mercedes I've been with for ever, but now they say they have a different marketing plan, going forward. I'm not making any new contracts to replace the ones that disappear.

So I need more money. I have to borrow more from the bank. Another million, then another. With every increase the interest jumps higher: 10 per cent, 20 per cent.

By the end of 2015, the start of 2016, I'm paying back lots of the loan, around 1.5 million euros. But when the interest rate is 25 per cent, the debt accumulates more quickly than you can bring it down.

Sleepless nights. Lying there staring at my bedroom ceiling. I can't see my way through this. I can't see the end.

It's putting stress on my marriage with Sharlely. This life is not the one I once had. The nice stuff round the edges, the days where you have time and energy for your wife and your son? That's all gone. All I am now is a ball of worry. My guts are tight. My face is lined. I'm never home, because I'm always out there trying to fix things – meetings, new introductions, anywhere I can maybe bring in a few more euros.

All the time, the interest piling up. A leaking tap becomes an overflowing sink becomes a flood cascading through the floorboards.

Work on the finca is taking time, taking for ever. And Arbuthnot are becoming more aggressive. A new man in the credit team, a change in the language they use towards me.

INSIDE

They turn more aggressive again. I don't know where to turn next. So I give them the finca, this big house, as security. They take over John Caudwell's interest too. They add this to their own.

It still isn't enough for them. They try selling the house and they also have no luck. It's worse for me, because the interest is insane now. Every month, every week – fuck, every day – I owe more and have less.

They want to increase the pressure on me, so they make an application to the court about bankruptcy. There is a hearing in March 2017.

I'm standing on the edge of a high cliff. Everything is falling apart. Stuff I don't even own any more is costing me money.

I find a company that invests in distressed assets. The distressed part is perhaps more appropriate for me right now than the assets bit, but they seem friendly, and they seem interested.

The next hearing is due in June. We're ready to tell the judge the good news: okay, we have found a company that will buy the assets, but we need another three months to finalise the contracts. The sums, for a moment, look simple to me. Arbuthnot will get the finca. It's worth 10 million euros. That pays off the monstrous amount I have outstanding to Arbuthnot. It pays off the distressed assets company. I start again.

I'm not there in the courtroom. They don't want me there. No need to give evidence, I am told. I don't even know whereabouts in London the hearing is.

I'm not worried. I've been told not to worry. There's a plan in place. This is all going to be sorted, right?

A slowing of the van, an impression of turns and decelerations. Brakes and gear changes and a halt. I was surprised by what I saw when I stepped outside. I was expecting another Wandsworth, an old Victorian building, dark and intimidating. High walls and suburban streets beyond. Huntercombe was different. Not modern, but maybe from the 1970s. Two storeys, wire fences rather than stone, green trees around and fields. An incongruous thought: it's kind of beautiful round here …

They searched us again in reception. I didn't even think about it this time. Maybe they were a little friendlier than Wandsworth, or maybe I was just used to it all. A veteran after five weeks. Waiting in a different entrance hall, noticing it was now the evening, recognising that it didn't matter how long this all took, because everything takes a long time, and you have these hours there for them to use as they wish.

Same body search, same issue with my Puma holdall. I passed it over without question this time. Take it, I'll see it again whenever I leave. As they walked me through I thought, it's more modern, this place. Not as filthy. This could be okay.

My cell felt smaller, when I was taken there by a severe female officer. A lower ceiling in a less ancient building. On the first floor at the end of one long wing. No great high landings as in Wandsworth, no nets stretched across underneath to catch the fallen. I was almost excited now, because this was something new. Hoping Huntercombe might be a little easier for me, getting the impression it was less dangerous and less anchored to a cruel penal past.

I didn't realise at that point that I would have to start again from scratch. That the privileges I had built up in Wandsworth

INSIDE

would not transfer with me westwards across the country, that the teaching maths and English and the trust in me as someone whose cell door could be unlocked each morning and afternoon had disappeared in transit.

I was focused more on my new cell. I noticed the low ceiling. Not a bunkbed this time but a single bed, by the wall on the left, same grey metal frame and blue mattress with its rubber cover. Light yellow walls, covered in scribbles and old phone numbers and jokes and wild rants. The toilet right behind the door, sink next to it. Not as much mould in the corners.

The window was a little bigger than my old cell. Maybe a foot wide and half as much again high. A layer of glass, a set of metal bars, a second layer of glass beyond. No curtains at all, just the springtime evening light coming in.

I looked at the trees, the woods. I could see a lot of green. That felt good. Okay, there's the evening sun, I must be facing west. Then I looked again at all those trees, and thought, if I can see out, then others will be able to see in. When the paparazzi find out I'm here, they're going to have a very easy time taking pictures.

Your first night is always uncomfortable. No surprises this time. I put out everything I had – the clothes on their shelves, the shoes under my bed. The Karl Lagerfeld book and the Barack Obama autobiography, the exercise books and the red biro and black biro. The list of names and phone numbers.

But always the shock of the new, the unexpected. The guards came the next morning and changed my cell to the opposite side of the wing. I was not the only one thinking about security. So I lost the trees and the evening sun, but I gained a courtyard view and with it the sun each morning. When you are awake early and there's nothing to do each night but rest and sleep, that's just fine.

I was also right at the end of the corridor. Semi-detached, if you want to look at it that way. I wanted to meet the man opposite and the one next door, but this was not like Wandsworth. My door was only unlocked from 11am to midday and then again from four to five. Servery time only.

That first day I assumed this was merely a beginning. They must know I'm already enhanced, right? I'm one of the trusted ones, I've got a job, I've got some privileges. By the third and fourth day of staring at that immovable grey cell door I was realising maybe I was wrong.

You can always hear the wardens' keys. The keys are the one sound that's consistent, from prison to prison, from morning to night. The staff unlock one side after the other so the whole wing gets opened in five minutes, and the first time 11 o'clock comes round and you hear the keys outside your door, you're initially very nervous because you know you're going to be meeting your new inmates.

I stepped out and looked left. The cell next to me was exactly the same dimensions as mine, but there seemed to be two men in there. One of them short and skinny, one of them enormous. It was the same in the cell opposite. Two men that looked maybe Turkish to me, one on the bottom of a bunk bed, the other on the top one.

You don't say hello, my name is Boris. I knew that now. You don't try to shake hands; you don't even make eye contact. The important thing is the first impression you give. So you put your shoulders back. You want to appear strong and tough, almost arrogant, like you don't give a shit. You keep your chin up and you look around a little bit, and you're careful what you wear too. It's hard to dress down in prison, but that's the strategy. Not the new polo shirt Lilian had eventually got through for me in Wandsworth and not the nice Puma trainers, but an old grey sweatshirt and the shoes I walked in with.

I was very sparse with my conversations, that first morning and in the first week. I stayed within myself. But I did keep checking out my new neighbours when I could, and the guy in the cell next to mine was hard to keep your eyes from. Not the skinny one. You could have missed him if he turned sideways. It was the big one; so big he was almost a giant – not just tall, but stacked with muscle like a body-builder.

They were an odd combination, these two. Both white guys, both speaking the same language, one I didn't recognise. As I walked behind them on the way to the servery that first day it was almost like looking at a father and his teenage son, except when they turned round they were both in their early twenties.

That wasn't the strangest thing. It was the giant's head. It was like someone had stuck it on his neck at the wrong angle, so he appeared to be looking at the world in diagonal. A picture that didn't make sense.

I looked and I thought and I wondered. Was he born like this? Did it happen in a fight, or has he been in a car accident?

I stood behind him and his cellmate in the queue for food trays at the servery, and I wanted to ask but was afraid to. By nature I'm curious. I'm interested in people and their stories. But I didn't want to disrespect him. Maybe it was something he was embarrassed about or didn't want to talk about.

He didn't know me, and I didn't know him at all. But then … two, three days go by. You're doing the same routine every lunchtime and early evening for dinner, and you're walking the same corridors in the same order, and you have no one else in the world to talk to. So there comes a time when you begin a little conversation about the weather or the football. I listened, and it was clear the giant liked sport. His favourite team was Real Madrid, and he loved Ronaldo. So we began to talk a little about that, and about Manchester United and Chelsea, and when we did I noticed he was actually very softly spoken. Good English, but as a second or third language.

And then, ultimately, it's an odd thing, but you are in prison, so pretty quickly after the small talk one of you is going to ask the big question.

– Why are you inside?

You're all the same in prison because you're all in prison, but because you're all the same you search for definition in a blurred landscape. It gives you outlines when you're all merging into one.

– He's inside because he's a drug dealer.

– He's inside because he killed people.

– He's inside because he's a paedo.

After a couple of days of talking in the lunch queue, the giant told me, without me even asking.

– Yeah, I was growing weed on my balcony.

Now I was confused. Is that still illegal in England? I mean, in California you can smoke it, in Germany too now. I thought, how big is this guy's balcony? He's got a proper weed-selling business, not just growing for his own kicks? He's got a flat big enough for a plantation?

It's not a one-way discussion. There was always going to be the same question for me. In Wandsworth nobody really knew what I'd done, exactly. And it was a complicated story – complicated for the jury, for the judge, the prosecution. Easier to be vague.

– Yeah yeah, I had a tax issue …

That was the wording I chose. But there is always another question that has to follow.

– How much time did you get?

The giant had been sentenced to nine years. So the more he spoke about it and the more we spoke about other things, the more sympathy I felt and the more curious I became about exactly how he ended up here and why he looked the way he did and why, too, he was so angry all the time. Not just prison angry, because I had seen lots of those sort of angry men around me by now – tired, frustrated, worn down. This was an anger he could hide, most of the time, and one never near the surface when you were talking football, but something that came smashing out of him in sudden explosions around certain situations and particular inmates. One moment he was calm and quiet and talking to nobody. The next he was throwing someone against a wall and using his fists and elbows and knees and getting hauled away by the guards. All of this with that youthful face and docile expression and soft gentle voice.

His name turned out to be Thomas. A straight, normal name. I called him Baby Hulk (to myself). That's who he reminded me of. And we both had the same problem, in that moment, which was that one of the main officers on the wing was a real prick.

I thought at the start it was just that he didn't like me. Always telling me to go back to my cell before anyone else. Not letting me go back for food if there was spare, when those around me were doing exactly that. A big guy, physically, a man I sensed knew the old me outside, and didn't like it, and because of it would treat me worse. A man who loved to say no.

I asked around. It sounded like he was one of the difficult ones. Baby Hulk was stacked with muscle because he loved going to the gym. This officer liked to stop him, or find a reason he could only go once a week. Not to prove a point, but just because he could. To exert some power. To make things worse for someone else.

It's all about respect when you're in prison. From the inmates, from the officials. Some of it is real and some of it is imaginary, but it all matters. And this guard showed no respect to me, and none to Baby Hulk. It was like we were pieces of shit on his shoe to be flicked away. The weather was getting warmer now, spring gradually turning into summer. This man seemed to take a pleasure in locking me up for twenty-two hours a day. In how little respect he could show me, in how little respect I deserved in this new place.

You spend that much time by yourself and it becomes a test of who you are and how much you can cope with. But this was worse than Wandsworth now. Worse than the first week of it all. I had been enhanced there. I had Jake and Charlie and I had my maths and English classes.

Here? I was nobody. I didn't expect to be Boris Becker, tennis player. I was sort of reconciled now to a new identity as a prisoner. As another man who thought he should not be inside but was and so what did it matter. But I did expect fairness. I did want to talk to other men. I wanted to see the sky and smell the grass and feel it under my feet, sometimes.

The officer liked to make it difficult for me to get food. He would hold me back as long as possible, tell me the kitchen was closed. When another inmate came in later than me he would let them through. Sometimes he would tell me I could no longer pick from the options. Take that one, it's all they have left.

I'd come across people like him before. I had a way of trying to deal with them. If you want to treat me like this, I don't see you any more. I walk past you like you're not there. I can listen when you say something, but I'm not acknowledging you.

I didn't know if it was going to help with this guy, but it was what I decided to do. And, in the same week, I met an officer who could not have been more different. This would be the one who ended up changing my life, not the prick.

His name was Andy Small. About my height and age, very fit guy, a lot of muscle. Light brown hair, a thick beard. Always in shorts.

He was in a navy blue tracksuit, which set him apart from the other officers in their black and white uniforms. But there was something else about this guy that made him stand out. A distinct outline, a confidence. A lot of keys on him, as if he had access to places other officers did not. He looked and spoke like a tough guy – the prison talk, a lot of swearing.

I was in the corridor, walking behind Baby Hulk and Tiny Tim on the way to lunch, when he first came up to me and took me to one side.

– I run the gym. I know who you are. Eventually, you're going to come to work with me.

This was different. Not trying to push me around. Not messing up small moments in a world where you only have the small moments. A couple of days later he came to my cell around ten in the morning. A time when I was lying on the bed, away in my own thoughts, nothing to do but cell dream.

– Boris, I'm going to show you around. I'm going to show you the gym.

Cell Dreams: The Fall

June 2017. I'm in the car when I hear the news. Doing a television job in Halle, Germany, where the grass court tournament is each summer. The one Roger used to win every year.

A call on my phone, on my way to Dusseldorf.
Boris, it's bad news. They made you bankrupt.
What do you mean? We have a plan. We can pay them. They know this.
Yes, it's impossible to understand. But it's happened.
The next morning I have a press conference to announce my new TV show with Eurosport, Matchball Becker. *All night I've been watching CNN news, BBC news, German news. All leading with the same story: Boris Becker – the wunderkind, the former Wimbledon champion – is bankrupt.*

I go to the press conference. Ten o'clock in the morning. Everybody is speechless, looking at me like I'm a ghost. Like I shouldn't be there. Then the questions start. Every single one about the bankruptcy.

– Guys, guys I'm here to talk about Eurosport.
Doesn't matter, of course. When I'm back in London, I meet the official receiver for my case. I'm told I will meet

INSIDE

the trustee for my bankruptcy in early September. My personal bank accounts are frozen. Okay. This makes sense. But I'm told I can use my company account for my expenses until that meeting in September – for food, for travel. If someone invites me somewhere I can go, as long as they pay.

It is catastrophic, if I look at it one way. I read it in the media every day. Such a juicy story. The millionaire big shot who lost it all. It's triumph and disaster, together. He must be a fool, right? Yet at the same time my company is doing well again. Well enough to pay my rent, my expenses.

I ask my lawyers. How do I live, now? My bank accounts are frozen. How do I put food on the table? How do I make my maintenance payments to my first wife and my second wife? How can I pay for my children?

And my female lawyer says, you're okay. Your company is solvent.

I don't know then how bad this advice is. I trust my lawyers. I pay all the bills I have to pay, the agreements I'm bound to, from my company's accounts. All the financial obligations I have every month.

Still today I am speechless when I think about what happened next. Whoever I tell the story to. I don't even want to speak about it to anyone in here, because people won't believe me, and I'm tired.

But that's what happened, and that's what I did. That's how it all came falling down.

No one had opened my door at this time so far. I was grazing on the empty hours, reading my books for a second time, watching the shadows slowly move across the walls. Of course I went with Andy.

I was yet to see Huntercombe properly. I didn't know the layout, hadn't been to the other wings. The system of Listeners here was not as comprehensive as Wandsworth; I wouldn't meet one for a couple of weeks. We went down the stairs from my level to the ground floor. Along the corridors, through what felt like a series of connected cross-shaped buildings, my cell and my wing out on the far reaches of it all.

The gym was at the end of a long straight corridor. Andy showed me through a big metal and glass door. I looked to our right and saw a sports hall. On the left I could see through another door into a small kitchen. A few more paces and I could glance into the locker rooms.

They were busy. Men who didn't look so angry. Men who weren't lying around, away in their own restricted fantasies. And then we walked into the gym itself, and for the first time in that place I felt the draw of the familiar and a wave of comfort from my long-ago life.

The roof was high. Maybe two storeys. You notice these things when you spend a lot of time staring at the low ceiling of your own room. A couple of rowing machines, a couple of static bikes, then a lot of free weights on racks at the back. Two Olympic bars for lifts and squats, a couple of weights machines – a chest press, a shoulder station, a leg-press machine.

There were posters up on the walls. The classics, the ones from muscle gyms in the 1980s. Arnold Schwarzenegger, in his posing trunks and tanned brown and squeezing a move so his tendons pumped and his veins stuck out. Denzel Washington, which I wasn't expecting. Then there were the words. Sentences and quotes: positive and inspiring and philosophical.

'It is not what happens to you but how you react to it that matters.'

'You have power over your mind, not outside events. Realise this, and you will find strength.'

That was the good stuff. The bad started with the smell. Sweat, fresh and old. No air-con, a small door at the end which was shut and no breeze coming through. Soft rubber floors that looked worn out and trampled.

I liked it. It reminded me of all the gyms I had ever been in. Maybe not the best equipment, the most flattering lighting. Definitely not enough stuff to go round. But dumbbells and big disks of metal and the clang and echo of it coming together and being reassembled and dropped back down onto that battered floor.

This was where Andy told me again: in a couple of weeks, this is where you'll be working. Then he said something else, in the same confident, no-nonsense way.

– You see these quotes? They're from the Stoics. It's a class I teach, and I think it's going to be one for you.

All these hours on my own in my cell, and now someone talking to me like they knew me. Like they had plans for me. Like they cared. I felt an unfamiliar emotion kicking up again inside. It felt like ... hope.

We kept walking, and I kept listening. He told me the names of each wing as we walked through them. He told me who was housed there, the nationalities and the schools of crime. This wing is called Howard. This one is Mountbatten. Yours is called

Patterson. It's not as dangerous as the other wings, Boris, we put you there on purpose.

On the way back to my cell we stopped to talk to a middle-aged woman coming the other way. The two of them obviously got on. She introduced herself as the head of the prison library. Then she said a very Andy thing too.

– Tomorrow, Boris, I will pick you up and show you the library, because I want you to work with me there.

The next day, again close to the 10am dead zone, she did pick me up. And the library wasn't huge, but it was good. A lot of books, a lot of old videotapes – VHS, like I was a teenager all over again.

There too was a really sweet guy from Ghana called Jeffrey. He told me his brother was also in Huntercombe, a big figure in the gym. Suddenly I could see a future for me. Okay, this is Friday. The start of next week, I'm going to have two jobs. I'll be in the gym, and I'll be in the library. My morning will be full and my afternoon will be full. No more on my own in that cell with its low roof and tight walls.

Monday came. I got myself ready. Good clothes. A wash and smarten up. Nothing happened.

Tuesday. Same routine. Nobody came.

On Wednesday, Andy opened my door. Right, here we go. But he wasn't coming to pick me up. He was here to explain.

– Okay Boris, they're being difficult here with you. Trust me, you're going to get what I told you, but you might have to wait a couple more weeks until you're enhanced.

– But Andy, I was enhanced in Wandsworth.

– Yeah, but it's different here. They're difficult with you. Leave it with me. I'll put in a good word but you'll have to stay patient.

INSIDE

So then I was back to it. Out briefly for lunch and that prick of a prison guard trampling on the small moments. Out again for dinner, and more food you didn't want but needed to eat. One day passing and the next beginning just the same and the day after merging in and nothing changing and nothing to set any of them apart.

A week in, I asked myself a question. Okay. How are we going to pass the time here? Hmm. Good luck.

If the gym had to wait, I could exercise in my cell. I paced it out. Two steps wide, maybe four steps from door to window. Same dimensions as Wandsworth, but with that low ceiling bearing down on you.

I created a little lap. Maybe the shortest lap I had ever exercised on, but this was the only lap I had, so it would do.

I began walking. Half an hour clockwise, half an hour anti-clockwise. Half an hour walking 12-metre laps kind of drags quite quickly, so I reversed it another way. Backwards walking, clockwise, anti-clockwise.

All those tennis courts I ran round! The baselines I tracked, the sprints I made from the leap of my serving motion to the net for a volley. The patches of green Wimbledon grass that turned brown under the soles of my shoes and then wore away to hard dirt. The bottomless blue skies overhead in Melbourne, the vast open stands at the Arthur Ashe Stadium in Queens, New York. The beaches in Monaco, the parks of central London. All these places I had pushed my body and been free and never even known it, really.

Hey, I could use the in-field part of this lap …

Lying on my back, doing sit-ups. Lying on my front, working my back. I tried push-ups for the first time in a long time, but a life of tennis is bad for the elbows, when you get past your half-century, so I held the Barack Obama book in my right hand and the Karl Lagerfeld book in my left and bicep curled them as if they were very well written weights. That's the thing about the incredible life of a president or fashion icon. There's a lot of words and a lot of paper and a nice heavy cover to hold them all inside.

I did the whole thing twice a day. Once in the morning, once in the afternoon. The highlight of my day, going dizzy in the outer edges of a concrete block somewhere in the English countryside.

Things I found out later. Henley-on-Thames was only seven miles or so away to the south-east, with its rowers and boathouses and pubs on the water. Wallingford was about the same in the other direction, all medieval buildings and small streets. You couldn't find two more film-set English towns, rolling in old money and comfortable charm. And here I was in a world in between but sharing nothing of that wealth and insulation from all the bad things in the world.

Something else: there had been a prison at Huntercombe since the Second World War. Back then it had been an internment camp for German prisoners. Maybe it was a good thing I didn't find that out for a while. I needed good omens in this moment, not echoes from a darker past.

So I waited for Andy Small, and I waited for my luck to turn. When you play professional tennis, you lose your temper a lot, if you are like me, but you have to learn patience too. Just because you are losing doesn't mean you are going to lose. Just because you are going to lose doesn't mean you ever give up.

I would say to myself sometimes, when I was two sets and a break down and sitting on my chair by the net post between games with my head under a towel: okay, Boris, always play until the last point.

Now, lying on my bed, one day merging into another on an endless slow loop, I stayed with the same message. Head always at the end furthest from the door, sacrificing a view of the small window for the protective animal instinct of having your feet between you and anyone coming in. Feeling the slightest breeze coming through the vent on the window, fiddling around with it to let more air in and then accidentally breaking it in frustration so it was jammed open, but not wanting to complain because while it was so bad being stuck in here all night and all day, at least it was my cell I was stuck in, and I didn't have to move again and empty it all out and set it all up and find another neighbour who maybe wasn't as softly spoken and intriguing as Baby Hulk.

I still heard the whispers on the prison telegraph. Strange noises and rumours, stories that made sense and many that didn't. You would hear about inspections, unannounced and unwanted, inmates finding secret places for the private and illicit. Someone saying with certainty the inspectors would be coming tomorrow, someone else saying they were on Mountbatten wing the day before and were heading our way. If you had something to hide you did so. If you didn't you kept an eye out for the others, because the safest place to stash something that could get you in trouble is in someone else's cell. Don't leave your door ajar, don't invite anyone in. Don't accept unexpected gifts, don't take anything that seems too good to be true. One guy a few doors along offered me his radio, one day. I said yes. I could let a little more of the outside world in. And then Baby Hulk saw it happening, and shook his crooked head, and took it off me and gave it back. A radio is seldom just a radio, if the inspectors are coming calling.

Something else you heard about, in the lunchtime queues and in the corridor walks. Something that everyone found interesting in a prison holding only foreign nationals. You could stay in the UK and you could fight this system, and then one day they might let you out and you could stay here and try to start your life all over again, if you thought it might work out better second or third time around.

But there was another way. Deportation. I wasn't quite clear on how it worked or how you made it happen, but I liked the sound of the maths that seemed to come with it. If you agreed to go back to the place you were born – if you could, if you were safe there – then the talk was that you only needed to serve half your sentence here. You then couldn't come back to the UK for a certain amount of time. But you could get on with your life, rather than seeing it disappear in dizzy laps and same-same days.

The one I talked it over with was Baby Hulk. I didn't have anyone else yet. Thomas, you're in here for nine years. Now that's a harsh judgement for growing weed on your balcony. So the question is, okay, are you going serve it all and stay in the UK and fight, or are you going to get through your four and a half and then go back to Lithuania to start again?

At first he was certain.

– No, I want to stay, I want to fight. Everything I have is in the UK.

So I tried walking through the alternative with him.

– Thomas, maybe it would be better to be deported back to Vilnius. Your family is there. You will be free. You can travel to anywhere but the UK.

INSIDE

You look back when you're in your fifties and you realise, as your own years accelerate past, the luxury of time you had when you were younger and never even realised.

– Thomas, you're twenty-five years old. I know a lot of things have happened to you but your world is still open. You don't like it here in Huntercombe. Why would you want to stay here so much longer? Okay, you could stay in the UK. But half of the time you're on licence, meaning you can't work and you can't travel. How can you feed your family, how can you spend your days, how can you do anything worthwhile? Even though you're outside, it's not much better. The chances are high you're going to do something stupid at least once, something illegal, big or small, and then they'll catch you.

You know how it is. Sometimes you give advice to people, and you truly believe that's what you're doing, when actually you're talking to yourself. I could feel Huntercombe all around me – its rules, its lost and angry men, the ones who were in here for something and no one cared what happened next. We were numbers in a system designed to work at the slowest possible speed. Each day you encountered things that made no sense and didn't function, and no one seemed to do anything about it. It ground on in the same way: the same time your door was unlocked, the same time the keys turned again the other way. Same food, same corridors, same ceiling to stare at.

Who did it work for? I couldn't figure it out. It costs money to lock people up like this. To patch up old buildings, to not patch them up at all but push more men in. The longer a prisoner served, the more money it cost. The more money someone somewhere was making.

It was late May, more than five weeks into my new life, and I was still naive. Who did it work for? That didn't matter. We were just in there, and the days could blur, and people might not change, or maybe get worse, and almost no one cared.

All you could say about it was that when you found someone who did care, or someone who had cared and kept on caring, it was like the rays of the sun on a cold winter's morning. You still felt cold, but you could remember what it was like to be warm.

Cell Dreams: The Revenge

It's not done and dusted. That's what I don't realise about Cleven.

I am bankrupt. I'm paying my debts off. I think we're there, or close to being there. And then he contacts my bankruptcy trustee, Mark Ford, and he tells a different tale.

This Mr Becker, he owes me 40 million Swiss francs.

I'm really confused now. We've had two court judgements saying this isn't so. Cleven is not on my creditors' list.

But it all starts to drag, and it all starts to get confused and confusing.

My bankruptcy trustee wants an English translation of the Swiss court's ruling. There isn't one. I think he can use Google Translate; he doesn't.

Three months go by, four.

A couple of old and forgotten friends get back in touch and ask how they can help me. One has professional ties with various African countries. He mentions the Central African

INSIDE

Republic. He says the president, Faustin-Archange Touadéra, is in Paris next week and is keen to meet us.

I ask why I would want to meet him, and what good would it do. He says, the CAR is a poor country. They want to use your contacts and your connections to bring in outside investment. They want to build a national sports programme with your experience.

I've always been fascinated by the continent of Africa. I've always supported various charities there. I played tennis with Agassi in Johannesburg in front of Nelson Mandela to raise money for the great man's foundation. I worked on projects for the Laureus Sport for Good Foundation in Africa.

So my heart is open. I agree to a first meeting. We have good initial discussions. The president and his minister of foreign affairs ask me to join them at an official banquet in Brussels. There, they offer me the role of cultural and sports attaché to CAR. We'll have weekly calls and meetings. As part of that, I'll be given a diplomatic passport.

I've been insolvent for more than a year now. This new role is not me trying to escape that. It's not going to magically reverse the court judgement of summer 2017. It's not going to conjure away my debts.

For two months I call people. I make connections. Then my bankruptcy trustee says he wants to auction off my memorabilia. I'm not sure about this. I'd really like to keep some for my kids: trophies, old rackets, shirts. Then my friend Ben Emmerson, a high-profile human rights lawyer, says – you know what, Boris, you might have diplomatic immunity with this new role, the trustee cannot sell your trophies off unless you agree.

He suggests we ask for a court hearing and let the judge decide. We do. The judge green-lights the appeal. We just have to provide the diplomatic passport for his approval.

Here comes the catch.

We wait for the passport to arrive. It doesn't, for quite a while. I haven't paid anything for it, so I have no proof it actually exists. When it does finally turn up, it's quite clear something is seriously off. It hasn't been signed by the foreign minister. It's a fake. There are political plots going on, and I've been an unwitting pawn in someone's power game.

I feel disappointed. I feel frustrated. Once again someone's promised me something, and it's turned out to be wrong.

So we go back to court, and we tell the judge we've made a mistake. We withdraw our request to stop the auction, and we apologise. I tell the trustee we're going to give him everything he needs to make it work.

Meanwhile, I reach an out-of-court settlement with Arbuthnot, the private bank. The finca in Mallorca is finally sold for the amount I owe them. That takes time too, because it's a company based in London and one based in Spain, and Spain works a little slower than London. It's May 2019, now it's June.

They do the auction of my memorabilia. Trophies, medals, a replica of the Davis Cup. My US Open trophy from beating Ivan Lendl in 1989 raises £150,250; in total, we raise almost £700,000.

It's a weird feeling. I didn't pay for these trophies. I won them. But I didn't play for a piece of gold-plated metal; I played for the glory.

INSIDE

It's strange to me that someone would want something they haven't earned themselves. I would never want Michael Jordan's NBA championship three-peat ring, because I'm not a basketball player and I didn't beat the Utah Jazz in the finals. What's a trophy if it hasn't come from your own sweat and talent and hard work?

Still. Keep paying the debts, keep paying the debts.

July, August, no one seems to work. So it's not done yet, but it's near. In September I give Mark Ford all the documents. I can pay back the money I owe by the end of the year. We can get the bankruptcy annulled.

Arbuthnot Latham send Mark Ford a letter. It is short and to the point, and concludes with this line:

'We write to inform you that on 13 November 2019 we have agreed a settlement, whereby Arbuthnot has acquired ownership over the Mallorcan finca called Son Coll in full and final satisfaction of our claim. We therefore consider that as a result of this executed settlement, our claim against the bankruptcy estate of Mr Becker has been discharged, and no further actions or claims shall be undertaken by Arbuthnot against Mr Becker in this regard.'

This is settled. I am free. Until – a week or so later – the trustee decides to accept Cleven's claim that I owe him 40 million Swiss francs.

I ask him. Why have you accepted this claim?

He says he is satisfied with the explanation that Cleven's lawyers have given him.

Two more questions from me. Okay, hundreds of questions, but two of the key ones.

– You accept this, even though he's lost two court cases?

BORIS BECKER

– How do you expect me to pay 40 million Swiss francs?

I try meeting Cleven. He doesn't seem to realise this doesn't work for him either. He makes his claim in London through a bankruptcy case, and he can never get the money he wants. I can never get an annulment. We both lose.

Now I feel like a man drowning in soup. Everything around me is crazy. I think, how on earth can an English trustee accept a claim from Switzerland that lost in court on two occasions?

Tennis is black and white. There's a winner and a loser to every point and every game and every set. The result never changes. No one can look back two years later and say, okay, that drop shot actually went long, this game is reversed. No one looks back at me against Kevin Curren on Centre Court in 1985 and says, hold on, I don't believe the score in the third set tie-break, I'm going to accept Curren's claim he was the one who took it.

So now I'm lost in this difference between my old world and the new. I can't navigate my way through its strange twists and turns. I can't make sense of its shifting lines and baffling calls.

I've always liked rules. I like certainty. Facts you can't change. 1988, Wimbledon men's final, Edberg beats Becker 4–6, 7–6, 6–4, 6–2. 1989, Becker beats Edberg 6–0, 7–6, 6–4.

I think I have a very strong character. I believe in what I believe in. If you fight me I'll fight back with what I can. If you win today, okay, you win today, but tomorrow I'm going again.

I don't know yet if this is a quality or a flaw, but I realise for the first time: this isn't helping me now.

INSIDE

I lose my faith in the system. In my dark moments I begin to wonder if I have been handpicked because of my fame and my name.

This is my lowest moment now. Forty million Swiss francs? This bankruptcy could be for ever. I can't pay that amount of money off, even if I work every day until I'm eighty years old. Despair and panic, racing round my head. I've lost. I've lost for ever.

I think: if I hadn't won Wimbledon aged seventeen, I would never have gone through any of this. The trust in older men to do my business, the habit of letting others run my finances.

If I'd never won it, if I was still successful but maybe number five in the world and still good, still reaching Grand Slam finals – these issues would never come to me. All this stuff I don't understand comes from the one thing I did.

I never wanted to escape it. But now I can't. One day in July, in the heat of south-west London, still controlling everything.

25/05/2022

Message with reply to: Boris Becker A2923EV Huntercombe
Message from: SPROTT A7210CT

Dear Boris
How's it going over there?

Have you settled in ok, do you remember how to use the kettle and make yourself a cup of coffee HA HA. You have only been gone a couple of days and I'm writing to you already. It feels weird not seeing you here, when we would go for walks around the yard or sit down to have lunch and a good old chat. You was only here for a short period of time but you became one of the

BORIS BECKER

boys. You inspired me a lot. You're a real down to earth fella. You did make us laugh HA HA.

Anyway Boris keep your head up, this will all be a distant memory soon. If I don't hear back from you I will call Lilian or get my dad to check in to make sure you're good.

Take care Boris stay in touch thanks for everything

Jake

CHAPTER 6

Washington, Tyne and Wear

Dear Mr Becker
I hope you are in as good a health as you can be. I have always been a big fan of yours along with me mother & mother-in-law since you won Wimbledon for the first time as a young lad of 17 years of age. I really thought Dan Maskell described you well just before the commentary of that match [when] you won your first Wimbledon saying he admired your physique & at 17. Also doing your acrobatic acts on court.

I also like your commentary especially at Wimbledon & hope the BBC still employ you when you return to public life as I will watch you & hope I can get a Centre Court ticket on men's singles finals day hopefully (joking aside). I used to be a driving instructor & once took a young chap from Durham University. He was from London & the Wimbledon area & when the tournament two weeks were on he used to work in a restaurant at Wimbledon which you used to use fairly regularly for a meal or cup of coffee. He said he often used to speak to you & found you a very approachable chap.

Well take care & hope everything goes well for you when you come back to public life.

Regards,

William

It was always about weaknesses on the tennis court. I'll look for yours and exploit them. You'll look for mine and then pull at the loose threads and stamp on them until it drives me mad.

When I played Ivan Lendl, when I played Stefan Edberg and John McEnroe, they liked to get me into rallies. They wanted to get me running from one tramline to the other, because they were better movers than me. You've seen Stefan in full flow – he had the glide long before Roger Federer, the same ballet dancer's art of sprinting flat out and making it look as if he were floating to the ball.

There was something else too, early on in my career, maybe a bigger weakness. My emotions were always on the surface. This could be okay, but they had to be controlled. Sometimes I let them go. I showed everyone my frustrations. That's when I lost my balance. That's when the guy on the other side of the net thought: yeah, keep shouting, keep swearing. I want to see you breaking your racket.

I got better at it, down the years. I could still figure out someone else's flaws, and I sure as hell went at them as hard as before. This is tennis, not a social date. One of our mothers is going to cry tonight, remember? But I could hide my emotions a little more. I could adjust to the opponent who came at me.

Okay, with one person I'm going to have to be one version of myself. Another person, they're different, so when I'm around them I will be another version once again.

INSIDE

But it takes time, to see how someone moves, to work out their strategies and shortcuts. As May became June, and the slow warmth of the English summer began to seep down the cold corridors, I realised I had a problem building with two prisoners.

They were Polish guys. It wasn't that I couldn't read them, more that you couldn't miss the signals they were giving you. They were aggressive and they were angry. They were confrontational, and they had power. They gave me the Hitler salute.

I had been told in Wandsworth, just before I left, that when I got to Huntercombe I should look out for a Polish guy called Robert. Boris, you can't miss him, full of tattoos, controls the gym, really. When I got there I didn't need to look out; he had already heard I was coming and made moves to befriend me.

This seemed okay at the start. He got me involved in conversations, he talked me through some of the unspoken rules. He owned a gym outside in the real world. We talked workouts.

You're seen with someone like that, and it sends signals that others understand. Robert is looking after Boris. You want to mess with Boris? You're messing with Robert too.

There is always a payback in prison. Nothing comes for free. Seven weeks in, I knew some of the unspoken rules too. But with Robert it seemed okay. I was no threat to him, and that was unusual for him. He talked to me about his case and his wife and son, and what he needed to do and what really happened to him in England. He told me why he wanted to go back to Poland; he told me a couple of secrets that I think he really wanted to share. Maybe he felt comfortable confiding in me because sometimes when you're talking to somebody you cannot always just pretend. You have to tell the truth with someone. Maybe that was my quid pro quo with him, and it kept me safe, and all was good.

But then he left Huntercombe – deported back to Poland. And the rest of the Polish were ... rough boys. I could sense their aggression when we walked through the exercise yards, so I changed my tactics without even consciously thinking about it. You just knew not to walk alone when they were close. You knew not to look.

Sometimes it would be in the queue for the servery, other times before the wardens opened an interior gate and you would be in among an indiscriminate crowd. They would stare at me a little too long, make comments I could hear to spice it up a little and try and get a reaction.

– You're the famous guy, right?
– You're the tennis player. I saw you on the news.

I heard it, I noticed it, and I tried not to react. Never looked back. Other times, when I would be walking past them in the hallway getting from my wing to the gym, they would be coming the other way, always in groups of five or six. Then it would start. Making the Heil Hitler sign, the Nazi slogans. Whether out of a desire to provoke me or some twisted sense of brotherhood I never found out. Just looked at the floor. Kept walking. Showed no emotion, no weakness.

All the time strategising, all the time thinking. When I was out of my cell, that was when I was vulnerable. But it was also when I could take strength. When I could think about the gym or the library or maybe this course Andy Small was teaching. This time I had to stay in balance. This time I could not lose control.

INSIDE

Sometimes having people who knew exactly who you were could be a good thing. Early on in those first few weeks in Huntercombe I was introduced to the admin team in the front office. Three middle-aged women I would become close to, all of them big tennis fans, all of them keen to talk about matches and players and commentators.

They were the ones who knew about the deportation conundrum. I could see how it made sense for Baby Hulk, because he had nothing in the UK but mistakes and enemies. Why wouldn't he want to leave? I had a daughter and a son in London, I had my work for the BBC. London was Lilian and walks in Hyde Park and Battersea. After a life of different hotels and the same old tournaments, it was the closest I had to a home.

So that was my line, instinctively. I want to stay here. I'll fight deportation. I was allowed an appointment with some lawyers, and they began putting the arguments together. I began getting my head around the acronyms: ERS, the Early Release Scheme. ERSED, not too hard, Early Release Scheme Eligibility Date. Then it got more complicated: HDC, Home Detention Curfew; ROTL, Release on Temporary Licence.

What I hadn't heard about, because you don't, unless it's your specialist field, was NABA 2022. The Nationality and Borders Act. British prisons were becoming dangerously overcrowded, and they needed to make space. So, from 28 June, the law was changing. Deportation would become a much more attractive option. Less time inside. Much less time.

An official Prison Service letter came through, early in June. A printed sheet of A4. I took it back to my cell and tried to make sense of it. The big numbers, the ones that could be made smaller.

Sentence(s):
29/04/2022 0 years 30 months 0 days
29/04/2022 0 years 18 months 0 days

Key dates:
Number of days in sentence: 914
Sentence expiry date: 28/10/24
Conditional release date: 29/07/2023
HDC (Home Detention Curfew) Eligibility Date: 17/03/2023
ROTL (Release on Temporary Licence): 14/12/2022
ERSED (Early Release Scheme Eligibility Date): 14/12/2022
Licence Expiry Date: 28/10/2024

There was a line at the bottom of the page. 'If you disagree with any of the above dates, please write down what you think the days should be and hand to your wing office.' I didn't know enough to disagree, but I could do the simple sums. If I stayed in the UK, the earliest I might be allowed out, to be tagged at home, would be March 2023, next year. An emotional time, around the time of my father's birthday. If I went for this deportation option, I could be with Lilian on Christmas Day.

But there was something that didn't quite make sense. My sentence had been given as thirty months and calculated as 914 days. My conditional release date was down as July 2023. That was as it should be – you serve half your sentence, so fifteen months. Agreeing to deportation should halve my sentence again. I did my sums: 914 divided by two is 457 days; 457 divided by two is 228.5. My first day inside had been 29 April.

I had a small pocket year planner. In red biro I ticked off the days. First pass at it I calculated I should be leaving on 26

November. That didn't seem right. But however I tried I couldn't get it to 14 December.

Did it matter if they were two or three days out? Right now it did. Both the theory of it and the practical. Every night inside was a night too many.

I needed good news, because I was still waiting for Lilian to be given permission to visit me in Huntercombe. No matter that she had been doing it regularly at Wandsworth. This is the way the prison system works. They move you, and they know exactly where you are, but they lose you too, in the system.

Lilian tried the old way. Calling the person she knew in the office in Wandsworth. They told her straight: we don't have visibility on his visits system now. But we can see he hasn't been enhanced yet, so there can't be any visits. When he's cleared, there is a website you can use. You put in his prison number, and then you can see the availability and the dates. You'll just have to wait for that point. And we can't tell you when it will be.

So now I had time on my hands. Too much of it. No visits, no gym time. The promise of a job with Andy and the course in Stoicism, but nothing more.

It can send you mad, all that time, all that silence. All that space for dark thoughts to climb into your head. I would have to be disciplined. I would have to put up my own internal defences. Those thoughts would always be out there, but I could not let them in.

I tried to take a step back from it all, when I was in my cell. To start trying to cope with it all. Calming myself down, doing everything more slowly – breathing more slowly, speaking more slowly on the phone, when I could get through to Lilian. All my movements in slow motion. Feeling my pulse steady, then settle, then start to drop.

Slowing it down, letting other thoughts gestate. Feeling them bubbling up and floating down.

– I've made some mistakes, in my life. This is the penalty I have to pay. I deserve what's happening to me here.

This was new for me, and it wasn't always comfortable. Resistance would kick in.

– Hey, I've got the message now. I've learned the lesson. I don't need to be here.

Then I would go back to it. Breathing deeply, breathing slowly.

– There are still things I need to learn. Maybe I do need to be here. If I don't, maybe I can find something here that can take me to a better place, when the end comes. Whenever that might be.

Sometimes it went further. I'd think about certain people I'd trusted who had let me down. Individuals I had put my faith in. This was their fault, not mine.

And then again the reflections. Slowing it all down, not fighting it, breathing it in.

– I can't blame these people. I wasn't careful enough. I didn't check whether they would actually do what they told me they would. I didn't check whether what they advised me to do was actually legit after all.

Moving into a new state. A promise to myself.

– This is my responsibility. When I'm done with all this, I'll take much more care. I'll look after myself in a way I haven't done before.

A promise, and then a question: what do I have to do better to be given another chance?

INSIDE

The way I've described this maybe makes it sound too straightforward, too quick. It was never quick. I would go forwards and backwards some days. I would have bad moments and feel the old anger rising to the surface. You can't live as we lived in Huntercombe and not be overwhelmed by frustration at times.

Cell Dreams: The Rival #1

I'm in New York, early autumn 1984. At Flushing Meadows, in Queens. Sixteen years old, thrilled to be at the US Open, tired after losing the final of the junior tournament to an Aussie kid called Mark Kratzmann but happy still, because there is tennis everywhere and this is what I'm about, this competition and this grand adventure.

This is the final Saturday, and it's an insane day. Two men's semi-finals, John McEnroe taking on Jimmy Connors over five sets in one of them, Chris Evert and Martina Navratilova going three sets in the women's final. It's the original Super Saturday, and I'm watching the other men's semi-final – Ivan Lendl against this cool young nineteen-year-old Aussie kid with black hair and a white headband.

Pat Cash.

I'm up there in the stands, still a boy. Still amazed by everything I see all around me. But this guy's actually doing it. All of us know everything about him. He's won the big stuff as a junior, he's done crazy things in the Davis Cup. He's just made the semis at Wimbledon, and it took Mac to beat him on the grass there.

I can picture him now, on that pale green hard court, white sweatband on his wrist, white shirt with the dark blue shoulders. Matching Lendl all the way, winning the first set, coming from behind to level it up at two sets all, saving a match point on his own serve at 4–5 in the fifth. Serve and volleying even on that court, punching his volleys away.

He loses in the final set tie-break, but I still find him amazing to study. I love the rock-and-roll look. I love his aggressiveness, his demeanour. He looks like someone who hates losing, who's obsessed with winning.

He looks like me.

And now this is weird, and I don't quite get it. When I win Wimbledon in 1985, I don't remember what he did, when I should – we are basically the same person. When I win in 1986, I don't remember either. I don't remember ever talking to him or practising with him and, in those days, that's weird.

Do we keep a distance from each other? Maybe it's because we're too similar. He can't be pleased that I'm taking his mantle off him, not when you love winning and hate losing like we do. He's the next big thing, and suddenly I'm winning two Wimbledon singles titles, and I'm serve-volleying, and I'm two and a half years younger than him. He likes the limelight; I like the limelight. But it's on me now.

Now it's Wimbledon 1987. I have my big loss to Peter Doohan, an Aussie no one is talking about as the next big thing. I'm number one seed, not that it matters when you have a match like this. Cash is eleventh seed. But he beats Mats Wilander in straight sets in the quarters, and then it's Jimmy Connors in the semis, and Jimmy is old now, for this

INSIDE

era, so Pat is through to the final against Lendl, and this time he's stronger and more certain and wins in straight sets, and then he celebrates like Pat Cash should celebrate – throwing his black and white headband into the crowd, climbing up to the players' box, shouting and swearing so loud that Princess Diana a few rows along must surely hear.

It's 1988. He's defending champion. Only seeded four, but that's because Lendl is number one. Wilander two, Stefan three. I'm six – behind Connors and only one ahead of Henri Leconte.

Pat's opening match is on Centre, because he's defending champion. He's also always a bit of a talker. In his press conference he makes a few remarks about me. Something about giving me a lesson, or showing how it's really done on a grass court. I give a little back; the press build it up some more. There is real friction there. I am twenty years old, he has just turned twenty-three. We are in our prime. We are designed for this and we have built ourselves for these moments.

We meet in the quarter-finals. I call this a tough one at this stage of the tournament. It's inevitable with that draw, but it also feels like it has to happen. It's the afternoon of the second Wednesday; he's in Sergio Tacchini, I'm in Fila.

I know I am playing well. I can see he's frustrated. I can hear it too. Pat uses language like I like to use language.

There is one moment where he has to chase a drop shot. He runs to the net, can't stop, puts his racket down on the grass like a walking stick and just tumbles over to my side of the court. And I know how this works, so I jump over the net too, and lie there on his side. Like a joke but not really a joke *too. Because this is tennis, and it's about winning not losing, and making their mother cry, not yours.*

So I roll over, and he's standing next to me, and he's Pat Cash, so he says the most Pat Cash thing.

– What the fuck are you doing here?

And I'm Boris Becker. Sometimes my character is to stir it up more. I never walk away from a knife fight. So I look at him and say something back, and he comes back at me again, and tells me to stick something I can't somewhere I won't.

I win in three sets. It's clear in the end, and it's a slap in the face for him. There are some remarks in the press conference from both of us. I make fun of him a little. And so we never look eye to eye, metaphorically, throughout our whole careers.

This is his last Grand Slam quarter-final. He ruptures his Achilles the next year. And he's always chasing after that, and we don't meet, and we don't talk, about any of it.

I couldn't always just live inside my head. Even in this strange timeless world the calendar that used to run my life would squeeze back in and make an impact.

Queen's was always a big tournament for me. The one I won as a teenager in 1985, the month before everything that happened at Wimbledon. It was the Stella Artois Championships then. I went in as a nobody and came out as slightly more somebody. Playing Johan Kriek in the final, ten years older than me and a serious player on grass, winner of two Australian Opens when the courts at Kooyong were the same surface as Queen's and Wimbledon. Me winning in straight sets for the first singles title of my career, Johan coming out with his warning afterwards: 'If he plays like that, he'll win Wimbledon.'

In an ordinary year the start of Queen's would always be an emotional one for me. A moment to look back, to reflect on a period that was happening so fast that at the time I could only look forwards. My nickname among the other German players at the time, the Red Baron – sort of because of Baron von Richthofen, the First World War pilot, but more for the Underground station we used for the tournament, Baron's Court, when I was winning my four titles there.

In retirement I always made time to watch the semis and the final. This year was different. Here in Huntercombe I had seen almost nothing. No internet, no Sky, no Amazon. I hadn't been able to watch tennis and often I couldn't even keep up with who was winning and who was losing, unless Andy Murray was involved or another British player had been beaten by a bigger name. Then you might see something in the sports bulletins on the BBC or ITV news. None of the wardens cared, and I barely knew anyone else. Baby Hulk had his own issues; Andy Small was in the gym, and I was not.

But when it came to Queens, I watched it all. Every afternoon that week, live on BBC Two. Every match, every point. With all that time to myself it was a gift from heaven. My door only opening for lunch and dinner, the rest of the day and night to burn. Matteo Berrettini won the final. That mattered less to me than the sounds and the dramas and the sweet familiarity of it all. It was the same when Eastbourne came on, a week later.

In those moments, tennis came back into my life like a rush of warm wind. I watched, and the hours went by.

This was my regime. Wake up, do my exercises. Lie back and dream. Get unlocked for lunch, walk in with Baby Hulk. Come back, exercise, read, think. Twenty-two hours a day all alone in my cell. Try to anchor myself to stuff that was going on outside. *Channel 4 News* reporting that Paul McCartney had turned eighty, so listing all my favourite Beatles songs, putting them in order. Watch some Mo Gilligan on BBC One, love his energy and talent. Turn my thoughts back to my own world and wonder when the hell this enhancement period would begin. It had been four weeks now, becoming five. I spoke to the main warden on my wing, but with that asshole it was always the same.

– Hey, excuse me, I've done the time now, I should be enhanced …

– No, that's not correct. You have to stay here another week.

I'd always talk friendly with him, not letting him see he was getting to me. Not giving him anything of me too. But I would make myself clear.

– You told me it was four weeks. Then it was five. Soon it will be six …

But I was slowly becoming better at coping. The familiar comforts of watching tennis, a growing ability to decode those strange transmissions in the static around me. Coming to know myself in a way I maybe had never tried to before.

I was living inside my head, and it was starting to feel like a good place, a comfortable place. I would think, okay, I'm fifty-four years old. I'm older but I'm not too old yet. There's Lilian, there's my kids, there are people out there who still love me and believe in me. Maybe there's still enough time for me to change and make it better. My life is not a 100-metre race.

INSIDE

There was a day, a month after I arrived at Huntercombe, still not enhanced, when the cell door was unlocked at 11am, and my first thought was, I'm not ready yet, give me another half an hour because I'm just getting through something mentally. A few days later I had the same thought in the afternoon. The warden opened the door at 4pm and I was completely at ease in my own mind. Almost talking to myself, but at one, too. Okay, I'm not hungry yet and I'm in this great thought. What should I do?

Every letter I received I would read several times. Slow it down, pause it halfway through, savour every word.

The one that arrived this morning was the game-changer. I was in as a gym orderly.

I would be working with Andy. My door would no longer be locked twenty-two hours a day. And I would be moving cells again, from the first floor down to the ground floor.

This was what happened when you were enhanced, when you had a job. You were never entirely trusted, but you were inside the machine. A small cog but part of something bigger than you, and that was better than being left on the side.

Packing my stuff up, a last look around, down the stairs and into the same room with the same furniture and the same layout. This time I was one cell from the end of the corridor. I glanced into the cell on the immediate right as I went through the door. The guy was big, serious-looking. An air of danger about him.

Okay, Boris, you know this. No speaking to anyone yet. Get your shoulders back, walk like you're walking onto Centre Court and your body feels great and your form is exactly where you want it to be.

So I kept my eyes down, until I was in the gym later that day. Getting a sense of how it would work, the machines and the matting, the mood and the groups. Baby Hulk gave me the floor information, keeping his voice down. This guy, he's called Ike. Big, big drug dealer. Cocaine, the hard stuff. He was worldwide. London, Nigeria, Germany. He's done twelve years already. Now he's in the gym twice a day.

I had a little look, when Ike was on the weights. He was the man from the cell next to mine. Early fifties, strong, moving the big weights easily. Respect from the others in there, people easing out of his way as he went from each piece of equipment but also stopping to talk to him sometimes. Him helping a few others with their workouts.

I was busy. Small tasks, menial ones. Mopping the floor of the changing rooms, down on my hands and knees cleaning the toilets. This made me kind of invisible too. So I could watch him, and after a few days I began talking to him, about the obvious stuff, the immediate. I asked about his workouts. He asked about my own. I gave him some compliments, praised his strength and lifting technique.

And that was the start of it. A few words, in that first week, and then, quite naturally, a few more, as we walked back to our adjoining cells, as we came in again the next morning. He told me about his job in the laundry. Now this was a good gig, partly because everyone needs clean sheets and clothes that don't stink, but also because of all the machines and the noise. You could shut the door in the laundry and you could speak. There were cameras, of course, but the churn of the water and the spinning of those big drums drowned everything else out. Inmates would walk in with their dirty clothes, stay in there half an hour and tell him all the stuff they wanted to say without being overheard.

That's a powerful position, in prison. And while Ike was a big man, and had done bad things, he wasn't menacing when he spoke to you. He was calm. He listened. He gave you little glimpses of who he might be inside.

He'd done his research. Nodding at me one morning as we stepped out from our cells into the corridor.

– Boris, your son is called Noah, my son is also called Noah.

My Noah was only a year older than his Noah. He knew about Barbara, my first wife, and he knew her heritage. He knew my sons shared some of that heritage.

So this was Ike, and the start of a cautious trust beginning to form between us. On the other side of my cell, on the right as I came out, was a smaller guy. Friendly, from the first time I saw him. Actually smiling, when he spoke to you. And he liked to speak – a lot.

His name was Shuggy. A Sri Lankan man inside for gang violence. I didn't know exactly what he had done, but he didn't seem to have any enemies inside. He liked the gym too, but there was no tough exterior with Shuggy. He smiled so often you got used to the sight of his big white teeth. And that had never happened to me in prison, not in Huntercombe and not in Wandsworth. Why would you smile when there was nothing to smile about?

He liked the gym, but God defined his day. Our cell doors were open from 7am each morning now, staying unlocked until 12.30pm, then open again from 1.30pm to 5pm. You got used to looking in and not worrying about the consequences.

In Shuggy's cell I could see a little altar. You would see him praying several times a day. If he saw you, there was no aggression. Just one of those smiles.

It was organised around national lines, a lot of the time, the allegiances and the power structures on the wing. There were the Poles, with their tattoos and their Nazi slogans. I was warned about the Romanians, but I got lucky there; I had my old connections to the young days, my coach Günther Bosch, my manager Ion Tiriac. Word always gets around, inside. In time they would come to me for help with writing English and reading it. Everyone wants something in prison.

Then there were the Albanians. Lots of people were scared of the Albanians. I wasn't – until I found out I had one in the cell just across the corridor from me.

Alex. Not a scary name, but a scary guy, when you heard about him. He had a bad reputation. A drug dealer, that's what the floor information said. Inside because he killed two men with a knife. Here's how the story was told: Alex in his house, taking coke, drinking alcohol, having sex. Two others from his gang, convinced he was stealing from them, breaking into the house and coming for him. Alex so high he went after them himself. Chasing them out of the house, down the street. Hunting them down, stabbing them both.

I stole glances at him, when I could. In his early forties, a long bushy beard that looked like he never trimmed it, not much hair on top of his head. Not as muscular as Ike, but strong shoulders, strong arms. You could tell from his demeanour and the way he held himself that if you looked him too long in the eyes, he was going to do something. Remember, in a fight it's always who gets in first. Alex looked like he always got in first.

He also seemed quiet, most of the time. Not like a man who could stab two people in the street, but then what did that look like anyway? He seemed to play chess a lot of the time. I enjoyed chess. I just wasn't ready to play with him yet.

So I spent time by myself, thinking things through, and I spent time in the gym. I saw Andy and I could see he was pleased I was there. He talked to me again about the course he ran in Stoicism. Another chance to escape my cell, another chance to move in Andy's circles. It all felt positive. I told him I would sign up.

And I spent a little more time each week with Ike and with Shuggy. Sometimes going into their cells now, for a few minutes at a time, not panicking if they came into mine and there was no warden nearby.

There was a lightness about Shuggy that didn't compute with his backstory. He and Ike had been together in Belmarsh, and they'd had it rough. Everything you heard about Belmarsh made you glad you weren't there: the conditions, the inmates, their crimes. The two of them made it clear how much easier it was for them in Huntercombe. Belmarsh was a bad place, probably the toughest prison in the country. Shuggy and Ike also shared the same attitude of the long-termer, those serving eight years or more. Just got to do your time, not make a mistake, and then eventually you'll be out. But those guys tell you something else too: when you're inside that long, prison never leaves you, even when you're outside.

BORIS BECKER

Cell Dreams: The Love #3

We take our distance, a little, me and Lilian for the rest of 2019. She is still deciding what she wants to do with her life, where she wants to go. She wants to fix herself, find her ground. She doesn't move to London until early 2020, and then she's in Highbury, in north London, and I'm in Battersea, just south of the river.

We reconnect. Slowly at first, and then Covid comes, and you have no choice but to speed things up or to stop them. You have nowhere to go, no other people to see. We can meet at her place or my place or in the middle, but all the restaurants are closed, and it is only us.

We meet in Hyde Park. Right across from the Mandarin Oriental. I'm waiting for her, looking around, and then suddenly she's there, jumping on my back. We walk in the park. We go for ever. Two laps, and Hyde Park is not a small park.

There is only one bar open. Everything else is shuttered up. We have a drink, sitting outside, and this is the first feeling of being in public a little bit, even if there is no one to witness it; the paparazzi and their cameras and shouts are also under lockdown.

We catch up on stories, on thoughts. Where we've come from, where we want to go. Things accelerate. She starts staying over, occasionally at the start, and then more and more. Soon I have some things of mine at her place, and she has some things of hers at mine.

Spring becomes summer. There is no Wimbledon this year; the pandemic sees to that. The BBC has no matches to show,

INSIDE

so they make programmes about the old days. They ask me in to the All England Club to film, and I take Lilian with me for the first time. Into the clubhouse, round the ground. I show her the trophies, the locker room. The players' entrance to Centre Court. There is nobody else there. It's eerie. If you want to hear the ghosts of your past, there is nothing else to block them out.

We stay in London, and we share more days and nights like this, and for the first time in my life I can build a relationship in private. No Instagram stories, not one picture. The paparazzi are out again, but they only catch us long distance in the park every now and then, and this is all different to me and new and welcome.

When we see the photographers, we talk about it. Lilian, this has been my life. It's not my fault, but they will come for us again at some point, and there won't be anything I can do about it. I wish it could be different, but it won't be, and you have to ask yourself if you can deal with it. I'm serious about my feelings towards you now, and this is how they will make it. If you want me, this comes with it too.

She looks at it all, and she accepts it. Our lives wind around each other a little more each day.

When Christmas comes, and suddenly London is in lockdown again, I escape on a late flight and spend the holiday with her in São Tomé. I meet her father; he gives me a huge bear hug.

Just before the holiday ends, he sits down with me outside on the porch, and says, Boris, are you okay? I tell him about my bankruptcy. I tell him it all. And he's okay with it.

Later on, when we are out for dinner, I ask him if I can marry her. He says yes.

He says, Boris, welcome to the family.

There was a way of behaving in the locker rooms when I was a player. Whenever another player was in there, you had to show your masculine side. Or what we thought back then was a masculine side. It was aggressive, antagonistic. Never friendly.

This was how it would be. You had your corner, maybe your coach with you. All the other corners also had players in. No one wanted the middle bench, no one wanted the space. It was corners or, if you couldn't get a corner, it was walls. All of it territorial. Don't come over here, I'm not your friend. Never any, hey, how are you? Never a handshake, let alone a smile or a hug. No eye contact initiated. Instead: look at me and I'll stare back at you. I'm happy to go into a fight with you.

My tutors in the early days were John McEnroe and Jimmy Connors. They were the guys who led the locker room. I would watch them and see how they behaved. And they were rude, and they were arrogant. Convinced about their place in the world, on the surface at least. Convinced this was their room and nobody else's.

Us young ones would look up to them. They were winning big tournaments and serious money. So we'd look at their act, like sons watching fathers, and we'd copy it and try it out for ourselves.

Never a question about any other way of being. You want to beat the other guy, right? Okay. So you're going to do everything within the rules to make sure you're in a better mental space than him. Sometimes you'll bend the rules. If it works, and you win the match, you'll double down on it again in the locker room afterwards. Drive home that advantage, that superiority. And if you've just beaten me after three or four hours, I won't be happy about that, so I'll be aggressive too.

Maybe it was helpful for me as a tennis player to be like that. Maybe that was me anyway. I saw something in McEnroe and Connors that I recognised within myself; I saw the excuse and let it free.

But it was not helpful in Huntercombe. It was not helpful in the locker room at the gym, where there were men who didn't care about Johnny Mac and Jimbo and any other skinny guy in perfect white clothing. There was no space, and no one was giving me a corner. It wasn't helpful when I was walking through the gym. I wasn't going to win the fights in here. I'm not stupid.

Instead I tried to enjoy it. Being kind of free inside the gym, within the rules of the role. Learning some new behaviours. Understanding what a gesture Andy had made by getting me a job in here. Everyone wanted to work in the gym. It was the coolest place. Where you wanted to be anyway. But there were only six spots as an orderly. Once you were in you didn't want to give it up. No one resigned as a gym orderly. You either had it taken away from you or you were released. Ike had the laundry, and that worked for him. The gym was me. There didn't seem to be much jealousy about it, either, because I was a former professional sportsman. It made sense.

Always the same faces, always Baby Hulk. I've seen a lot of athletes work out. Ivan Lendl was the first fitness fanatic in tennis, and I watched him. Edberg was so fit, Sampras and Agassi too. I saw Federer and Nadal working out, and those two were something else. And that was even before Novak Djokovic. Novak was a beast.

But Baby Hulk? With this guy it was like the Rocky movies. He was like Drago. He had a very different type of workout which nobody would dare to do. A lot of bodyweight stuff, all the usual lifts with free weights, but also something else. He would stand by the pull-up bar and brace his arms against the side. Then he would lift his torso and his legs until his whole body was at right angles, held out like a human flag.

The first time he did it the whole gym stopped – big guys, super strong, everyone staring at him. Then he did it again. Down to the ground, up again. He did five reps. Then he did ten.

Not everyone in the gym worked out all the time. Some just did it to get out of their cells, to have a change of scene for an hour. To chew the fat with someone in the same mess. But there were lots of strong men in there, and all of them liked to deadlift. They liked to bench-press even more. It was the standard you judged yourself and others by. In that gym, heavy metal was always the soundtrack.

But this was different. A new consensus on the floor: don't fuck with this guy, he's by far the strongest in the gym.

Bench-press? Sure, you're powerful. It looks good on your body, that muscle. But the secret in a fight is who punches first and who's the quickest, not who's the strongest. I've been in a couple of fights, and you don't underestimate size, but it's not the size of the ship but the rhythm of the ocean that counts. If you're quick you'll beat anybody who's bigger than you.

He took his shirt off sometimes, Baby Hulk. That stopped the place too. Not just for his build but for the imbalances.

INSIDE

One shoulder was up high, the other dropped down. Whether this was because of the strange angle of his head to his neck, or the head was at a strange angle because of the shoulders, I don't know.

He chose to tell me about it a couple of months later. One of the six gym orderlies got his release and a space came up, and I got Baby Hulk in so he could spend even more time in there. By then he trusted me.

He had looked like this from birth, he said. And of course he was the butt of many jokes as he grew up. He was ridiculed and embarrassed. So he built up this body, this machine, to defend himself. To impress people. To stop the jokes.

I liked this about him. How he responded to the way the world treated him, the layers and depths he had that his strongman exterior might make you overlook. But there was an aggression there too. I felt he had a good heart. I saw it when I talked with him over lunch, or between sets in the gym.

I saw as well how quickly the heat could rise within him. It was as if all the mockery down the years had piled up inside him, like some toxic landfill, and now it only took one spark to set light to it all. He hated paedophiles. Everyone hated paedophiles; in a place of rogues and outlaws, they were considered their own special category of moral pariahs. But Baby Hulk really loathed them. He wanted to kill them. Not just attack them, kill them.

I felt the years between us. My hot-headed days were over. I didn't want to fight anyone any more. You can have that corner if you want it. You can bare your teeth and be the masculine one, if that's what you think it's about. So I would try to discuss things with him.

Like a lot of the white foreign prisoners at Huntercombe, he could be racist. I didn't know whether he really felt that way, or if it was just part of being in the group he felt he belonged to. I would challenge him on those views. I had to be careful, because he had quick hands to go with the strength. But I could talk to him about it. And if we were in the kitchen and he raised his voice and started to come at me a little, because that was his way when he wasn't thinking, I could say to him, Thomas, Thomas! Hulk! And he would snap out of it and think it was funny and come back to himself once again.

There were lots of lost and lonely men around us. That took me a while to appreciate. I just saw the way it played out: Poles hanging out with Poles, Romanians with Romanians, Albanians always together. African men with African men.

Sometimes it wasn't race but religion. Maybe the largest group of all were the Muslims. They were active and they were together. On some days the gym would be closed and requisitioned as a mosque. On those days it wasn't the wardens but the other inmates who told you to stay away. This is not for you. Don't be interested. Don't go looking.

You didn't argue. I listened a lot, more than I was used to doing in my life. Sometimes it made you uncomfortable. Sometimes it left you trying to work out sums that made no sense.

Alex, the Albanian in the cell opposite mine, talked to me more when he saw Ike and Shuggy trusting me and inviting me to their cells. He kept mentioning the chess. With our doors unlocked for so much longer, you had more time to stretch out the conversations. It wasn't just practicalities like shower groups and lunch and watch out for this thing and that person. It was who you were, too, or who you wanted to be seen as.

With Alex there was never any remorse. One afternoon, when he was telling me again about his chess games and how I should play, I asked him when he thought he would be out. I asked him what he thought he might do. And he just shrugged. Boris, we are drug dealers, that's what we do. We do nothing else. When I'm out, I'm going to go back to my job. That's what I'm going to do.

I don't know if he felt Huntercombe was teaching him something or not. Maybe he didn't feel the need to change. Maybe he couldn't. Maybe he was just a realist. Drugs made him money; drugs bought him a car and house. With a guy like Alex, you don't ask him these things. Inside you don't push buttons you don't have to push.

Shuggy? He was different. I kept looking for the darkness in him, for the past that had brought him here. In Alex you could sense it in his intransigence. Shuggy genuinely appeared harmless. He seemed to have accepted what he had done, getting into a gang fight when he was eighteen, being part of a crew who had killed a man, even as I struggled to connect him to a guy who could hurt other people so wantonly.

Ike? He liked to talk about God. He was part of the Christian group, and he often stood up to speak when they met on Sundays. He would preach without sounding like a preacher.

I couldn't feel any violence in him, any bad thoughts. There was no talk about what he might do when he got out, at the end of his twelve-year sentence. He was focused on each day in this place. His job in the laundry, his role on Sundays. The inmates around him he thought of as friends.

People often fight their past in prison. It's the narrative you hear on every wing and in most conversations.

– They stitched me up.

– I didn't do it.

– I got a bastard judge; they gave me too much time.

Ike was one of the exceptions. One of the first to say, yeah, I'm guilty. I did it. One of the first to understand that you have to accept who you are, or who you were, to get through the long years ahead.

But none of us were truly at peace. All of us were battling our own weaknesses, our own private selves. One evening, just before lock-up, Ike came to my cell. You couldn't shut your own door; the wardens would see it as a sign of you hiding something they didn't want you to hide. So Ike sat on the toilet behind the door so nobody could see him, and he looked at me and told me he couldn't take it any more. I've been inside for twelve years, Boris, and it's too difficult. I don't know what to do. I don't know how to get through it any more.

This big man, strong and powerful. The drug dealer with connections everywhere. The preacher who seemed to have forgiven himself. Sitting on my metal toilet, crying his eyes out. Opening up to someone he barely knew.

CHAPTER 7

Tavistock, Devon

Dear Boris

I am writing to you just to let you know you have not been forgotten and that you are in my thoughts this Wimbledon fortnight. It must be very difficult for you and I hope you have found a way to follow it.

    I was the same age as you when you first won Wimbledon, and you have been a huge inspiration to me. I play tennis for pleasure only but my son has seen some success, making the local tennis academy. I understand the level of commitment and sacrifice it takes to achieve what you did and I admire that.

    I know things have taken a bit of a wrong turn for you, but I know you will bounce back. I hope you are experiencing some kindness and I hope it's some comfort to you to know you are still in people's thoughts. You are not a bad person – just made a few wrong decisions, which we all do.

    Best wishes

PS I have a nine-year-old pug called Boris named after you, not the Prime Minister.

Late June now, two months into my incarceration, and my life in Huntercombe was starting to take a shape. Three hours or so working in the gym, Monday to Friday, me usually getting one of the two daytime shifts, 0815–1130, or 1345–1630. An hour each day Monday to Friday in the classroom with Andy for the Stoicism course. Four hours out of my cell, plus lunch, plus dinner. Better than a cell. Better than before.

A life that you could live, not wish away. For now, anyway.

The gym made sense to me. It was the one place of freedom, where you could immerse your head in weights or running and rowing, where you could talk to other prisoners or just relish two hours out of the hole, as we called our cells. The worst punishment, or the most effective deterrent, was to be banned from the gym. We all cherished our time there.

But it was a while since I had been back to school, and that's how the Stoicism course worked. You were taken to a different wing, to a room like a classroom. Rows of chairs for the inmates, Andy at the front with a chalkboard. There was an incentive to stay, as there always was in prison; if you sat through the entire hour, or hour fifteen minutes, and you contributed, got involved, you were allowed to go to the gym for an hour afterwards.

It was a good inducement, and it needed to be. They were not natural classroom inhabitants, the men around me. A few young ones, nineteen or twenty-one years old, first-timers. They looked a little more open to it. Then others who were clearly ticking off an hour of dead time. Men on their third or fourth spell inside, wise to the rules and ways round them, as set in their position as the walls and fences around us.

We were given a booklet when we walked in that first morning. This philosophy had changed Andy's life; now he wanted to

INSIDE

share its power with others. He had felt its positive effects on him, and he thought it could do the same for those of us struggling inside too.

The booklet was A4 size, clear plastic cover, bound with black rings. I picked it up and turned it in my hands. Maybe an inch thick, capital letters in black on the cover: HMP HUNTERCOMBE. STOIC PHILOSOPHY COURSE. Under that was an image of a Greek warrior in silhouette, holding a circular shield and a spear. Overlaid on the soldier was the same quote I'd seen on the wall of the gym.

'It's not what happens to you, but how you react to it that matters.'

Then a name. Epictetus.

I turned to the first page and began to read.

>The purpose of this programme is to try to show you a better and more importantly happier way to live both in and out of prison. You are required to fully engage in the course and get involved.
>
>This might be the most important course you have ever done and can completely change your life!
>
>Before we explore some basic concepts of how to find contentment, we need to have an understanding of human responses to potentially difficult situations.
>
>Luckily our ancestors learned to run away when they spotted movement in the long grass. The ancestors that didn't run away were eaten by a lion!
>
>Natural selection has hard-wired us to respond in extreme ways to different situations. This response has served humanity well for over 99 per cent of its existence. It has helped us run away, fight to the death and breed voraciously.

Fortunately these hard-wired skills are seldom required today. Unfortunately these skills work against us living good, happy and productive lives. The problems we find ourselves in are nearly always created by ourselves, by our chimp. Our 'chimp' is the part of the brain which takes control of the handles when we are: angry, hungry, frightened, threatened and pretty much any other emotional situation.

The chimp in us is a very powerful animal and useful if a situation is genuinely life-threatening. However, at all other times it can destroy your life.

Prisons are full of people who cannot control their chimp.

So, how do we control our chimp?

This was how it began, and how it would be each morning. Andy at the front, leading us through a section. Asking us to reflect on our own experiences, to share if we wanted to. Nobody did at the start, and some chose never to. When we were asked to discuss an idea, or a quote, it was never truly like a school. With some of the pupils you could feel the resistance and you could feel the hard edges. They had been shaped by forces beyond this room and were not malleable to anyone else.

That first day touched something for me. I learned several new English swearwords, and how to combine some more familiar ones into fresh combinations. They didn't talk about paedophiles, they talked about nonces. You want to know where that word comes from? It's another prison acronym: Not On Normal Courtyard Exercise. Inmates hated paedophiles more than anyone else. Make sense now?

I remembered about keeping your eyes down from the gaze of some others. I was also intrigued. On the second page of my booklet was a diagram of the human brain, annotated to show the difference between the prefrontal cortex and what it did (empathy, insight, emotion regulation) and the limbic brain (fight, flight, freeze). Then a line underneath: *Indulging our limbic brain usually ends in trouble. We must allow the information received to get to our prefrontal cortex.*

More explanations on the next page.

> The name Stoic comes from the Greek word for 'porch'. This was what ancient Greeks sat under when they discussed life and how to live.
>
> Following Stoicism was the way many people lived their lives from 250 BCE to 500 CE. Some religions use Stoic practice to provide the framework of their doctrine.
>
> The Ancient Greeks and Romans understood that if our 'chimps' are not controlled they will cause havoc to our lives. The problems we face in life are almost always created by ourselves. If we learn how to control and manage our chimp we can live a happy and productive life. We will look at ways to effectively manage our chimp and perhaps find purpose to our life.

This was the exercise for the first day, as spelled out by Andy.

'Think of a film character or real-life person you think is someone worth admiring. Winston Churchill, Nelson Mandela, Bruce Willis in *Die Hard*. In extreme circumstances – war, terrorist attacks, imprisonment and facing death – they all understood they couldn't control the situation but they could control their response. They are all "Masters of Self". So, how can we use Stoic practices to be like these Masters of Self?'

I could feel some of these questions sticking to me. I had been the same man for a long time. I had also been shaped by something else, and it had begun a long time ago. From when I first truly took hold of tennis, from when tennis took hold of me, it had always been about winning. About being the best. Not someone near the top, not someone in second place, but the best. The best player, the best coach, the best partner.

When I had the feeling of being the best, I wanted to repeat it. I tried to work out the qualities that had got me there, and I identified them as discipline, control and consistency. But there was something else that came before all of them, and that was commitment. Without commitment, I couldn't see how you had the others. You had to be committed to consistency, you had to be committed to being disciplined, you had to be committed to be controlled.

So life begins to be formed around all this. As a young player, regardless of anything happening around me, my Monday and Tuesday and Wednesday would always be the same. All about commitment to the aim. The other attractions and distractions? They can't matter as much. If they do, you're not winning, and if you're not winning, you're not truly happy.

But it could never be this simple. Even as a young man, two Wimbledon titles before the age of nineteen, I could feel the friction within this tight world. A question that could be both an incentive and a provocation: what are you willing to do, what is your sacrifice?

And as I grew older, and other men won Wimbledon, and I lost in finals I thought I should have won, the balance grew more unstable. Was I always disciplined? Fuck no. Did I mess up? Fuck yes. Was I always consistent? No. Could I win seven matches across the two weeks of a Grand Slam? Absolutely.

I thought back to those days. You could feel like the king of the world, if you wanted to. Not just hotels but hotel suites; cars with drivers, people screaming at you as you went from one to the other. Adoration at the court. You had so much money you didn't know how much money you had, just that there was enough to get yourself whatever you wanted. Whatever that might be.

I thought: back then, in my head, I was strong. But I was weak, too weak sometimes to say no.

Maybe in any generation there's a price to pay. I had seen in young players in the last few years how social media had softened some and damaged others. Living two lives, one for yourself and one for Instagram. Losing control over the first so you could show strangers how you were really meant to be. Monetising your private time, inviting everyone in, all the time.

In the 1980s and 90s it was the real world that came to you. Parties and drinking and drugs. With me it was more the late nights and girls. Knowing I would be tired the next day for practice, but in the moment knowing I wanted to be with this girl until three, four in the morning, wanting a release, wanting to escape from this disciplined world that had been constructed around me. I would do it, and then suffer the pain of the 7am wake-up call.

I still practised, but was I as good? No. Did I benefit from that 9am practice? No. So I paid the price. I didn't do it every week, otherwise I could never have won, but I still did it, and I didn't regret it. I wasn't committed to commitment.

Could I look around this classroom and think myself better than the others? Sure, these men were flawed. You could see their weaknesses. But I was weak too.

We were all paying the price. We all needed a new way of being in the world. Of being malleable, once again.

Cell Dreams: The Trial #1

It's late summer, 2020. I'm at the rented flat in Battersea.

I get a call from the concierge. Someone downstairs asking for me. I don't know their name, so I don't want to go down. I have to be careful.

Two days later the caller comes back. This time they explain who they are. They give me some documents. And this is the start of the criminal case.

I don't go to prison because I'm bankrupt. I don't go to prison because I don't pay my bills after I'm bankrupt. This is a problem I don't understand: I am on trial partly because I've continued to pay my bills.

I don't see it coming and my lawyers don't see it coming, when I feel they should have spelled it out more clearly, but it accelerates fast and it's never back under control.

A first hearing. My lawyers are relaxed.

– Mr Becker, this will be quick and easy. The judge will ask you twenty-nine times, because there's twenty-nine different counts, whether you're guilty or not, and so you say not guilty. And then, after half an hour, we're done.

But it's not like this. After fifteen minutes the judge is already talking about an ankle tag, because she thinks I'm a

INSIDE

flight risk. She thinks I'll try to leave the country. This is not half an hour. This is not easy.

I give up my passport. The bills from the lawyers start arriving: £100,000, £200,000. I ask them where the ceiling is here. They say, this could cost £1 million.

I change lawyers quite quickly after that. I'm bankrupt. I owe people money already. I can't owe more people even more. The same estimate comes back; I change lawyers again. I'm told my new QC has never lost a case. These are more like my kind of numbers.

The trial date is set for spring 2022, six weeks away. In the four weeks before, we work on the case all day every day. The prosecution drop five counts of the twenty-nine; we're down to twenty-four. Better numbers again.

But I'm not good. I'm not sleeping. While I'm allowed to earn money, half of it has to go directly to the trustee. The rest has to cover my rent, my bills, my child and spousal maintenance. All my expenses.

I can feel the stress in my head and in my chest. Squeezing from every direction.

Always so wired. So wired. Can't stop thinking, can't control where the thoughts are going. Moving to a smaller rented flat, signing only a six-month lease because we don't know what might happen by then. Drinking at night to shut it off, but I mean, how many beers can you drink?

There's fear there. Of the unknown, of what might happen if this trial doesn't go my way.

This is when the long walks start. First thing in the morning, sometimes twice a day. To clear my head at the beginning of the day, to process it all at the end. A fast walk, when my hips and knees allow, so I breathe hard and I sweat. So I'm tired at night and can maybe force myself to sleep.

I had another key belief, as a player. People would sometimes talk about moderation. Like it was a good thing, this sense of control over your actions, over what you wanted. Don't go too far, don't go too hard. You'll break things.

But I could never understand moderation. I was a believer in all-in. If you want to win Wimbledon and you know that means six hours every day until you get it, you play six hours every day. If you want to go out for the night, let's go out on Friday night, and Saturday night, and Sunday night too.

All this had worked for me. To achieve greatness, you have to be passionate, but you need to go further. You have to be borderline crazy. Obsessive, relentless, cruel, dismissive. It's either full speed or nothing, otherwise you don't get to where you want to go.

Sitting in the prison classroom each morning, reading the pages in my book, listening to Andy, I could feel myself slowing down. I could feel myself stopping, a lot of the time, and that was weird, like I was watching myself in a movie. I had achieved greatness. I had won three Wimbledon titles, two Aussie Opens, the US Open. Two Davis Cups, an Olympic gold medal. But where was I now?

I looked around this small room, at the tired faces. I looked at the walls and the small windows. Either I was some strange exception, a great man surrounded by lesser men, or I was not an exception at all. I fitted right in. And if I did, why was that? Some fierce internal engine had always driven me – a kind of

INSIDE

relentless intensity that never let up. It had taken me to Centre Court at Wimbledon. Maybe it had taken me here, too. I thought this craziness was my greatest weapon. I go all-in. Maybe I had turned this weapon on myself.

So I kept reading, each morning. I kept listening.

> Epictetus, Marcus Aurelius and Seneca used logic and reason to find a better, kinder and happier way to live. Using the techniques we study, you too will be able to free yourself from the shackles of chimp-led emotional thinking, which most probably landed you in prison.
>
> The first thing we need to consider on the road to self-mastery is our thoughts. Thoughts become the first step towards action. If a thought we have is incorrect it is very likely that the action we take will also be wrong.
>
> **Characteristics of thoughts:**
> Just because you think it doesn't make it true.
> Just because you think it doesn't mean you have to believe it.
> Just because you think it doesn't mean you have to act on it.
> Just because you think it doesn't mean it is the 'real' you.
> Even though thoughts do not have to be acted on, repeatedly dwelling on a thought will predispose you to act on it eventually. Don't set yourself up for failure by starting down that trail.

Always these quotes, at the top of a page, on Andy's chalkboard.

> **Marcus Aurelius:** 'Everything we hear is an opinion, not a fact. Everything we see is a perspective, not the truth.'

Epictetus: 'Show me a man who though sick is happy, who though in danger is happy, who though in prison is happy, and I'll show you a self-master.'

Shakespeare: 'Nothing is either good or bad but thinking makes it so.'

And then the simple sentences, in bold. The challenges.

Make sure you understand this:
Watch your thoughts, for they create your actions.
Watch your actions, for they create your habits.
Watch your habits, for they create your character.
Watch your character, for it creates your life.

You want to talk about all these things, when they're being thrown at you, and you're juggling them. I would see Baby Hulk in the gym, and at weekends, when the cell doors were unlocked, I would go back up to the first floor and visit him. I would look into Shuggy's cell and see his smile and find it impossible not to smile back.

But it was Ike that I found myself naturally drawn towards. He had a radio in his cell, and he would listen to music a lot in the evenings – good music, loud music. Stuff from the 80s and 90s. I would compliment him on his musical choices, and often he would invite me in, and sometimes he wouldn't have to, because I'd find myself walking in like it was a normal thing.

Sometimes it would just be me and him. One of us sitting on his bed, one on the small chair. Sometimes it would be Shuggy too, which meant one man sitting on the toilet. There was never room for any more, but at weekends there was always a new face in there – someone Ike had known in the old days, someone else who knew he knew things because he worked in the laundry, and that's where these secret things got talked about.

Ike had respect from people. For his job, for his size. He wasn't Baby Hulk, but he was a big man, and muscles mattered in Huntercombe. They bought you admiration and they bought you deference.

I got a little of it by association. Those men who would come by to visit Ike and then see me in his cell. See us together at lunchtime, or in the same corner of the gym. What I didn't know is that it wasn't entirely luck. I would only find out later that Andy Small had told Ike to look out for me. Whether this was because he'd worked out that I needed protection, that I was still an innocent stumbling through an uncharted landscape, or because he had plans for me – a role he wanted me to play that would work for him too – I don't know. Maybe a little of both. But he saw us talking in the gym, and he knew where our cells were, so he talked to Ike too.

– Listen, look out for this white guy. He needs your help.

You can't be naive, in prison. You can't look at something the way you used to do outside and think you know it in here because you knew it out there. I couldn't forget that Ike was in the last year of a twelve-year sentence, and he got those years for a reason. But, even when I tried, I struggled to see this Ike who welcomed me into his cell – who came into mine to let it all go – ever visibly slipping back into the old Ike.

I felt I could trust him, as much as I could anyone since I had been led down from the dock at Southwark Crown Court. I didn't have doubts. Maybe that was me going all-in again. But there was the way he was with me, the way he was with others.

His devotion to God, the prayers in his cell. The speeches he made in the church services on Sundays. The way he looked at me when the priest asked me if I would also read from the Bible, occasionally.

I had been brought up Catholic – that southern Germany thing. The services here were across the Christian denominations. There were about twenty-five or thirty of us who were going along, most weeks. What else are you going to do on your Sunday morning – take the dog for a walk, wash the car, prepare a big Sunday roast? I was happy to do the occasional reading; I saw it as a good thing to be picked, and I thought it displayed confidence, to the inmates I didn't know, that I could get up and speak in public.

They liked the Old Testament stuff, in the main. The meaty stuff, more dramatic, more inclined to the black and white. And when I had read and Ike had read, and that part of the day was all done, we would go to the showers together. With Ike I could almost feel safe. I knew that when the shower room door shut behind us, there was a big man with a reputation between me and anyone else. And Ike had been in Huntercombe so much longer, more than three years now, so he could tell me which shower worked, which one was broken, which one had enough hot water and which had none at all. Shuggy would join us too.

The ground floor of Patterson, strength in collective numbers.

I said you couldn't prepare a big Sunday dinner. That turned out to be wrong, because Ike began inviting me to his cell for lunch. He had no more way of cooking food than I did. No hot-plate or saucepans, no knives and forks. Just a kettle. But somehow, with just a kettle, he would cook up a feast.

He called it fufu. A West African speciality. Balls of maize, rolled in his hands and boiled until they held their shape, dipped in a sauce of vegetables and stock and flavour.

He ordered the ingredients from the canteen menu, paid for it with his wages from the laundry. You weren't going to get rich, working in prison. When my monthly balance sheet came through, it was all spelled out: £1.05 per shift, notated for each day you were on duty. Even on the days when I tried to do two shifts at the gym, which didn't come off very often, you could see the funds you had creeping up only at the slowest rate: £31 in total, up to £35, then back down again to £28 as you paid for your phone calls and TV and those things you ordered from the canteen list. But Ike got the food, and I understood the honour I was being given: my neighbour, sharing his bread with me. The respect, the friendship. All the other inmates he could have eaten with, the ones who could maybe pull favours for him. So I ate with him, and because I knew he liked Diet Coke, I bought a couple of those for him from the list with my gym wages and I took them along and hoped they were cold enough to enjoy.

The unspoken pleasure of it all. First Sundays, after church service, then sometimes Saturdays. Hanging out, talking stories, eating together.

Cell Dreams: The Trial #2

This is how I try to deal with it, before the trial. I speak to Lilian. Lilian, this is like me playing a tournament. It will be repetitive. The Monday and the Tuesday and the Thursday, it's the same game every time. This will be two weeks and people trying to take me down and I have to come through. So we'll treat this like the old days.

We'll wake up at the same time each day. We'll eat the same things. We'll call in to that same small Italian restaurant, and we'll eat food designed to give us energy. We'll leave the drinking alone.

I feel ... focused. I feel closer to some sort of control. I'm a little quieter, but for good reasons. Processing a little more, planning and strategising.

I tell Lilian how I was during Grand Slam tournaments. I would never sleep in the same bed as my girlfriend or wife. So now I will sleep in the small bedroom we've kept for visits from my son Amadeus. Even though I could be going to prison for seven years. Lilian, I have to concentrate, I have to sleep, I have to be ready.

The flat is small. Probably the smallest flat I've had since I was a teenager. One and a half bedrooms. In Amadeus's room there's just the single bed and a cupboard. The kitchen is tiny, the bathroom is smaller. There's room for one person and that's it. So we walk Hyde Park's well-known parts and its quiet corners.

We end up sleeping in the same room. It turns out to be better that way. Who knew? But we stick to the same routines, the same wake-up. At night I want to watch football and tennis on TV, but we don't have satellite channels, so I watch YouTube highlights instead. Sport took me to this place, but it also helps me escape.

INSIDE

The last week of June, heat building in the low corridors and small rooms of Huntercombe. Something else beyond, coming round to me as it always had done: the start of Wimbledon.

How strange it felt, this summer, to be so far away. Not to be driving in to the All England Club a few days early to see the old place, to meet old friends and pick up my commentary rota. Wimbledon changes each year but so subtly that only the insiders can see the joins. Even when it's close to forty years since you first stepped on to Centre Court, the snap of your serve still sounds for you, the slide and grip of that grass under your feet. This was like being away from home for Christmas, or watching your kid's birthday party on Zoom. I was too close and too far away, all at the same time.

I didn't know then what a special Wimbledon it would be. The connections that held me to those courts, to the white lines and dark green grandstands. I was glad I would be able to keep an eye on it, on the TV in my cell on the summer evenings, on the big TV on the gym wall if everyone was behaving and we were permitted to switch it on. I wondered how my BBC friends were preparing. Sue Barker and Tim Henman, John McEnroe and Andrew Castle. I thought about Novak Djokovic, and whether he could win his fourth men's singles title in a row.

I hadn't expected to ever coach Novak, when that relationship came around, late in 2013. A call from his long-time agent, Edoardo. I'd made some remarks in commentary about Novak's court positioning, about how he was letting his matches in the early rounds of Slams go on too long, and was too tired mentally and physically, deep in the final. Not in a disrespectful sense, but because I had been there myself. I knew it.

So we met in a restaurant in Monaco that all the tennis players know: Avenue 31. And I didn't play games, because there was no point for either of us.

– Novak, we're wasting our time if I cannot be honest. It's just the two of us here. I have to tell you what I think, whether you like it or not. I don't know who your groups are and what they tell you, but if you want me to help you, I need to be honest, and you need to be honest about what's bothering you, why you're not the same as before, how your private life is, how your professional life is. If I don't know what's wrong, I can't help you.

I don't think he had heard anything like that for a while. No doubt from his father, but success changes the atmospheric pressure around anybody. You don't even know it's happening, but you gradually slide into your comfort zone. You get buddies telling you all day long how great you are, and I was not going to be Novak's buddy.

And it worked, for three years. For both of us. In those Wimbledon final wins over Roger Federer in 2014 and 2015, when he had never felt comfortable playing Roger on Centre Court because of how Centre Court felt about Roger. How Roger knew that place and had owned it – for a long time; how he could serve and volley, could rally, could slice. How hard it is to find a strategy against a player like Roger Federer, in the one place Roger Federer loves more than any other.

Winning in five sets in 2014, when Roger had won the first set, and everyone knowing that Roger never lost at Wimbledon after winning the first set. The whole BBC crew, everybody, saying in the commentary box, in the studio: 'Roger, the perfect player, the perfect man in this form, Novak doesn't have a chance.'

Winning in 2015, after an interruption for rain. When I thought Novak might be losing it, mentally, and I ran from the players' box down to the clubhouse during that break, even though I wasn't supposed to go in, knowing no one would stop me. Thinking, I've maybe got ten minutes here, and deciding to let it all go. I don't think I had ever spoken to any player the way I did with Novak, in that locker room. Being really very aggressive with him and making him wake up. Novak, you are giving this match to Roger, and you can't do that.

Maybe something clicked in that moment. Maybe it was the words, maybe it was the luck of the rain break. Maybe him listening to me differently. But our journey was moving. Winning four majors in a row, the final two of 2015 and the first two of 2016. Six Grand Slam titles in total while we were together, fourteen ATP Masters 1000 titles.

We stayed close, even when the coaching came to its natural end. When I worked with other players, when I coached with the German national team, there was always a time he'd call up.

– Boss, I need to talk to you. Watch my practice. What am I doing?

I would always tell him what I thought. We would talk about expectations and how to cope with them. The bond remained. A mutual understanding that in an emergency he could call me and I could call him.

Maybe that's what was on his mind, as Wimbledon came around that year. The reigning men's and women's champions do a media conference, just before the tournament begins. In his, Novak told the reporters he was thinking about me.

'Even when we stopped working, our relationship kept going in the right way. I have been in touch with one of his sons, Noah, and asking if there is something that I could do.

'It's terrible. I'm just very sad that someone I know so well, and of course someone that is a legend of our sport, is going through what he's going through. We know how long he has to be there. So I just hope that he will stay healthy and strong.'

People heard about this, in Huntercombe. When I called Lilian that weekend, we talked about it. How good it felt to be remembered, when you thought everything was moving on without you. I said to her: this is hard on me, but it's hard on you, just the same. You should go watch Novak at Wimbledon. Call Edoardo, I'm sure he'll get you a ticket.

Of course Edoardo said yes. I'll get you two tickets. There's just one condition: if Novak wins this match, you'll have to come every time.

I knew this rule. I liked it. I'd experienced it too, when I was part of his team. So when Novak walked out on to Centre for the opening match on Monday afternoon, as the champion does, Lilian and Noah were there to watch him take on South Korea's Kwon Soon-woo. Such a fantastic gesture, such an emotional moment to know my partner and son were there on Centre Court, supporting my old friend as he supported them.

I was on orderly duties in the gym that afternoon. I got there in time to see that Andy had put the tennis on the TV. The players were warming up. That's when Ike and Baby Hulk came over to me.

– Boris, they've just been talking about you.
– Who?
– The BBC people. They say they're missing you.

INSIDE

Lilian told me about it later. John McEnroe, right at the start. 'Boris, we love you. We miss you, man.' Sue Barker, nodding and smiling. 'We do indeed.'

Of course it was a small thing. I think they also got into trouble with some people. Why is the BBC sending greetings to a convicted criminal?

I just knew it changed things for me, that week. Just as it did when I found out, much later, that my fellow commentator Andrew Castle had said something similar at Queen's the fortnight before. 'I've had a real moment of missing Boris. I know he's in prison and I know why. Boris, we look forward to welcoming you on your return.'

I got a different look from people, that Monday. That week. Before that, a few inmates called me the tennis guy. But most of them didn't know. Didn't care.

Now I had a profile. A little respect. The TV in the gym stayed tuned to the tennis, even if the sound was muted for the matches. I was working but I was staring at the screen all the time I could. Watching Novak and his movement and him winning the first set, waiting for the camera to cut to the players' box and there's Lilian, suddenly, and there's Noah, wearing my jacket, maybe even my shirt ... definitely my shoes ...

I couldn't hide it now. I was looking at the screen and smiling and spinning out a little, too. Since this was prison, the talk around me didn't cut corners.

– Fuck, you've got a hot chick, how did you do it?
Knowing I had to roll with it, when I replied.
– Hidden talents, my friend, hidden talents ...
Then other comments.
– That's your son? The Black kid?

A different sort of respect, now. Okay, so that's how your family is … A kind of new acceptance and recognition from all the Black inmates.

Cell Dreams: The Trial #3

There are things you expect in a trial and things you don't.

The experience of standing in the dock. Of going to the witness box. Feeling the eyes of the judge and the prosecution, of the jury. Thinking, this isn't like before. I can't win this crowd over like I used to. This is not my game.

The walk in each day, Lilian by my side, holding her hand. Great banks of reporters and cameras set up opposite the doors at Southwark Crown Court, the shouted questions, the noise of the feet rushing towards you, cameras focusing and firing.

So I breathe. Inhale through the nose, exhale through the mouth, very long and very slow. I lower my pulse. Inside the courtroom I focus on the faces in the jury, try to read who's with me, who's not with me.

These are the charges read out. Nine counts of failing to hand over old trophies. Seven counts of concealing property. Five counts of failing to disclose estate, including properties in Germany and London, shares and a bank account. Two counts of removal of property. One of concealing debt.

I listen as the prosecutor reads out loud from her notes, in her formal language.

– It is the prosecution case that Mr Becker acted dishonestly with regard to a number of his assets, that in

INSIDE

various ways he effectively hid from, or made unavailable to, those responsible for identifying the assets. There is a consistent policy throughout the history of bankruptcy legislation, which goes back hundreds of years, that bankrupts who play the system, act in bad faith, should be punished and that, in short, is what the prosecution say Mr Becker did here. The issues boil down to everyday issues of dishonesty and knowledge. That is what we say is at the heart of this case.

I can sense the atmosphere now. Count 4 feels like the big one. Of taking money from my company to pay my ex-wife, my child support, my knee surgery, my rent. To pay the lawyers who advised me that this was all okay. I thought it was okay. If I don't make these payments to my ex-wife, I'm breaking the law in the US. That seems obvious to me.

It's three months, this period when it happened. Between being made bankrupt in June 2017 and meeting the trustee on 13 September. When he told me I shouldn't do what I was doing, I stopped.

The rest of it? It's my mother's house in Leimen. It's the mortgage on it. It's me owning 75,000 shares in a company called Breaking Data, which sounds great, but the company is worth almost nothing. Those shares were sold by the trustee for £9,000. You really think I'd intentionally hide that amount of money?

All of this was told to the trustee in September 2017. I made a mistake. I didn't know it was a mistake. When I found out, I stopped.

These nine counts of failing to hand over my tennis trophies. Two of my three Wimbledon men's singles titles, my

1992 Olympic gold medal. The Australian Open trophies from 1991 and 1996, the President's Cup from 1985 and 1989. My 1989 Davis Cup trophy, a Davis Cup Gold Coin won in 1988. These are the ones they couldn't find when they auctioned all the others off.

And this feels like a weak point because we have no evidence. My short answer is that I don't know where they are, which is hard for them to believe. I try to explain: when you win a trophy at seventeen or eighteen, the trophy doesn't matter. It's the title, it's you winning the match, it's you becoming number one. You couldn't care less where the lump of shiny metal is.

Now I'm finished playing, it's the other way round. At my age, I want to show my kids: this is the Wimbledon trophy, this is the US Open trophy. I want to explain to the jury that if I could find these souvenirs tonight, I would show them to my children tomorrow.

I know this doesn't sound good. It sounds confusing. But it's the truth, and I want to tell them.

The prosecution completes its case. The defence does the same. And now we wait for the jury – first for the Easter break, then for their deliberations.

It could be one day, it could be two weeks. You don't know. Going into the court each day, no steer or inkling from your lawyers which way this could go.

A Friday morning, just after the Easter holidays. So tired now. Three days in jury limbo, all played out.

We're having a nap in the chairs in the corner of a windowless room off a corridor when my lawyer comes in. Boris, we have a verdict.

INSIDE

Now your heart falls to your feet. The blood in your face and hands feels cold.

This is the final game of the final set. This is the moment the ball falls. My side of the net, or theirs.

Next day the good news kept coming. After four weeks of trying, Lilian and Noah could come to visit me in Huntercombe for the first time. Noah was still wearing my jacket and shirt and shoes from the day before, but he's my boy, so that was fine with me.

We had two hours together, the usual stipulated limit. The same process for them coming in: giving ID, leaving everything they had brought with them in a locker, going through security with sniffer dogs and then me standing up at a small desk right in the far corner, and the two of them coming over, and us hugging each other.

My partner, my son. Of course I kept putting a brave face on things. But it was less overwhelming now than it had been in Wandsworth. I actually had things to hold on to: the job in the gym, Wimbledon, the Stoicism classes. Ike and Shuggy and Baby Hulk. I asked Lilian and Noah questions, before they could ask me.

– How was Wimbledon? How was the journey?

Lilian bought us snacks from the little kiosk in there. From an Italian inmate called Giovanni, who had been a lawyer on the outside and apparently had a sideline advising fellow prisoners on the inside. A rare chance to enjoy a fizzy drink and not have to calculate what else that meant you couldn't have. Keeping the conversation light, at the start. Amore, this looks better than Wandsworth, it's greener out there, right? Amore, your natural hair colour is growing through, after years of bleaching it, and it's amazing – it's not really white, and it's very healthy, and I think you should keep this style, it's more authentic.

But it was always hard to be comfortable. To be truly normal. The CCTV cameras in the corners, cross-referencing each other; the microphones you knew were listening. The tables set up so you could sit opposite each other but never side by side.

The wardens were understanding, in this liminal space. They allowed you to hold hands across the table, and to hug at the beginning and at the end. Not too close in between, so nothing could be passed across, yet respectful of how much we all needed this brief and unnatural interaction. Every time it happened I could feel the longing between Lilian and me for an authentic intimacy. For the comfort and courage that only physical contact can bring. I could sense, on some visits, that she would be taken aback by small changes she noticed in me: slightly strange haircuts, because grooming was a DIY process inside and another inmate hacking away with something blunt was never the true salon experience; a different scent to the old days, because I had no cologne of my own but would always try to trade something with someone else on my wing so I could have a splash of theirs, to be slightly more presentable. I would try to look good, laughably, for our meeting, in the least battered tracksuit I had available. Always trying to make the best from the scraps I had. Telling stories that would indicate I was in good spirits. Let me tell you what Baby Hulk has been doing, last weekend I ate fufu and it was tasty and nutritious – you should look up the recipe.

INSIDE

And when Lilian and Noah left that day, I was heartened by the thought I might see them again the next day, when Novak played his second-round match on Centre, and Novak – being Novak – would want them there again and organise another pair of tickets.

Conversations were happening now that could not have taken place before. Inmates I hadn't spoken to coming up to me in the gym, where the TV was now always tuned to Wimbledon in the afternoons. People asking me who was going to win the men's singles. A lot of support for Novak from the eastern Europeans, a lot of love for Rafa Nadal, because he's Rafa Nadal. The wardens asking about Andy Murray, until John Isner's big serve was too much for him in the second round and their attention switched to the other British man making progress through the first week: Cam Norrie.

Novak beating Thanasi Kokkinakis in straight sets in the second round, Miomir Kecmanović the same way in the third. Tim van Rijthoven, comfortably, in the fourth. Each time Lilian was there, either with Noah or Elias, and each time I would spot them in the players' box, and I would rollercoaster through the same conflicting emotions. Finding it intensely hard, in some moments, because they were so close but so far away. Missing them more for being there but not with me. The pull of the old currents: oh man, I should be in those seats with them, oh my God, look where I am instead, this is so terrible ... The swooping uplift of the good stuff: hey, I can see them, and they're having a good time, and this court, this arena, is still connecting me to things that no other place in the world can.

Here's the thing when you're an elite tennis player: you train yourself not to look back. Only look forward to the next challenge, the next contest. Looking back gets you stuck. That bad stuff behind you? Ignore it. Shut it away. Everything that isn't about getting to the next level is a distraction.

Inside, I had begun to change. To reassess, to turn over what lay in my wake. Almost the opposite to the old days: don't look too far ahead, because it might all become too much. Stay in this day and worry about nothing else.

Stepping backwards was helping, in lots of ways. You can't move forward if you're still tethered to something in your past. It could become too much sometimes too. Thoughts could tumble over themselves, pick up speed, run away in the quiet lonely hours. *I should be there, I should be there. The whole world is destroying me, the media have witnessed my funeral. These things people are saying, the things they have written – it's the worst I've ever had in my life, and some of it is deserved, and some of it is not, but what have I ever done to these people? The Wimbledon champion who has to watch it on TV in prison – I get it's a great story, but there's a person behind all this who still lives and breathes, who has children, who has a mother. I've made mistakes, but this cannot be a fair price to pay ...*

When you feel like this, you are touched by the smallest of gestures. By a little comment here or there that someone else might not even notice. That there was still someone like Novak Djokovic who was thinking about me and taking care of my family, that Sue and John and Andrew said they missed me. I felt like I was still a part of something. Not all the old bonds had been severed. Maybe I would be able to go back one day. Today was not for ever. The past and the future might come together in harmony once again.

INSIDE

So I immersed myself in the quarter-finals and I tried to pull from them all the consolation I could. Novak up against Jannik Sinner and going two sets down, and the prison gym getting antsy, and then Novak doing Novak to come through 6–2 in the fifth. Norrie coming through another five-setter against David Goffin, the home crowds going crazy. Nick Kyrgios working his way through to the semis, all attitude and cool temper; watching Rafa fighting and fighting against Taylor Fritz, coming through injury and pain and all sorts of doubts to win on a champion's tie-break in the fifth.

In those matches, in the tight seconds where contests turn, I could sometimes pretend to myself that I wasn't in a prison gym, mopping floors, scrubbing toilet seats. I could feel myself in the commentary box, low down on the angle at the back of Centre Court, headphones on, lip mic in my hand. I would find myself commentating, sometimes inside my head, sometimes to the inmates who would come stand at my shoulder and ask me questions. Telling them, even when Novak was two sets down and Sinner looked to be away, that Novak could still win. Pointing out the critical moments towards the end of the third set. Staying late in the gym for the Fritz-Nadal match, spotting when Fritz was tightening up. Thinking about who Novak might play in the final, being afraid of Kyrgios because he's a crazy guy and might just beat Novak and so wanting him to have a proper contest in the semis, where he could lose or get exhausted. Okay, I know Fritz a little bit, he seems to be a nervous guy, he seems afraid to me. If he stays nervous here and bags it, then an injured Nadal is somehow escaping this quarter-final, and when he's up against Nick in the semis he's either going to be at half-strength or he won't be able to play at all. If Fritz beats Nadal, at least Kyrgios has a match, right?

All these thoughts focused on a distant place, such an escape for those hours. I felt happier than I'd felt in months, but sadder, too. Seeing my partner and my son, close but not close enough; watching the player I had coached to Grand Slam titles, aiming for another. Emotions I'd kept tucked away, coming up on my blindside. Tears, sometimes just below the surface, sometimes bursting through.

Prison never truly leaves you alone for long. It's the system that rules you, and any brief respite you find will never last as long as you might hope.

Thursday, 7 July. The women's semi-finals, Elena Rybakina against Simona Halep, Ons Jabeur versus Germany's Tatjana Maria. I wanted to watch, but the guards had another idea. You could see how it made sense to them: they wanted a basic tennis court marked out in the exercise area, so who else would you order to paint the lines than the guy who spent his life sprinting around them?

I went out into the sunshine and took my brush and marked it all out and painted. And the currents from my past came at me and pulled at me and dragged me back, and out there in the afternoon heat I felt something and knew it: 7 July is my date. This is the day I won Wimbledon for the first time. Seventeen years old then, the world all there for me. Fifty-four years old now, so much of it behind me. Only the unknown ahead.

Friday came. Novak against Norrie in the first semi-final, not on shift in the gym so watching it on the small TV in my cell. I never thought Novak could lose, even when the first set slipped away from him. I didn't believe Norrie was good enough, mentally or tennis-wise. I didn't see enough weapons to truly hurt Novak in a semi-final. He could take a set, maybe two, but I didn't think he had the self-confidence and, well, balls, to beat a player like Novak at this point in the biggest tournament in the world.

I wasn't afraid of Norrie. I was afraid of Kyrgios. Rafa's injury had indeed been a bad one, and Kyrgios got a walk-over. Then I was very nervous for the final.

Sunday afternoon, in my cell again. Waiting to see Lilian on TV, waiting for Novak to step onto court.

I wasn't commentating now. I was coaching. Sending good heart and advice through the ether to SW19. Just making sure he got the memo, making sure he understood how to play.

You get to a Wimbledon singles final, and you have to do a lot more than play tennis. It's a question of whether you can overcome your own demons, your latent fears. Every man or woman who reaches this point has been a kid dreaming of this moment. Are those dreams going to drive you on or swamp you? I had been impressed by Kyrgios and the way he had overcome the obstacles in front of him. The Stefanos Tsitsipas match in the third round where he had been a set down and handled it. He was old-school. He liked to get in your face. I liked that about him, and it's why I thought he was dangerous. He really didn't seem to care who was on the other side of the net.

He won the first set. The contest was too quick for Novak. Nick was winning his points too easily; he got one break of serve, and that was enough. Novak hadn't started to battle.

I sat there on my narrow bed, in T-shirt and shorts on a sticky afternoon. I was hoping that in that second set, every service game for Nick took a little longer. He gets to 40–30, he gets to deuce. He has to work harder to win his service games. I was hoping Novak could hold his.

At the beginning of that second set Nick had chances to get an early break. You're a set up with a break and you can run away with the second, and then it's a long way back. Nick likes to go for broke. When it's going for him, he can accelerate away from you fast. So I knew this set was key for Novak to make it a match, to make it a competition. The longer it went, the more chances for Novak.

And that's how it was. In prison, there's a way you communicate excitement. When you're pleased, when you want to celebrate. When you want the whole fucked-up place to know about it. You can't text people, you can't organise a party. So you bang on the wall. You bang on the door. You bang things together – cups and cutlery, chairs and beds.

On my first night in prison, in those first few weeks, it had been the screaming and the distress that filled my ears. Now the noise was just as intense, but for a different purpose. When Novak won the second set, all I could hear throughout my wing was that banging. Ike and Shuggy next door, Alex opposite. All the others down the corridor on the ground floor, Baby Hulk and his mates on the next floor up.

They were all watching. They were all with Novak. They were all with me.

Novak took the third set. The fourth went to a tie-break. Feeling confident now. Even if Kyrgios levelled up, the fifth set – that's Novak's territory. In the deciding set of a major, you don't want to play Novak. He takes it personally.

Into the tie-breaker. The first few points are always important, because Novak is a frontrunner. He smells blood when he sees the finish line. He gets better where a lot of guys actually get worse because they're afraid. They don't know what's behind the finish line. Novak does.

So, I wasn't afraid any more. And when Novak won, and raised his arms, I stood up and I raised my arms too. And as I did so, the noise along the wing broke out again, louder than ever before.

The banging didn't stop for ten minutes. On walls, on doors. With cups, with chairs.

It had taken me two weeks to educate them that this was my man, and now I realised. They had understood.

I stood there and I cried. Everything coming out – the tension, the doubts, the stress, the hope. The love I felt for Lilian and my children, the love I felt for Novak. For Centre Court, like a portal that July afternoon, bringing us all together.

You can't shut your door. But I pushed mine closed so no one could see me, and I listened to the banging, and I listened to it echoing across Huntercombe. When the door opened, it was Ike, then Shuggy.

– Wow, Boris, your man won, he won …

Everyone coming by. Embraces and slaps on the back. Smiles, in a place where you always hid everything away.

I thought about all the things I had learned about Stoicism, when night came and my door was locked again and all was quiet. Wimbledon is for Stoics. Train your mind and you will win. Play until the end. Don't give up in the third set, don't give up in the fourth. Fight until it's over.

These brief moments sustain you in the days and weeks afterwards. They carry you through the darkness you know is coming and all the stuff you don't. That Sunday night I was still

BORIS BECKER

locked up in a tiny cell a hundred miles from those I loved. My life was inside. But I was flying, too. I was flying.

Dear Boris,

I wanted to write to you to say how disgraceful it is that you are in prison. I watched the coverage of the Queen's Tournament and I am watching Wimbledon, and I hope you know that all the commentators are behind you. John McEnroe, Andrew Castle, John Lloyd and Sue Barker, have all wished you well on air and all of them say they miss you. We all do!

You were a great iconic champion, who has graced the above tournaments. It's not the same without you in the commentary box. I hope you are managing to cope in prison – it must be absolutely horrendous – and that each day is 'notched off' as another day done and a day closer to freedom.

I hope that you are getting lots of support too. I will always defend you, and I'm sure all tennis fans do.

Sending very good wishes to you,

Rosemary

CHAPTER 8

Dublin, Eire

Dearest Boris,

I hope my letter finds you well and coping with how things are in your life now. Remember, you are loved and respected and gave so much joy to tennis fans! I just wanted to write to say I think about you in prison, and wish for you to get out soon and put it all behind you.

I'm a published author and have written eight bestsellers. Why don't you put pen to paper in there and write a book?

Anyway, just wanted to say 'hello', and hope you're doing okay!

With all my love from Ireland,

Caroline

A clarity, in the aftermath of all that Wimbledon brought. I loved living in London. I wanted to go to the All England Club again and to walk out onto Centre Court. But I didn't want that as much as I wanted to be with Lilian. Not as much as I wanted to be able to see my children and embrace them, to wake up early on a sunny morning and walk out into the dew and the blue skies, not stare at it all through a small dirty window.

I wasn't wasting my time in prison. It felt like I was using it now, rather than it using me. But I had to be outside so I could begin again. I wanted to be the one making decisions about my life. All those years and the control had come from somewhere else. From tennis, from agents, from financial deals. From parents, before all that.

So I talked to my deportation lawyers, and I looked at all those acronyms – ERSED, HDC, ROTL. I looked at those dates, printed in black ink on the prison letter I had received in June.

Number of days in sentence: 914. Sentence expiry date: 28/10/24. Conditional release date: 29/07/2023.

I looked at the line below. ERSED (Early Release Scheme Eligibility Date): 14/12/2022.

It was simple, now. I would agree to deportation back to Germany. Even if those dates weren't exactly right, and it slipped a few days, as it always did in prison, there was an end I could imagine to all this. Christmas with Lilian, with my family. London could wait. Centre Court had its roof now; it wasn't going to change much more before I got back.

I signed the forms and circled the date on the calendar at the back of my diary. And I set about finding fresh ways and new people to help those intervening weeks and months accelerate by.

It was Shuggy who introduced me to Balak. Another Sri Lankan, another man who had spent time in Belmarsh. Balak was in for fourteen years. Floor information said he had been part of a gang that killed a teenager. The origin story was vague and complicated – committing his crime aged eighteen or nineteen, moving to the US, starting a family, and then the FBI tracking him down, four or five armed agents coming for him at night and extraditing him to the UK. Agents who were rough with him, according to the stories.

I didn't know how much of that was true. He seemed slightly different to the others, when I spent time with him. A little bit intellectual. He said he had been a business agent in the US. He said he wanted to study and set up another business. You hear lots of stories in prison; it passes the time, it makes you feel good about yourself, it makes you feel like you're moving forward. So you hear these things and nod, but you withhold judgement inside. You work with the tangibles, not the dream.

With Balak it was chess. That was what brought us together. He had a beautiful set, maybe the best on the wing. He was good, too. Everyone wanted to play him. His cell was busy at weekends, and soon I was in there on weekend afternoons.

We helped each other, in some ways. He had a couple of hearings about his possible release date, and they didn't go well. One postponement, then another. I tried to keep his spirits up and offer a little practical help from my own experience. What he should say at the hearing, what it helped admitting to, the steps that make up this formal dance. We talked about the stuff I'd learned on HDC and ERSED. We discussed body language.

Through these conversations and the hours of chess we grew closer more quickly than we might otherwise have done. Which made it uncomfortable when I found out, in conversation with others, that not all Balak said could be trusted. There was the backstory, and how much of it was true. There was what he might be planning next. Some said he was going back to his old ways of making money. Others just pointed out the inconsistencies. Considering he had been locked up at a time when the smartphone was in its infancy, he knew an awful lot about technology. Almost a hands-on knowledge.

He was a sharp guy. I got that from his conversation and his aptitude for long, challenging games of chess against a variety of characters and styles. He could be fascinating at times – drawing you in with his intellect and erudition. But he knew things about the internet and coding and social media that didn't make sense for a man who had been imprisoned for as long as he had. I began to wonder if he was one of the inmates with access to a mobile phone. If he somehow had access to the internet.

I decided to hold a little space between us, but I kept the chess games going. I'd always enjoyed playing. My style was the opposite of my tennis game: defence-orientated, trying to take matches deep, happy to slow down my opponent like someone might if taking me on on a clay court. Sometimes I would attack at the start, trying to push the other player into making mistakes, but then I'd sit back and wait. There were three or four opening gambits I liked to use, my way of quickly working out whether you could play or not. And then I would play for ever. Hours and hours for one game, up against a clever mind like Balak. He was a better player than me, although I learned quickly from his moves. My reactions were always good and I understood that chess is a repetitive game. You have to study your opponent and remember their preferred patterns of play. I was consistent. The longer we went, the better my chances got. We'll play until I win, right? I could grind Balak, and at times he would lose patience. You could see it flicker across his face: another hour? This motherfucker just never gives up …

INSIDE

The weeks were falling into their own pattern. Andy had been correct about the Stoicism classes. I did find myself naturally drawn to them. One Monday morning we began with a discussion about one of Epictetus's better-known quotes. 'Happiness and freedom begin with a clear understanding of one principle. Some things are within your control. And some things are not.'

On the chalkboard were two headings, with a list under each.

Up to us:
Our opinions
Our dislikes
Our reactions
Meaning of things
Our goals
Our behaviour
Loving
Respecting

Not up to us:
Actions of others
The past
Our body
Family of origin
What others think
Being loved
Being respected

You read these things and they were often challenging. You held them up to your own life and the way you had been and sometimes that made you feel uncomfortable.

A few days later it was a worksheet we had to fill out. Lines of instruction at the top of the page: 'For those things that you can do nothing about, an attitude of acceptance is most helpful. Acceptance does not mean that you like what is happening or that you agree with what is happening. It means that you can emotionally accept the reality of the situation without bringing harm to yourself or others.'

As a player I had always been a fighter. You gave it everything until the last point. You refused to believe the reality of a defeat, even as the sets piled up against you and your body strained and failed. You accepted none of it. You railed against those who seemed to accept defeat as inevitable – umpires, opponents, sometimes crowds. Sometimes your own flaws. You swore and you threw things and you raged against the dying of the light. Acceptance? That was giving up. That was death.

But that's only half true. That was never the whole of me. It was the version of Boris Becker that worked on lots of days. Other times I could look at it differently. Peter Doohan, beating me in the second round of Wimbledon when I had won the last two championships and beaten him in straight sets at Queen's two weeks before and nobody could imagine any other result than an easy win. Telling the press afterwards. *I didn't start a war. Nobody died. I only lost a tennis match, nothing more.*

On the same page of the book was a flow chart for us to follow.

INSIDE

Event (coming to prison)
⬇
In your control or not
⬇
Acceptance (do this quickly)
⬇
Find a benefit (good) for you

Further down, a quote attributed to Reinhold Niebuhr: 'Grant me the courage to change the things I can change, the serenity to accept the things I cannot change, and the wisdom to know the difference.'

This one stayed with me, beyond that day, beyond that week. Some of the lines in the course booklet were practical, and those were the easy ones to implement. 'Our journey towards the good life starts with making our beds every day and making our room as tidy as possible.' Okay, sure. This makes sense.

The ones that stuck were the challenges. The uncomfortable ones. The ones you wanted to run away from, sometimes, and hold on to tight, on other nights.

Busier days, fuller evenings. As Wimbledon finished the women's European Championships were beginning. I had always loved football. Growing up with Bayern Munich, being drawn to Liverpool by the charisma and raw energy of Jürgen Klopp, keeping an eye on Chelsea, my local team when I lived in London. I hadn't watched as much of the women's game, and I wished I'd seen more, as this tournament picked up pace.

Good old BBC. Matches most nights on one of the two main channels, another magic trick to make those lonely evenings accelerate away. Something for us all to talk about the next morning that wasn't about what was happening around us. What wasn't happening. Even in my cell I could get a sense of how big this was for England – the crowds, the atmosphere in the grounds, the growing sense of belief around the national team's chances.

Of course I followed Germany's progress. But I was incarcerated in England, so every one of their group games was live on the TV. I liked their style of play. I liked their Dutch coach Sarina Wiegman. Some nights I couldn't wait to get back into my cell to watch their matches. I started humming 'Sweet Caroline' on my way to the gym.

I got the vibe from a little way out. This final's going to end up as England against Germany, isn't it? It's like a gentle karmic dig at me. And when Alexandra Popp scored those two goals to get Germany past France and England hammered Sweden, I realised something else. I was in a prison full of foreign nationals. Ninety per cent of them hated England, because England was the reason they were locked up. So pretty much every man around me, bar the wardens, wanted Germany to win. I'd never felt so supported.

But then. Popp injured in the warm-up, Ella Toone opening the scoring for England. Silence on Patterson wing. Lina Magull equalising late in the second half, cheering and banging on doors all the way along. Chloe Kelly bundling in the winner in extra time, and when the final whistle went, a different kind of banging. Boos and jeers and discontent.

But I was okay. What could I do to change the result? Nothing. Not me, in this cell, all alone on my bed. Tracksuit on, two paces to the sink for a glass of water, two paces back. I didn't have a choice about accepting it. It just was.

INSIDE

Someone else, coming into my world. When Andy had first taken me round Huntercombe and I'd seen the prison library, there had been that calm Ghanian man, Jeffrey. He had told me about his brother working in the gym. This was Frank, and now I was in the gym most days, I was getting to know him through Ike.

Frank was an orderly too. The same sort of menial tasks, the same familiarity with the gym vibe. He said he was in his mid-forties, but he looked good – nice build, fit, confident in himself. You got the sense pretty quickly that he was an influential guy, that he knew a lot of people in this place and he knew the good guys and he knew the bad guys.

They were fraudsters, him and his brother. Jeffrey was younger, and I wondered if maybe he was struggling a little more, because he talked less, and he stayed in the library a lot of the time. So I was surprised when he approached me one day and said he had a book for me to read. The cover was a Black guy in a pristine white military tunic. It was called *Can't Hurt Me*. The guy on the cover was David Goggins, a former US Navy SEAL. The blurb described him as a kid from poverty, prejudice and physical abuse. It mentioned he had once held a Guinness world record for doing 4,030 pull-ups in seventeen hours. Kind of made sense why they liked his book in prison.

It wasn't a big place, the library. Two small rooms on each side. The woman who ran it, the one I had met on that first tour with Andy – she was good. She could break through the usual barriers between inmate and staff. She might offer you a cup of tea, occasionally. She would get us playing word games like charades. You could see her intentions in those moments: dial down the danger, get us to work together in a social environment. She spoke to you as a person, not a prisoner. But then she left, at the end of July, and the guy who took over was not the same. Cooler, more formal. I barely went back, after that.

This was how things were. The good stuff happened in little backwaters and corners. The good people were few and seldom stayed. The system marched on, oblivious to it all.

I asked at one point, when I still hadn't realised all this, when I could talk with the social worker. That was my naivety. There was no social worker. There were practical classes you could do. You could learn to make food, learn to sew.

There was nothing to stimulate your mind. You couldn't go to a history class, you couldn't learn a foreign language. A charity came in once with musical instruments. That lasted one Saturday.

I had been an education orderly in Wandsworth. I was glad; it burned through empty hours. But the maths was at second grade level. It was basic addition and subtraction. If you want to learn English, you probably don't want to be taught by a German, but my grammar and vocab was better than that of 99 per cent of the other inmates in Huntercombe. Some of them barely had a word. Learning a language in a new country makes practical sense – even more so when you're a small piece moving through a complex legal machine with arcane words and phrases. Some of the Eastern Europeans I tried to help in Wandsworth didn't pick up a single sentence in the four weeks they had with me. I had to fill out their answers for them. What was the point of it? There was none. And it was hard not to be angry, when you saw that and felt it.

– Boris, I think you need this book. It has really helped me control my demons in here.

That was Jeffrey's line, when he gave me the David Goggins book. He was in for ten years, so he was someone to listen to. I didn't get the same vibes as I did from Balak. With Jeffrey I sensed a naivety. A little bit of a lack of knowledge about the world. Like his brother he could tell me about Huntercombe, because that was what he knew. The people, the rules, the connections.

This lack of connection to the outside world, this immersion inside – it made sense to me, as I saw it in prisoners around me, but it didn't mean it was right. There were no actual newspapers in the prison library, just a prison one. It was like they didn't want you to know what was going on out there. Like they wanted to lock your mind away too.

Those acronyms again: HDC, ROTL. No wonder, when you got out on licence or negotiated a release, you could fall so easily into the old ways. A lack of knowledge, an absence of options or alternative skills. What was prison for? Sometimes it was hard to work it out. Punishment, yes, but sentencing could seem arbitrary. Rehabilitation? I could see almost none of that. If you wanted to change, you had to do it yourself. And how could you change, if everything around you stayed the same?

I was deep into my fourth month, and it was becoming clearer to me. Prison is about survival. That's it.

I was in the gym with Andy when he first mentioned it. A Stoic convention he was bringing to Huntercombe. Guest speakers from outside the prison, a couple of us converts inside. An audience of inmates and officers from this prison and others too.

I knew how Andy worked now. He was always two points ahead of everyone else. Setting up his next winner even as everyone else was scrambling around on the baseline.

So I could tell his plans were formed and they were going to happen. A stage set up in the visitors' room, a day to show the power of Stoicism and how it could soften the most obdurate of inmates. How good it could be for our education, our behaviour. How it could maybe be a way out of prison. He told me he was inviting an Australian businessman, a guy called Justin Stead. A very successful man, the founder, with his wife, of something called the Aurelius Foundation, which Andy said promoted Stoicism in prisons and business and with young people. Then he told me something else.

– Justin's bringing a guy I think you know.
– Oh okay, who?
– Pat Cash.
– Tennis Pat Cash?
– Yeah. He's a friend of Justin's, and he's a Stoic, too.
– Pat Cash? I thought he was sex, drugs and rock and roll …
– Sure, he had a few issues. But he's changed things around, and he likes all this stuff, and he's part of our group now.

At first, I didn't know how I should handle it. Did I want an old rival to see me like this? A guy who was free, and me in here with nothing and no clothes and no power? I felt uncomfortable. My old life and my new, bumping up against each other again.

And then Lilian pushed me about it, when we spoke on the phone that evening. Why would you be embarrassed? This is a different you. What do you have to hide?

What do you have to lose?

INSIDE

Cell Dreams: The Rival #2

It's the early 2000s. I'm back at Wimbledon, this time as a commentator. I'm in a suit and tie, because it's the All England Club, and you respect their traditions and their rules. Pat's there too, also working for the BBC. I've never ever seen a tie on him, and he's not wearing one now. Black leather jacket, spiky hair, earring. That's respectable too, in some ways: he doesn't care about these rules, he's being true to himself. And it's a fun place, Wimbledon, when you're working on matches for the BBC. You hang out with the other old players – Mac, Connors. You catch up over a beer.

But Pat and I are never catching up over a beer. We say hello but we're not really talking. And it stays like that, for a long time, as you hear the stories about him – a separation from his wife, an expensive divorce, the two kids. That's when I started feeling for him a little bit. I know those feelings. I know this life.

Then I'm in New York one time, coaching Novak, after Novak has been in the final. There's a night flight back to London. I see Pat. For the first time in our lives, we actually sit down and have a beer. Or rather, I have a beer. Pat doesn't. That was one of the things I don't know about, at that time. I don't know about most of his demons.

So we talk, and we look each other in the eye, and we are ... normal with each other. Like men of our age, not rivals. Not fighting for the same prize. I hear about some of the things he has overcome, and I feel a great respect for what he has come through.

When we see each other after that, something has changed. Now whenever we see each other at Wimbledon there's a conversation and there's even a sort of bond. When I go back to commentary after coaching Novak I don't take the mickey on air any more. I'm more careful and more respectful.

I began to notice something, as August came around. Or rather, I noticed I was noticing more. Tuning in to the hidden vibes and the songlines, becoming a small part in the flow of floor information.

I was known as the tennis player, now, after Novak and Wimbledon and John McEnroe and Sue Barker, but there was a lot of stuff about me that hadn't made it through. The relationship troubles, the business struggles and the scandals that spread across both. There was quite a lot that felt good about that. Almost as if I could start from scratch when I gave small parts of my story to those on my wing I was seeing regularly. In the outside world, wherever I travelled, everyone I met seemed to know me. You could see the flare of recognition in their eyes, the preconceptions. Oh yeah, you're the guy who did *that* ...

Inside it was different. You couldn't read about me in the newspapers. It was harder to google someone. There was almost an innocence in how you could tell your family story. You dropped in a little detail, waited for the reaction, and then, depending on their response, might give a little more. As the time you spent on the same corridors grew, and you walked to the servery together, or stood in the queue, another layer might be added to an anecdote, another family member introduced.

INSIDE

I began to trust some, and others began to trust me. Ike heard things in the laundry, Jeffrey in the library. I would hear things in the gym. As we moved between jobs and cells the lines would join up and the stories spread.

And it could be fast. I was at work one morning when the lines started humming. There's been a drugs bust. They're searching the far wing. They're coming for Patterson next.

Hearing it and being able to do something about it were two different things. You can't rush back to your cell from the gym. If you're in your cell you can't keep them out. They come when they come. You take it slow and you walk back at the end of your shift and see your books have been opened, your mattress turned over. For some people, the backs of their TVs taken off, their packets of food tipped out. The storm passes through, and the floor information begins again.

– Hey, they found some stuff.

– Who did it?

– That prison officer. Got it off his girlfriend. Left it in the toilets in the visitors' hall, in the basket for wastepaper.

All this stuff, these undercurrents and subplots, was beginning to bring me back to something I used to do so well. When I played tennis for a living, I always believed I was good at reading my opponents. Same when I played poker afterwards. I could put them into a category: who is this person, how do they react under pressure? What are their strengths, what are their weaknesses?

The more I played them the better I got at it. Okay, so this guy defaults to aggression. This one, he's conservative, he's careful.

I was never 100 per cent correct. I wouldn't have made the

mistakes I did otherwise. Sometimes I took things for granted. I assumed someone would always behave the way they had. People can slip and they can surprise you.

I was very good on the tennis court. Afterwards, at times, I got too comfortable. I became complacent. A little bit lazy. Not when I was young and hungry, at the start of my career. My toughest opponents then were Ivan Lendl and Stefan Edberg, but I felt I quickly had their number. I knew what to do in order to beat them.

Lendl? I attacked his backhand return. Didn't matter if I got passed once or twice; it was a real weakness to exploit. Mentally, since he's a perfectionist, I had to ruffle him a little bit. I had to get him away from being so computer-like and get to his emotions, because he didn't know how to deal with that. My plan didn't always work. Sometimes you're not good enough. Sometimes I wasn't able to deliver on my own strengths. But a lot of the time it did work.

Stefan? I knew I was more powerful. I knew I should avoid playing tennis with him because he had such finesse, such good footwork – he could out-manoeuvre me. I had to be quicker, harder. I had to shorten points, because he liked the longer rallies. He liked the space and time. I had to be aggressive. I had to take away his time.

Inside Huntercombe, I could feel myself tuning in again. To all of the disparate characters around me: officers, inmates, staff. Being able to read an element of their character and personality helped me gauge my own behaviour. Working out who I could trust. Thinking about who might appear solid but had a weakness that could see them slip. Where to be careful, and when to step back.

INSIDE

But you could fool yourself sometimes. This was not Wimbledon, or Flushing Meadows, or Flinders Park. It was a dangerous place. When your cell door opened, you were behind enemy lines. You could show a private truth to some men sometimes, but you also had to put on a mask. To go blank again, to feel your way around. Who you can look in the eye, who you really shouldn't. Who you can make a joke with, who you have to be careful with. And if you don't work it out pretty quickly, you're going to get into trouble.

So it was when an American prisoner arrived on the wing in early August. Patterson was a popular place. Floor information had it as the safest place to be, and when a prisoner was transferred or released and a cell became free, inmates on other wings would try to apply for the spare cell. I'd have people coming up to me in the gym: Boris, could you put in a good word with your wardens? Could you help us get in there?

This American arrived. White guy, chubby. And the lines started buzzing.

– This new guy, he's a paedophile.

– Yeah, he hurt little boys.

I got a sinister feel from him. Baby Hulk wanted to kill him. I didn't want to hurt him, but I didn't want him anywhere near me. When time came for lock-up, most of us on my section of the ground floor would shake hands with each other. A sense of brotherhood at the day's close. A way of ending anything that had taken place that day. Acceptance and forgiveness.

I never shook the American's hand. I never responded when he tried to talk to me. When we walked to the servery, I fell out of step with him and put myself somewhere else in the queue.

My crimes were not like his. I felt that and I thought the others on Patterson did too. Often they were confused. Boris. You didn't kill anyone; you didn't deal drugs. You're not a people-smuggler. Why are you in here?

I didn't want this to be a weakness. To have someone studying me and thinking, this guy's a lightweight. We can get into him. He can crack. But I wanted to be seen as someone else, too. Someone you could trust. Someone whose hand you could shake.

And then it hit me, one afternoon. I was playing cards with a convicted murderer. Why would you play cards with someone who had killed two people with his own hands? I had seen the chubby American at lunchtime, sharing a table with three other inmates, talking to them. How could you sit and talk with a paedophile?

Why? Because we were all the same. We were dressed the same. We ate the same food. We slept the same broken sleeps. These distinctions I was drawing between the tough men and the weak, between those with crimes I could accept and those with heinous moral flaws – none of it mattered.

No man better than any other. No one cleverer than anyone else. Tired men, angry men.

That was the read, when you saw it clearly. Everyone is equal in prison. It's a democracy of rogues.

INSIDE

Cell Dreams: The Love #4

Lilian and I are trying to move forwards at our own pace, but the world doesn't want to move with us. In August 2021, I have to leave Battersea. The bankruptcy order digging in. They're going to kick us out.

Sometimes you have time to decide on your own. Sometimes it comes rushing at you. Okay. Do we want to move forward, do we want to go further? Lilian could move back to her place. But there is something solid between us now, something we don't question. A togetherness, a shared idea of where this might go. So we move into a new flat in central London, and even though it's the smallest place I've ever stayed and there's barely room for one person, let alone a big man who used to live very differently, it works.

The world comes for us once again. It's clear that life could change for ever at the end of March. There is a worst-case scenario now, and it's me going inside. Will it happen? We don't know. But we know it might, and it could be a month, or it could be much longer. Enough to change everything.

Friday, 8 April 2022. The verdict is reached. This has always been real, but now it's upon us. I start to fast-forward. I don't know if that's a talent or weakness, but I can feel what is about to happen, and I know what I have to say. We have no choice any more. This is a very open and vulnerable and honest time. There is no time to bullshit.

Listen, you're my closest ally. If the shit hits the fan, if I'm incarcerated, you don't have wait. You're too young. You're at the beginning of your life. If they lock me up, it could be two years, it could be five, it could be seven.

I love you, but I don't expect you to wait.

And without a second thought, she looks at me and says, what do you mean? We are a team, we're going to do this together.

There is no 'give me an hour'. There is no 'let me sleep on it'.

I'm really serious now. I say it in a different way. Hold on, let's take a moment. You're a young woman. You can think about it. We have to wait for the sentencing, and maybe we get lucky, but if we don't, they'll take me straight from the sentencing into the cells.

I look at her, and I can see something I don't expect. This is easy for her. There is no doubt in her mind. This is instinctive.

She'll tell me later. This is when I understood, mi amore, that this is really it. I'm not going to leave you. I'm going to stay with you. Fucking hell, I really love this person in a deeper way. I love you, and you are my own. It feels part of me.

That's what she tells me she feels, in that moment.

Taking responsibility. That was the theme in the Stoicism class, one Monday morning in mid August. Our old friend Epictetus, the most quotable man in ancient Greece, back with another pearl: 'A man is responsible for his own judgements, even in dreams, in drunkenness, and in melancholy madness.'

That was the provocation. Underneath was the challenge:

INSIDE

Mistake: An error caused by poor reasoning, carelessness, insufficient knowledge

Excuse: Something used to evade a consequence; deception, trick or scheme

Lie: A false statement or impression made with a deliberate intent to deceive

Blame: To put responsibility onto another

Responsible: Accountable; able to meet obligations; reliable to dependable

I had been different men at different times in my life. In my teenage years I couldn't care less where I was sleeping and what I was doing. For me it was just about winning. A single goal and a simple creed.

Then you win, and money follows, and you get a taste of luxury. You start to understand that a Ferrari is a cool car. You discover there are girls who will talk to you who wouldn't have talked to you before. You learn that the presidential suite is the biggest and most luxurious room in the hotel.

You get comfortable. And without you realising, suddenly all this is normal. You take Concorde from London to New York, just to watch a basketball game. Not even to play tennis. Then you do it again, and many more times, and it becomes second nature. You don't even value it any more. It's just what you do. Sometimes you think, everyone should be able to do this.

But I never lost myself in it all. It didn't define me. I never thought that just because I could fly Concorde then I was better than anyone else. I knew those plane tickets were expensive. I just thought, hey, what the hell, it's only money. I was a millionaire at seventeen. Every year another couple of million came in. Affordability was not a word I had to worry about.

Money never made me good or bad or more important or less important. If I had £10 million or was broke, I was still Boris Becker. So when my bankruptcy happened, I didn't feel like a bad guy. I didn't feel like someone you should disrespect. And I wondered now if this instinctive attitude was saving me in prison. I had lost it all, and I was still surviving. I was still getting out of bed each day; I was still eating. Still talking to other men, still sharing experiences. In return, no one was looking down at me. Prison is the ultimate non-judgemental environment. All of us in the same clothes, eating the same food, sleeping the same broken sleeps.

I was responsible for my own judgements. For my own mistakes, excuses and lies. So I began to think about where all this came from. The people and events that formed me.

I thought about my mother. She had been a refugee, in the Second World War. Living in Brno, in the old Czechoslovakia, when the Russians came in from the east, and pretty much packing up what she had overnight, with her mother and stepfather and siblings, and escaping west on a horse and carriage. Ten years old, travelling day and night until they reached a refugee camp in Leimen.

These experiences change you. They feed into your personality and how you see the world. From my mother to my sister and me came a strong sense of self-belief. Just because you are living through bad times, you are not a bad person. With hard work and discipline and being consistent, you can change your circumstances. Always the emphasis on family, on sticking together when otherwise you might fall apart.

INSIDE

My father? An architect and part-time politician for a conservative party. Yet on weekends a free spirit, a man who would fall in love with a girl from the refugee camp, who loved to listen to jazz music, whose favourite musician was Louis Armstrong.

My mother had an inner strength. Even now, in her eighties – a little lost sometimes in daytime TV and gossip magazines, finding it hard to navigate between the present day and old memories – there was a stubbornness and a refusal to give in. Back in the day when I played badly or lost a match I should have won, there was a robustness in her response. Son, what are you complaining about? It's a tennis match, not your life, and not my life.

She was right. When you have fled your home with almost nothing, when at every checkpoint you reach they're looking at your papers and could send you back to the Russians, when you're going somewhere you've never been before and you have no house and no food and no bed – what's a tennis match, what's a game where you lose your serve?

As the Stoicism classes reached their final few weeks, there was one more key session we did. It was titled 'Victim or Survivor?' That's what I thought about, when those of us who had completed the course assembled in the gym one afternoon to be called to the front, one by one, and be handed our diploma certificate by Andy.

Which one was I? My parents had always given me the freedom to choose. Even when I was thirteen, fourteen, they let me go out at weekends. Into bars and clubs at fifteen, never being told to come home by 9pm or 10pm, jumping on the last train back from Heidelberg to get home by midnight. They didn't tell me not to drink or to be scared of drugs. They didn't worry I would fall in with the wrong crowd, and they never questioned me the next day.

From that trust and that space I made my own decisions. I didn't drink alcohol, not at fifteen. I didn't come down to breakfast hungover or miss it entirely in bed. Before all that I was an altar boy, and if that sounds like a joke, with all the things I've done in my life since, I was there every Sunday from the age of eight, breaking bread for the priest, pouring the communion wine, dressed up in a different kind of white outfit. There is a lot of belief in Catholicism. You get used to holding on to something that a lot of other people reject. All these things that set you apart, and each of them has consequences in your adult life.

Had I chosen tennis or had tennis been given to me? My father was an architect. He built the tennis court that I started playing on. My sister was four years older than me, and when she was seven years old and I was three, she was my first coach. I was given a Dunlop racket, but it was too heavy and too long, so my father cut the shaft in half and wrapped on a new grip and I began to play. Growing up and going to the club every day of every week, as natural and instinctive as eating and drinking.

You have that kind of upbringing and there's going to be a result. The older you get doing these things the more unlikely it is you will change dramatically. If anything, you're going to go back to where you started in the first place. Choice? My parents put me into a football team, they put me into a swimming team, they put me into a skiing team. I wasn't bad at the others, but there was something special about me and tennis. My sister was a good player too, but she became a better swimmer and a better skier. They didn't push her into those, and I don't think they pushed me into tennis. I picked it up more quickly, I got really good at it and it became my passion. It became something I owned and obsessed about. I worked at it so hard. I kept the belief. That was truly me, and at the same time it was also a boy formed by the long-ago experiences of his parents.

One more thing I wondered, when I was back in my cell that night, holding the certificate Andy had given me to mark the end of the six-week course. I'd loved every lesson. It had been a while since I'd won anything, and I liked the wording: *This is to certify that BORIS BECKER has successfully completed the Epictetus Self-Mastery Programme and is hereby recognised as an official member of The Epictetus Club.*

Tennis is an individual sport, almost all the time. You have a coach, and sometimes you have a doubles partner, but when it matters, it's you on your own. No one else can help you make that forehand. No one else can decide where you put that serve.

I'd been forced to look out for myself. That had to be the result. And maybe that was why I'd always found it so hard to ask for help. I thought I had to fix every problem. That if I really focused on something then I could find the solution, sooner or later. I always spoke for myself. The big decisions I debated with nobody, ever. I didn't like the idea of calling on anyone else. Not a friend, not a coach, not my parents or sister.

Victim or survivor. Maybe I was neither. Maybe I was both.

* * *

We took our escapes where we could, that summer. In the gym, in the library. On the three astroturf tennis courts I'd painted in the second week of Wimbledon, playing football, when the wardens allowed it, me watching from the sidelines with my bad knees, the others slipping and sliding in trainers, not caring if they got too hot or if it was tipping down with English summer rain. You thought someone was going to break an ankle or wreck a knee for sure. No one cared. My fellow inmates were just going for it. Throwing themselves into tackles, trying to forget about everything outside of this game, this challenge.

Football was a topic most of us could return to. Everyone had an opinion – slagging off each other's teams, their players. A safe place to go in the queues and servery.

Then Andy came up to me. Boris, listen. You've never been here before, so you don't know, but every year we have a football championship. Teams from each wing, six men on each side. Everybody loves it. You want to be involved?

You have to make the most of everything in prison. So of course I said yes. I couldn't run, because my knees were bad, so they made me the manager. Not a player-manager, like the other ones, because I couldn't run around, but a proper touchline manager. I spoke to the heads of the different wings, and they gave me the names of the players, and I asked about their abilities, and I put together teams that sounded fair and balanced. I gave each team a set of coloured bibs. Even that planning part was fun. When your mind is racing to bad places, turn it to something else.

The tournament was to take place the next Saturday, when no one would be working, and you didn't have to be back in your cell outside meal times. Our team from Patterson was not the strongest. But we had one very good – albeit slightly overweight – player from Somalia, and I thought that gave us a chance. He was in his third spell in prison, and everyone knew him, so I made him our captain. He loved to talk football and knew everything about the Premier League and the Bundesliga. He also knew all the players in the tournament. I told him he would be our striker, but he could help me pick the rest of the team. Find the goalkeeper, the midfielder.

I was keen to get Baby Hulk. Not just because of his size, although when he was running at you with the ball, nobody wanted to tackle him. He was a good footballer, and he was super fit. When you saw him playing badminton in the gym he would reach everything. When he played basketball, he would grab every single rebound. A huge jump on him.

I didn't win that battle. Everyone wanted Baby Hulk. He went into a different team, because he was on a different corridor. But that side were a mess, arguing all the time, fighting over who was playing where and who should be passing to whom. We were the organised ones. Two at the back, two in midfield, our Somalian up front. A very good goalkeeper. A Brazilian in midfield, because any team with a Brazilian playmaker will do okay, right?

My managing style was less Klinsmann and more about consistency and discipline. Making sure everybody played their role, held their position and shape. Not the striker wanting to be a playmaker or the playmaker wanting to be the striker.

It worked for us. Five teams in the tournament, and ours kept winning matches. We made it through to the final.

I had a favourite T-shirt in my cell. Lilian had given it to me. I never wore it, because it was red and attracted too much attention. But it was a cool top. So, before the final, I gave it to our Somalian striker. I said to him: bring it home as a winner.

And he did. He was awesome. We were rock-solid. We won, and we celebrated like it was the World Cup. And then, for our prize, we got to play against a team of the best prison wardens. Of course it could have gone wrong, because this is a chance for revenge, to settle slights and scores. So I talked to the boys. Listen, don't make this personal. This is a game, and we want to beat their asses, and that's all good, but let's not start a fight. Let's show them by beating them.

We won that one too. And at the end, my Somalian striker wanted to give the red T-shirt back to me, and I told him, no, it's your shirt to keep now. That's how the weekend played out. A good moment, in a bad time.

All these small things – being a gym orderly, doing the course, the conversations with my striker and Baby Hulk and Ike and Jeffrey, looking after the football team – were changing things for me. Back in my cell that Sunday evening, in the darkness, listening to the night noises around Patterson, I felt like maybe I had a role. A part to play in it all.

I was sort of in between. I could listen sometimes, and I could make things happen, elsewhere. Not big things, because that was outside my control, but little things that mattered. I hoped I was respected by the prisoners but respected by the wardens too. Not all of them – that guy on my wing who treated me so badly when I first arrived was still on my case. I was still giving him nothing. I could handle him. But the prisoners realised now that I wasn't going to snitch. If you want to smoke, if you want to drink alcohol, if you have a mobile phone – I see it and I hear it, but I'm not going to tell anyone else. The prison officers were starting to use me as they had used Jake and Charlie in Wandsworth. Quiet words rather than big scenes. Boris, this guy is really misbehaving, could you talk to him, because otherwise he could lose his gym rights. One more mistake and he's out.

There was a phrase Andy kept returning to in the Stoicism classes, an ideal. He talked about being a master of self. Someone who could move past being a victim, accept responsibility, see and correct his errors. Build up trust from others through responsible actions.

That was all in my mind when he came up to me in the gym on Monday morning and asked me one thing. Boris, you've completed the course. Would you fancy teaching it now, too?

> Dear Boris
> I thought I would write to you and ask you if you could apply for the very hard job of helping Emma Raducanu. She is in desperate need of an experienced person and with the right guidance I am sure she could win more titles.
> In my view what has happened (i.e. winning the US Open) has gone to her head and taken her concentration off tennis. Too many distractions outside is making her lose focus and perspective on the urgent issue of getting properly fit and listening to someone like you and taking notice!!
> What you have achieved in your career and then helping Novak Djokovic is amazing. I am sure without you helping Novak he would not be the player he is!
> I hope you are coping with your time OK in HMP and look forward to seeing you coming out next summer or sooner. If you could apply for the coaching job I am sure it would go a long way to helping you stay here in England. I certainly want you here

using your skills and good advice to a young lady who is 'doing it all wrong' at this time! I am sure there are still a lot of fans who support you.

    Regards,

    Paul

CHAPTER 9

Cheltenham

Dear Boris

I very much missed your Wimbledon commentary this year and I hope that your knowledge and wise words will grace the airwaves again before too long.

In the meanwhile I wrote a letter to the *Daily Telegraph*, the same week Boris Johnson resigned as Prime Minister.

My letter has just been published in a booklet of letters entitled 'Here We Go Again'. I am sending you a copy of the letter just to let you know that you are still very much remembered with affection by tennis fans!

All the best,

Nick

As September drew closer, I had things to look forward to. There were so many letters coming in now that almost every morning brought good wishes from someone I had never met. I even got a sense that the wardens were starting to resent how much post I was getting. Too many trips to my cell door and back. Too much admin.

I didn't want to be one of those prison clichés who ticked off their remaining time in tally charts scrawled in pen on their cell wall, but I had marked my potential deportation date in my diary, and when I turned the page for each month it felt good to be only three pages from the big red cross. I had my gym role, four times a week, and I had the teaching to think about. Of course I'd said yes to Andy. More hours outside my cell, but a chance to pay back too – to the man who'd done more than anyone else to make my Huntercombe world a better place, to the men all around me. To what I had learned, and how it changed me.

And I had Lilian, too. She was now allowed to visit three times a month. We knew the system by then and we understood how to gently move it along. I would fill out the application form – add her name and our relationship, and then the date and time. I'd still give the wardens on Patterson a reminder, because information could always be slow reaching them, and they might be late, so you missed out on precious minutes of your time together

– By the way, tomorrow, two o'clock, please open my cell because …

At quarter to two the next day the key would turn in the door. You would wait in the corridor, and then they would guide you through the corridors to reception, and next to it the visitors' hall. Those three rows of tables, a chair on one side of the table for you and two on the other. You knew other inmates could eavesdrop on your conversations, if they wanted to, but you didn't care. You didn't want to listen to them and they didn't want to listen to you. You only cared about the person in front of you.

With Lilian the two hours would fly past. With the others who came – old friends from Germany, former German footballer Günter Netzer, my GP, Dr Renbeck, two old friends from Munich, Manfred and Willi – it could be much harder. They were shell-shocked by what they saw and what they heard. Boris, you mean there are killers here, there are paedophiles? But this isn't Wandsworth, I thought it was better ...

They couldn't help but ask more questions. Boris, what did that guy do, what about that one? And when you told them, although you wanted to change the conversation, they would look even more uneasy.

– Fuck, what happens if something happens in here?

– Well, there's a couple of guards, and it probably won't, so ...

They didn't know what to say for the first half an hour, the newbies. I would have to run the conversation. I'd have to think of topics for them beforehand. Show them that I was doing okay, that I wasn't going to die in this place, even if it could feel that way sometimes.

I wanted to enjoy the visits. I wanted to take something from each one – sustenance for the days ahead, support. But it could be exhausting, looking after these well-meaning people. It took away from my energy rather than bolstering it. Without really meaning to, I began to filter it down to just Lilian, and to my sons Noah and Elias when they could.

Sometimes you had no choice. I had a message from Jürgen Klopp, the Liverpool manager. We knew each other a little and got on. He was a man who always boosted your energy. You couldn't help but feel better after an hour in Klopp's company. But the prison service wouldn't let him come. We tried once, and they turned it down. Too much publicity, or something. We tried again, a month later. Same answer. We had to settle for speaking on the phone instead.

The teaching came more naturally. I had the course leader at the front of the room, sometimes Andy, sometimes another warden from the gym, and I would sit to the side. As we began each section in the book, he would ask me to speak about my experiences with that chapter. I would stand up, try to make eye contact with the inmates, and open a discussion about what we might learn that day.

It could get pretty heavy pretty quickly. Some of these men were diehards. They had been in prison three or four times already. Their point of view was very different to mine. Their stories, if they shared them at all, were raw and graphic. They had chosen a life of crime, and a few words from me wasn't going to suddenly transform their outlook. It was the first-time offenders, as it had been when I was a student in the class, that I was more optimistic about. The kids in their late teens and early twenties, where you could see your words landing and thoughts forming.

These talks began in the classroom but would sometimes carry on outside, as some of these young men began to look at me in a different way. Problems brought to you to solve, things you'd never imagined but were now in front of you, because you were no longer just an inmate, but someone in a position of authority and trust. One kid, asking me to stay back for a moment after a class.

– Boris, I mean I don't know if I'm sick, but I have to masturbate every day a couple of times, I mean is that good for me?

And he was sincere, so then without changing my expression or starting to laugh I had to give him an honest answer about what I thought was good or bad. Another guy had heard about Lilian, and people had seen her in the visitors' hall, and the assumption seemed to be that she was from Brazil or West Africa but had connections with Portugal. He waited for a quiet moment in the gym before coming up to me.

– Listen bro, I mean I trust you and everything, I got these diamonds. I've got these diamonds in Portugal, I know you're going to be out in three months, so I'll give you the address, you keep them for me, I trust you, and when I come out, we'll meet up and I'll give you 10 per cent, yeah?

This was a harder one. Of course I had to say no. I didn't care he said they were worth millions of pounds. Whatever. But you can't say no straight away, because you don't want to offend him. You don't want him to think you're disrespecting him, or – worse – that you're going to snitch. So I had a couple of conversations with him, non-committal, friendly.

The first time:

– Listen, you know, things are dangerous for me too. I don't go to Portugal, my girlfriend yeah, she's from São Tomé and Principe, which was a Portuguese colony, but she's not actually from Portugal.

The second time:

– Thanks, I get it, but it's not for me right now. I'm sorry I can't help you this time.

Gradually, more inmates and stories would come my way. There was one guy, very tall, very friendly to me. I liked him. He was direct but cool. I asked him after a while – you look civilised, you don't seem angry, what are you doing here? And he told me. He was a people-smuggler.

– Boris, it's not that I needed money, I had a serious job before and everything. But the financial offers are so rewarding, I made so much money every week and you know what, I'm going to do it again. I'm going to do my time here, get these three years done, and afterwards I'm going to be more careful but it's too good not to. It's a joke how much I can make. Half a million or so every month. If I make five, six million pounds a year for five years, well then I'm done.

He gave me his whole game-plan of how he smuggled people across the Channel from France and the Netherlands to England. On to London. He was okay about it. No moral issues. Just enjoying the money, and the organisation. Not thinking about lives, or danger, or coming back here again.

I listened to it all. That was where I was now. I listened, and passed no judgement, and I listened some more.

Cell Dreams: The Defeat #1

It's Wimbledon, the summer of 1991. A wet June, tennis on the middle Sunday for the first time to get the backlog of rain-affected matches cleared. But the courts stay hard and fast, and so it's a tournament for the big servers, for the boom-boom boys.

I'm feeling good. A semi-final on Centre Court against David Wheaton, who has just beaten Andre Agassi in the quarters. The kid Agassi is playing here again now, after the

INSIDE

years when he refused to come, because of the All England Club wanting you to wear all white, and Agassi doesn't follow other people's rules. But Wheaton's big serve and the fast grass is too much for him, and then my big serve and the fast grass is too much for Wheaton, so it's another final for me, and it's going to be Stefan Edberg for the fourth time in four years.

Of course it will. His semi-final, on the Friday evening, is against Michael Stich. Michael's not Stefan. He's not a rival, not a threat. I'm always very supportive of my fellow German players. When a Davis Cup teammate plays well in a Slam, meaning he'll go to the third or fourth round, I'll be almost coaching them.

– Okay, this is the next guy, you have to watch the backhand but the forehand da da da …

Never really expecting them to be somewhere in my part of the draw in the second week. So when Michael comes through the first week of Wimbledon this year, I'm the same. I am 'great, Michael' and 'super' and 'watch this guy'. I am talking, talking, not at all thinking: he's in the bottom half and I'm in the top half so if he goes all the way through, we could meet in the final.

Then this strange thing happens. Stich keeps serving fast and powerful too. Stefan breaks him in the first set and wins that one, but it's the only break. I mean in the whole match. Stefan holds serve in all twenty-three of his service games, but it doesn't matter, because Michael wins three tie-breaks.

You can tell Stefan is confused. He's lost without losing. But I'm happy. I know what this means. Come Monday, I'm going to be back at number one in the world. I'm overtaking Stefan. My rival. The threat.

Saturday afternoon, I'm really happy. For me, the tournament is done. I'm not thinking about the final, and I'm certainly not thinking about Michael.

Why would I? He's a year younger than me, he's never made a Slam final before, and I'm three Wimbledon titles in. When I was coming up through the junior ranks, he wasn't even there, because he took a different route. He stayed in school until he was eighteen. They called him the smart one, because the rest of us German boys finished school at sixteen, but everything about him is different. He's dark-haired, I'm fair. I'm from the south, like most successful German tennis youngsters; he's from the north.

He looks different, and he speaks different, too. When he starts playing well as a senior, he's not part of our first Davis Cup winning team in 1988. That was me and Carl-Uwe Steeb and Eric Jelen, winning it against Stefan and Mats Wilander and Anders Järryd. When we repeat that win against Sweden in 1989, it's the same German team.

So now it's Saturday, and I'm thinking about Sunday night. I'm thinking about what I might do when I win. You always make these deals with yourself, the night before big finals. What does this mean for me? How might it change me? Where do I go after this?

I'm in the garden of my nice, rented house in Wimbledon. You book it for the fortnight, you're confident you will need it. It's a warm evening, and I'm alone.

And I start crying. I think: when I win tomorrow, I'm going to retire. Do it Björn Borg style, go out at the top – Wimbledon champion again, number one in the world.

INSIDE

Tomorrow is going to be my last game of tennis. I sit there in the warm evening sunshine, and I cry.

When I looked at myself in the little plastic mirror in my cell now, five months in, I noticed the subtle changes to my appearance. My hair was darker now. The last of the bleached tips had long since grown out. My face was thinner, and when I pulled my tracksuit bottoms on each morning, I had to tighten the waist with the drawstrings. My knees, never great, were more inflamed than ever before. When I walked – hips bad, knees bad, ankles aching – I had developed a slight roll from side to side, a nautical gait more suited to HMS than HMP. My shoulders were sore each morning and my spine and neck stiff. It was getting hard raising my right arm much above shoulder level.

A change in my body but a new way of conversing too – teaching the classes, listening to the stories afterwards. Men's tennis had been an alpha world for me. It was a place where you put on a front and showed no weakness. Even when you talked to the media it was with a plan. You hid the real you. You were indomitable. You were fearless.

This could not be the same. It was letting people in. It was keeping secrets. Sometimes it was like therapy.

Andy had been right, when he'd told me what Frank had said to him: the only currency you had in this place was your personality. If you kept a strong character, you could survive here. And if you could survive here, you could surely survive anywhere.

When I was a teenager and I won Wimbledon, I was a son of a bitch. I was in your face. You fight me, and I'll fight you. How long do you wanna play? I'll play you all day. I'll play you tomorrow. I'll play you when it's too hot and I'll play when you want to stop.

As I grew older I became softer. I became comfortable. I settled into my life of luxury, and I moved away from what made me strong in the first place. Now, in Huntercombe, these other young men coming to me to talk, I began thinking again about young Boris. About what set him apart, about how he would have reacted in the same conditions as these teenagers.

I had no doubts, back then. I couldn't care less. Couldn't give a shit. I just went out there and did it. Didn't matter who you were or where we were. That's what, at seventeen, got me through a Wimbledon final against a twenty-eight-year-old.

What had softened me? They start offering you things pretty fast after you win big. They offer you a couple of hundred grand to play an exhibition somewhere you don't want to go. Chattanooga. The young Boris always said no. No interest.

At twenty-six years old, it changes. You start thinking, for that kind of money, I'm going to find a spare weekend. Everyone like easy money. Chattanooga, why not?

I changed back then because I became part of one system. The young men around me now were caught up in a system of their own. Could I help them change, for the better this time?

I hoped so. I hoped I could be part of that change. So I listened to these stories, and I was straight-faced – poker faced. I didn't move, didn't judge, wasn't surprised. No whistles of shock, no outrage. Mainly to keep the stories coming; sometimes for selfish, or pragmatic, reasons too. It helped me, being part of the inner circle. Maybe I would need one of them tomorrow. Maybe someone would be getting at me and I'd have to call on the tall guy from Holland or the quick young kid.

I also had to challenge some of the opinions coming at me. Never attack them. That wouldn't work for anyone. But I could raise questions. I could make statements to give them pause.

– Listen, sooner or later every criminal will be caught. There are only very, very few who haven't been caught. We love Pablo Escobar's story, right? All those drug kingpins, the lifestyle, the money. Which of them is still here?

Sometimes I could do the maths for them.

– So you came in here the first time at twenty-five years old. Now it's your third time and you're forty-seven. Has it been worth it?

There was the politics, or, more simply, the way the real world worked. There was a Nigerian prisoner who hated what had happened to him. He was anti-Britain and anti-America. He talked up Russia and China. I tried to raise what might have happened had he been caught for drug-dealing in either of those one-party states. How they treated Black people. What the prisons might be like, if you even got that far. I would say: I know no country is perfect, and there's a lot of things wrong about Britain and America. But given the choice, would you rather live in London or New York, or Moscow or Beijing? That made him go quiet for a fair while.

Sometimes it was business lessons. Business logic.

– Okay, so you're selling drugs and you make … well, how much would you make on average?

– On average, in a month, I'd make fifty, sixty grand. No taxes, Boris, no expenses.

– Okay. So if the average salary in Britain is about £2,000 a month, right … how many years in prison now?

– Yeah, I've been inside for eleven years.

– So let's work it out. Eleven years in prison you didn't have any income, right, so in eleven years with an average job you make £2,000 a month minimum, but you're smart and you work hard, so it's probably closer to £3,000 a month. That means you make about £35k, £40k a year. In eleven years you make about the same. You know where I'm getting with this, but you're in prison. And this is if you have an average job. You could do better. And you see your girlfriend, or your wife, every day you want to. You get to see your kids grow up. You can see as many women as you like, if that's for you. So what's worth it?

I would have to take their side sometimes. Tell them, the only thing you cannot do is be caught. Whatever you do, just do it better. You have a hell of a life in London, just don't get caught.

You never got through straight away. There were no eureka moments. You just had to start the conversation.

Andy was helpful to it all. He would ask leading questions in the class or in the gym.

– Boris, you've met pretty much everyone in the world, haven't you?

– Well …

– Did you meet the Queen?

– Yes.

– Did you meet Arnold Schwarzenegger?

– Yes.

– Michael Jordan?

– Yes.

And the response came back from the prisoners. Fuck, who are you? Then the follow-up: what the hell are you doing here?

INSIDE

That's when I worked out I had to give them more of my story. Tell them I had made mistakes. Who was I to judge them? Sure, I had an unbelievable ride. I had the fame and fortune, all the girls and everything. But I made mistakes, and look where I was now.

– Me? I lost everything. Was it worth it? No. I'm going back to the same kind of cell as you.

The critical part of it was showing them I knew. I could empathise. I had to show them I had accepted my part in all this. That I was reflecting on it all and being honest. That I wanted to do better, next time.

Maybe I had been asking the wrong question. Or rather, there was a follow-up question I had to ask too. It wasn't just whether I could help some of the young men in this system change for the better. It was whether I could change again too.

These were lives I had no experience of. Towns I had never lived in, parents not like mine. Sometimes no safety net, if it went wrong once. Friends who took you to places you never wanted to go.

I thought about Jake, the Listener from HMP Wandsworth. He was born and raised in Hackney. What were the chances of him making it big? Slim. What were the chances of him getting to Mayfair? None. It all seemed quite arbitrary. There were plenty of bad men in here and plenty of bad choices. There was also too much wrong place, wrong time. If the shit hit the fan, and you had a bad moment, or a drunken night, or a bad friend …

We talked a lot about comfort zones, about complacency. Of course it's easy to stay with the street gang you've known since you were ten years old. But if four of the five are involved in illegal activities, chances are something's going to happen to you. Maybe you have to change your group of friends, if that matters to you.

The moral ground was lowering for me. I was finding it harder to pass judgement on others or say that something similar would never have happened to me. What could you ever know for sure, in a place like this? A lot of us in there never really admitted all of what we had done. You came up with a lesser version, or a cleaner one.

They always say you should never ask a career gambler if he's just lost. Well, you don't ever ask an inmate what he's really done. This is the other part of the acceptance phase, once you're dealing with your own guilt: everybody is in here for a reason. Very, very few are genuinely innocent. Experience gradually teaches you this. And once you get to that point, judgement goes out of the window because you realise, well, I haven't told them all of what I have done, or how I was caught. I could debate my particular crime all I wanted. I could argue that in Germany it wouldn't have been a custodial sentence, I could argue that in Italy it would have been a fine.

It didn't matter. It was a crime. There was no longer any doubt about it.

So I thought again about the reasons why young Boris was so determined and so unafraid. It was my personality and it was my character. Some of it I was born with, some of it people taught me.

In those classes, teaching and listening, I was young Boris again. I wasn't comfortable, but I wasn't afraid, either. I felt it, and the men around me felt it too.

INSIDE

That was a powerful thing for me. The more classes I taught, the more stories I listened to, the more the dangerous guys in the prison came to me, walking with me and looking me up in the gym.

Young Boris won Wimbledon because he wasn't afraid. What an accidental talent that had been to possess! What a gift it could be to me here. When I could get through to the loose men and the lost, I felt something bigger still. There was a connection, when I could never have dreamed of such a thing. Criminals became confidants. Bad men became human.

All of a sudden, I was part of their group. I could feel their strength. They could feel mine.

Cell Dreams: The Defeat #2

I know I am in trouble when I lose the first set to Michael, and I don't really deserve to win it, and I just feel ... tired.

I have a mask on, when I'm playing well. I can pretend to be someone you don't want to play: super-confident, aggressive, ruthless. Your worst nightmare, staring across the net at you.

Today my mask has slipped. And when your mask slips, you can't take it. You can't take the pressure, you can't take the difficulties, you can't take any of it any more.

I am not prepared at all. That's what I realise. Yes, I did the warm-up, I did everything else I needed to physically. But mentally? I am already gone.

I am never calm, the whole afternoon. I am agitated. I am nervous. I speak to myself loudly in German in disbelief. What is happening here? Boris, what are you doing?

The second set is the key one. Just for me to get into the match.

I lose it on a tie-breaker.

It's not even a tight one. It's a pretty easy tie-breaker for him. I mean, if I lose it's one thing. But I'm hardly able to put up a real fight. I'm giving him, almost, the match.

This is not me. In so many other matches, even losing, I have fought until the end. Today? I am weak. I am soft.

Michael has match point. He hits the ball, he falls to his knees and celebrates. I go to the net to shake hands. This was going to be me. Wimbledon champion for the fourth time. The new world number one. I mean, the story was already written ... and Michael has won it. Even the umpire is confused. He leans into his mic and says, 'Game, set and match ... Becker!'

So I'm in the final in 1985 and 1986. In '88, '89, '90, '91. Six out of seven. But now, after today, something is broken right here with me and Wimbledon. I've accelerated past my own narrative.

When I lost early to Peter Doohan in 1987, I could rationalise it. Compartmentalise it.

Not now. Not here.

I think: I'm losing the plot here. I think: this sport is no longer healthy for my mind.

Something has to change.

You could never get too comfortable in this place. If ever you let yourself believe you'd cracked it, that you were safe from all the things you'd feared before, something would come along and wake you up again.

INSIDE

The chess games with Alex had continued. With his cell being opposite mine, I spoke to him most mornings and evenings. I thought of him as my neighbour. As normal as anyone else in there.

I was out in the exercise courtyard one morning in late August, walking my laps, thinking my thoughts. The days cooling now, the skies closer. Alex was there too, which rang a few alarm bells, because you were only supposed to be out for fifteen minutes, and he had been there for a while before me. A warden had spotted it too, one of the younger ones who no one really liked – too officious, not experienced enough to know when to step in and when to let things ride.

Alex was smoking. He looked in his own world. The warden stopped him and told him he should go back to his cell. Nice enough at the start, but Alex looked straight through him and kept walking.

Now the warden got angry. Raised his voice. Alex turned and began to argue back. The warden put out his hand and shouted. And Alex looked at the hand, and then up at the warden's face, and then – no warning at all – headbutted him flush in the face.

Point-blank, boom. Blood everywhere. He knew how to do it. And the speed of it, and the shock, because this sort of casual violence had never been part of my world, was like an aftershock that came at you and hit you too. Like someone was shouting in my face. *Fuck, Boris, you are in a bad place! Don't ever disagree with anyone. Don't get into any conversation too deep. This is always there. You could be next ...*

That night I was happy when the cell door was locked. I felt safer, even though there was no Alex opposite me. He was in solitary confinement for three weeks. A cell in a distant part of the prison, no TV, no books. Alone the whole time, even when you were let out for a shower. No servery with anyone else; food brought to the hatch in your door, and pushed through, and nothing said.

It could send you mad, in that place. There was no artificial light for you in the morning or in the evenings. Just the daylight. And the days were shortening now, and when it gets dark in your cell at 7pm, because the window is small and dirty, then it's a long night ahead. You'd hear stories about men going crazy. About men who went in there angry and came out even more aggressive. Less socialised, more untethered. Caged animals, for the time they were in there.

I left it a long time after Alex's return before speaking to him about it. After a long game of chess, when I hoped he was calm, when his mind had returned to a better place. I asked him why he had done what he had. He shrugged. He said, Boris I just hate these guys so much, and I just can't help myself. It's this second nature of mine. It's who I am.

That was Alex's spell in solitary. My own would come a different way.

I'd been told in Wandsworth about the misery of Covid, during the first lockdown in 2020 and then the second in 2021. How it turned a bad place into a hellish one, where you had no contact with anyone else. Locked away with nothing to look forward to and no one to share it with. No visits, no gym, nothing.

But you began to hear about second and third waves, late in this summer. All those people socialising in the better weather. The hundreds of thousands together at the women's European Championship matches. I'd watch *Channel 4 News* at 7pm each evening, and they were mapping the weekly increase in positive tests. It felt inevitable when floor information reached us in the gym one day: there's three inmates tested positive. They caught it from a visitor. We're all going to be tested now.

So, for about three or four weeks, once a week everybody was tested. The full nasal swab. They would give you the stick, you would put it up your nostril, and they would take it away. The first three weeks mine all came back negative.

The fourth time, right at the end of August, I came back positive.

As soon as that test came back red, that was it. You were confined to your own cell for ten days. My job as a gym orderly was suspended. There was no teaching. I couldn't even choose my food, let alone go out to get it. The wardens picked what I ate, the wardens brought it to my cell door.

They let us out to shower at 6pm, all of us who had tested positive. No conversations with Ike, or Baby Hulk, or Jeffrey. A random collection of men you half knew or wanted to keep a different kind of social distance from. If we wanted, we were allowed a short walk in the courtyard. Others would vape. Everyone seemed to vape, in Huntercombe. And then you were locked up at 7pm, and you had to sit in your cell until 6pm the next day, when outside the sun was shining, and your wing mates were out, and everyone was talking, and you were in a world of silence.

I had my suspicions. More of them than I had physical symptoms. Was I feverish? No. Was I losing my taste? No. I felt the same the day of my positive test as I had the day before, and the same as I did every day after that. The floor information was blaming the prison staff. They were the ones bringing it in from the outside. They were the ones going to football matches, going to pubs with their friends, hanging out with their kids.

I wondered how positive I was. I thought about the warden who had never hidden his dislike for me. He seemed to hate everyone who was relatively new, wanted to establish an extra degree of power over them. Maybe this was his way of getting at me. Could I prove them wrong? Another no. I was down as a positive, so I was inside again, and it was worse than ever before, because I was accustomed to the gym now, and I looked forward to teaching, and going back to the old ways was so much worse than before.

Occasionally Ike and Shuggy would sidle up to my door and pass on a message or a quick hello. You weren't supposed to, but they tried. So each day crawled, and each day merged into the one before and the one after, and I tried to kill time and had nothing to help me but my own thoughts.

We can be a remarkable species, humans. We can get used to almost any situation, including prison life. You can start low and build yourself up. You can go from thinking there's no reasonable future, to surviving, and then finding meaning in things you never knew were there. But when you have been low and built yourself up and then you suddenly sink again – that's the hardest thing of all. The first time had been Wandsworth. I had survived that and become an English and maths teacher and got used to it. At Huntercombe I had to start again. Those terrible first four weeks on my own, no purpose and no hope. Doing the course, finding the gym, finding teaching. And now, from out of nowhere, back to the loneliness. Back to the powerlessness.

INSIDE

I struggled to read, now. I couldn't reflect. I was done with prison – that's how it felt.

I thought: I have learned my lesson. I've had the epiphanies. I know what I've done, I'm remorseful, I get the message. I know what I want to do when I'm on the outside. There was no point in re-evaluating my life. I had done that before.

So I watched shitty programmes on TV, and I stared at the ceiling, and I looked forward to every phone call. I looked forward to Lilian's voice and I looked forward to any daft stories she had of gossip or entertainment or sport. Stuff that didn't really matter at all and might distract me as a result. Might put some thoughts in my mind that were different than the ones I had the day before.

I tried to lose myself in memories of better times. Of things so far from here that they seemed almost impossible. Playing golf with Michael Jordan in the Bahamas, with Charles Barkley and Wayne Gretzky.

Sometimes I would almost try to walk through a round, shot by shot. The time we played the same tournament, early in January, and Bill Clinton and Morgan Freeman and Julius Erving were there. There were always cigars, when you played with MJ. Clinton would blow you away with his speeches. Doing the charity dinner after the golf, and talking without notes, and the longer he went the better he got.

A cell in Huntercombe is about as far away as you can get from the Michael Jordan Celebrity Invitational on Paradise Island in the Bahamas. Maybe that's why I tried to take myself there again. Me as a golfer; not as I was as a tennis player, but Mr Consistent, taking a three-wood off the tee, nice approach, solid two-putt, everything decent and nothing spectacular. For the US superstars, for Peyton Manning and Barry Bonds and Derek Jeter, it was all about the bragging rights for the longest drive. I was never part of that group, but that was okay. The sunshine and the cigars and the early drinks allowed you to find your pleasures where you wanted them.

Wherever I went in those days I travelled with my golf bag. Now I had nowhere to go but the sink and back. Bill hadn't called; MJ must have been busy. If I wanted to go anywhere, it would be in my mind.

September came to Huntercombe. My Covid test came back negative. The Stoicism conference was actually happening. I was in the visiting room, standing by a small stage Andy had put up, wearing my best Puma tracksuit.

I spotted Pat Cash as soon as he walked in. Leather jacket and jeans, of course. We had five minutes before we were due on stage, and we talked. Smiles and hands on shoulders. I got up on stage and did my bit on Stoicism. Pat did the same. Two old players, back in the same space together.

When we finished, it changed again. He was a guest, I was an inmate. I had to go back to my cell. But before I did, we had half an hour. A good half an hour.

He asked me how I was doing, and sincerely. I asked him the same. He said Stoicism helped him, I said, sure, me too. All the time, these similarities and connections jumping between us.

– Yeah, this happened to me as well.

– Yeah, I know what you mean.

– Man, that's hard, isn't it?

And when we said goodbye, there was something new between us. I walked back to my cell and I thought all about Pat Cash, all over again. How as athletes we all have our own agendas and chips on our shoulders and long-ago childhood weaknesses. You battle the version they show you on the court but you never see the fights they're having on the inside. Maybe Pat was hiding a lot of stuff for a long time. The rock 'n' roll look, the playing guitar in a band with John McEnroe. The arrogance and the swagger, when all the time maybe there was a shyness and an insecurity.

I made the same mistakes back in the day. I was provocative and aggressive, of course I was. We were young men and young men lived a certain way. When I played Pat, that was part of my strategy. I will wear you down. I will break you apart, and I will stand over you and celebrate when I do.

And I thought: so maybe don't judge so much, any more. You don't know their inner demons and their fights. You have your own, too.

I thought: if I played Pat Cash now, I wouldn't do that any more. The old shit. It's possible we can share a stage without giving each other shit, without getting embarrassed.

He's a better man because of what he came through. I could be a better man too.

BORIS BECKER

29/07/22
From Lilian

If you can keep your head when all about you
Are losing theirs and blaming it on you,
If you can trust yourself when all men doubt you,
But make allowance for their doubting too;
If you can wait and not be tired by waiting,
Or being lied about, don't deal in lies,
Or being hated, don't give way to hating,
And yet don't look too good, nor talk too wise:

If you can dream – and not make dreams your master;
If you can think – and not make thoughts your aim;
If you can meet with Triumph and Disaster
And treat those two impostors just the same;
If you can bear to hear the truth you've spoken
Twisted by knaves to make a trap for fools,
Or watch the things you gave your life to, broken,
And stoop and build 'em up with worn-out tools:

INSIDE

If you can make one heap of all your winnings
And risk it on one turn of pitch-and-toss,
And lose, and start again at your beginnings
And never breathe a word about your loss;
If you can force your heart and nerve and sinew
To serve your turn long after they are gone,
And so hold on when there is nothing in you
Except the Will which says to them: 'Hold on!'

If you can talk with crowds and keep your virtue,
Or walk with Kings – nor lose the common touch,
If neither foes nor loving friends can hurt you,
If all men count with you, but none too much;
If you can fill the unforgiving minute
With sixty seconds' worth of distance run,
Yours is the Earth and everything that's in it,
And – which is more – you'll be a Man, my son!

Stay strong, Amore!
   Love you!
      L

The poem is 'If' by Rudyard Kipling, originally published in *Rewards and Fairies* in 1910.

CHAPTER 10

Email a Prisoner
Prison Message 57881
Message with reply to: Boris Becker A2923EV Huntercombe
Message from: Andrew Castle

Hi Boris

I got your number from Lilian after seeing her at Wimbledon. It was so strange to be working without you at the tournament and so many people have missed you in so many ways.

I thought this was a good time to contact you because England just beat Germany in the Women's Euros! Are you able to watch TV as you wish? I really don't have much idea what your life is like at the moment.

I just hope that you are feeling okay and that you know time will pass and somehow something good will come from it. You have a wonderful family and many great friends who will never desert you.

How do you fill your days at Huntercombe? I understand from a friend of mine who works at Wandsworth that you had your own cell and that you had a job. Apparently that is not always the case. I know that must have been a brutal first few

INSIDE

weeks, and all I can tell you is that you were at the forefront of my mind.

We have a grandson to enjoy, which is a thrill. It's hard to imagine falling in love with anything more than him.

I wonder if you have had relatives from Germany come and see you? I'm not sure what the visiting arrangements are but I would like to come and see you. Of course this is entirely up to you. Please let me know your thoughts.

My email is xxxxx. I hope this service works. Again I'm not sure what access you have to email/phone etc.

For the moment Boris, take care and hang in there. I look forward to hearing any news you have and let me know how you are. Sophia and I send our love.

Andrew

Nothing about prison is normal. Not the things you do and see, seldom the people you meet.

I loved getting Andrew's letter. It meant a great deal to me. I didn't take up his offer of a visit because I knew how exhausting these new ones were for me now. When an outsider came, it broke through your bubble. It was like being interrupted by a shout of encouragement in your service action – a good thing in the wrong moment. The letter was enough: his friendship, his support. I was in a place where you didn't have to see friends face-to-face to keep a relationship alive.

People try to make prison normal, of course they do. In the construction of routines, in the ways they find of padding out some of the sharper edges. A lot of it is pretence. After almost six months, it felt habitual to take a shower with six other men. It felt quite conventional to spend every evening on your own, watching TV programmes you didn't actually want to be watching. It still wasn't normal. It was just routine.

But people tried. You could see it in the number of mobile phones being used on the wing. It wasn't just a few rogue inmates who had one; now I was aware of it, more prisoners seemed to than not. A phone meant Instagram and Twitter. It meant emails. It meant photos from your loved ones. You could have a life with your phone at night.

You could keep running any business or scam you had out there, too. There was the little Italian-English guy called Giovanni who seemed to know everyone in Huntercombe. Small, early sixties, bald head and glasses. Because he was a lawyer, that gave him clout. Quite a few prisoners went to him with their legal issues. The word was that he was still running his law firm from inside. That seemed crazy when I first heard, but then you saw how many people were talking to him in the servery, and you saw how easy it was to get away with a smartphone, and it began to make sense.

He came up to me one morning, as autumn kicked in. Told me we were kind of in the same boat, because he was inside for business offences too. You talked to him and he talked back at you more. He had a PhD from Cambridge; he had friends in high places. There were a lot of stories and a lot of big names. At various points he told me about Rupert Murdoch, Yasser Arafat, Hugh Hefner, Ayatollah Khomeini and Mohamed Al-Fayed. He talked about football with the confidence of someone who had been involved in the game. He said he had been a director at Dundee FC and nearly bought Norwich FC.

He was due for release soon. From what he said, it sounded like he could have been out on parole earlier, but he

INSIDE

wasn't happy with the settlement the Home Office was putting forward.

– Boris, it's not worth it for me. I'd rather do it from inside. I've got everything I need.

It was good to meet people like him, just so you could remember that normal meant something else in here. That when you went past an open cell door, you should never look in. You don't want to see things you're not meant to see. You walked down the corridors, and you always looked wide. All anyone had was what was inside their cell. Their privacy, their own cramped space, but also their secrets, their treats and their scams. The soft extras they wanted no one else to see.

But I still made mistakes.

The most powerful group inside Huntercombe, even more than the Albanians, were the Romanians. They ran the upstairs floor on Patterson. When I'd been up there at the very start, you could see how different things were for them. How different other prisoners were around them.

They controlled that part of the wing, pretty much. They were closest to the prison officers; they had the best cells. In one of the cells were two bunk beds and two singles. The door was always open: they were wing orderlies, so they could move in and out as they pleased. They always had a lot of food, they had a big television, they had a large glass-backed mirror. No one else had that. No one else had their influence.

I'd had Romanians in my life. My first manager, the one who controlled everything for me, for a long time, Ion Tiriac. My coach, when I was a teenager and when I won Wimbledon those two times: Günther Bosch. The man I called Güntzi.

Those Romanians inside didn't know tennis. But the old connections had been enough to break the ice when I had first encountered them. The one who talked the most was called Bogdan, a young guy with a long past. He had killed two men with his hands when he was eighteen years old. Now he was thirty-six, and he still had plenty of time to serve.

He looked dangerous. Covered in tattoos, a reputation that followed him through the corridors. When I first met him I couldn't stop thinking about the numbers. More than half his life inside. How has he survived, how is his mind? Yet although it should make no sense, we got on well. I could speak to him. He could speak to me.

What he couldn't do was read and write English. That was true with several of his group. Another of them came up to me, quite early on, and shoved a piece of paper in my hand.

– Listen Boris, I have this document but I don't know what the fuck they mean. Read it for me, because I trust you. Then can you write for me in English?

He asked me to go to his cell. Normally this would never have been allowed. So I asked one of the wardens. They asked me why. I told them: one of the Romanians wants me to read a legal paper for him. And they let me go. Not even asking how long I would be, or checking on me when I was in there.

That was the start of it. Writing for this guy to the immigration office, reading to him the letters he received. Bogdan heard about this pretty soon and asked me to do the same. At some point, chess was mentioned. They told me that one of their gang was a really good player, someone they said could beat me. We played one weekend, and I won, and they kept challenging me, and I kept winning – more often than not.

INSIDE

They told me afterwards how they felt about that. Boris, if you're this good at chess, you must be pretty smart. Also, to play against us takes balls. So we trust you, and we need you now.

Of course you couldn't say no to them, even if you wanted to. I wasn't completely stupid. So I read them their letters, and I wrote replies for them, and that was my protection from the Romanians. I was never one of them, but I was with them.

It was a whole lot better than being against them.

One weekend afternoon in early September, I got a little bored. I didn't look wide, as I walked down the wing. I looked into a cell.

It was a different group of Romanians, playing poker. Now I like poker. I did it professionally, for a while, in the post-tennis years. I asked if I could sit in and watch. A little later, they asked if I wanted to play.

No one has money, inside. Not coins and notes. We played instead with matches. Each match represented £1, the first afternoon. The next time we played it was £10. But you didn't worry, because you were used to playing poker, and you could read other players, to a certain extent, and it was a good way to burn through some hours and to focus your mind on something else.

We kept playing, and matches kept going into the pot. Three matches, six matches. Another afternoon the matches had become £50 each. All of it abstract, all of it under control. It wasn't about money. It was about a distraction. Losing myself in a small pleasure, for a little while.

– Okay, so I'm down £70, but it's only £70, and the game is early. My hand is good, I think I can tell what he has, and what that one might do.

That was when I started to lose, and I kept losing. Sometimes when I was in good positions, sometimes when I didn't see it coming. Not always losing to the same guy, but often to two of them, and I noticed they were talking together afterwards.

These afternoons could go by fast. If you didn't look up you could be three hours in and a lot of matches down – £100, £150 … How much were these matches worth today again?

It was a shock when they told me, as I stood to leave one Saturday.

– Hey. You owe us £500.

Now £500 was nothing to me when I played poker outside. It was almost always abstract. When it wasn't, it was just a tap of the credit card or a quick signature on a line. Inside, £500 was a lot of money. It was your weekly allowance for about eight months. Even if you were earning the maximum as an orderly, as I was, it was fifteen weeks of everything you had. No money for phone calls, no funds for the canteen list. No breakfasts, no ingredients for Sunday lunches at Ike's. Nothing.

What do you do? Think about it a lot, when they say to you, listen, you have to pay up or win big next time. They weren't aggressive the first or second time I saw them after that in the canteen, but on the fourth or fifth occasion, I could feel them staring at me. I felt they were circling around me.

Then, one afternoon, two of them came to my cell. A simple message: when are you going to pay?

I knew what that meant. I also had a good idea of what might have led to this situation. In poker, if there's six guys on the table, and five of them know each other, and one is an outsider, and the dealer is an inmate, and there are no overhead cameras

Exploring the streets of Leimen with my mother, Elvira. Recognisably me, I think.

I loved many sports, but tennis soon became my number one.

It's not just about winning, but it turns out that winning is fun.
See if you can spot the other young tennis superstar.

Everything changed the July day I won Wimbledon as a seventeen-year-old.

I went all-in, as a player. What was the point in moderation?

I wasn't ready for the aftermath of 1985. But then, what teenager would have been?

Sometimes Stefan Edberg beat me, sometimes I beat him. There was so little between us.

I didn't even consider the possibility that Michael Stich might beat me in the Wimbledon final of 1991. When he did, it recalibrated my world.

Andre Agassi was the one who really changed things. Suddenly I was no longer Centre Court's darling boy.

My mother with my two eldest sons, Noah and Elias. A happy time and still a happy picture for me today.

It all started so well with Hans-Dieter Cleven. It wouldn't finish the same way.

Southwark Crown Court, where so much of the past thirty years caught up with me.

HMP Huntercombe. I knew only the cold walls and fences inside.

When I heard that Lilian and Noah had been invited to Wimbledon by
Novak Djokovic, it kept me going for weeks.

I had no idea who Giovanni Di Stefano was, when I first met him. A bad man in a bad place.

Ike and me on my 56th birthday in Milan. A wonderful man in the hardest of places.

Working in the gym at Huntercombe gave me purpose and pride. Physical education officer Andy Small (*left*) believed in me when very few others did. Georgia Stead and Pete Bryan are with him.

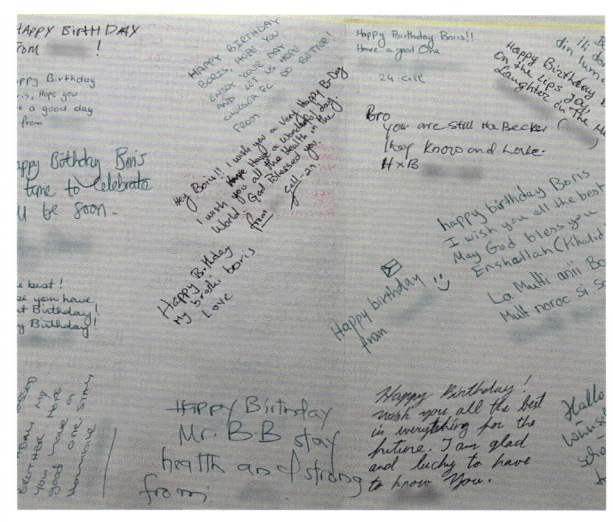

The birthday card I received from my fellow inmates.
It brought me to tears.

With Lilian and her family a few weeks after my release. I kept thinking about all those I cared about who were still inside.

I had to go for a walk on my own, that first New Year's Eve. I was too full of emotion and confusion and tears.

TOP LEFT: The happiest of days: our wedding ceremony at Cervara Abbey, officiated by Lilian's father, Victor Monteiro.

TOP RIGHT: Noah, Elias and me on the big day. I think the Becker boys are looking pretty sharp.

RIGHT: The woman who saved my life. I owe Lilian everything.

BELOW: The extended clan on both sides of the relationship. We felt surrounded by love.

INSIDE

... I should have worked it out. But I thought too much of myself. Of my abilities.

Bogdan had seen me with these other Romanian men. He came to my cell afterwards.

– Boris, this guy's a little crazy. You got to pay up, it's prison rules. And you got to find a way soon, because otherwise you're going to see how crazy he can be.

I called somebody. Not Lilian. I didn't want to worry her. I called somebody and they gave a friend's bank details from the outside and I made a transfer through them to pay off my debts. That was the end of those afternoons. That was the end of the poker.

This was how it was. You learned about yourself, and what you can do, and what you cannot do because you were never forced to before.

I never cooked, when I was younger. My mother did it all when I was a boy. By the time I was in my late teens it was players' restaurants and hotels and meals in the kind of places you go when you have money; people know this and recommend places and you go and eat and see all the other top players in there too. Now, here, in this cold and uncompromising place, there were men the same age as me who were cooking meals in their cells as if they could work magic spells. Ike with his fufu, of course, but others too, as some men were released and fresh faces took their place.

In late July, an Italian called Paulo had arrived on our wing. Short dark hair, quite fit, lots of tattoos. Charming, in a typically southern Italian way.

He was in for fraud, was the word, although I knew myself that this could mean anything you wanted it to. We talked football at first, the German and the Italian. The World Cup was coming up that November in Qatar, and Germany had qualified because Germany always qualify, and Italy had not, even though they were European champions, because that's how it goes in Italian football too.

We hit it off, me and Paulo. Not just for the football, but for the other small connections you look for. I talked about Lilian, how she had been born in Rome and brought up between Italy and Portugal, why she loved Italy so much. He told me about Napoli, where he was from. He told me he was a cook. He told me he dreamed of opening a restaurant back home, whenever it was he got out.

After a few months, there was trust between us. That's when he invited me to his cell. Boris, I like you, I will cook for you. Let's see if you like my food. So I walked down the corridor and I looked inside again and went in.

I have eaten a lot of pasta in my life. When you're a tennis player in the eighties and nineties, bananas make up maybe 20 per cent of your diet, but pasta is at least 50 per cent. I felt I had eaten the best pasta I was ever going to eat. And then I went to Paulo's one Sunday lunchtime, and I had pasta and a sauce that was incredible. Better than any expensive hotel. Better than any of those restaurants round the corner from the expensive hotels.

He was sharing a cell with somebody, so the food was split between three of us. The portions were small. But it seemed impossible he could make all this in his kettle. In the sauce was garlic and fresh tomatoes. There was pepper and parsley. All of it chopped with the small, blunt plastic knives you got from the servery.

I guessed he had ordered the vegetables from the canteen list. But he had no saucepan. He had only one kettle, and that was small, maybe big enough to boil the water for two cups of tea. Was he holding his finger down on the on button, and keeping it boiling? Was he making the sauce, then boiling the pasta, but then how was he keeping both hot, and why did nothing taste burned, and how could it all be at just exactly the right texture and consistency – not chewy, not sloppy, not a mixed-up mess?

Paulo's pasta, Ike's fufu. It was miraculous to me. But we all needed our diversions. We all needed our obsessions. They could get it right because that was their thing, in a day where you had nothing else to do. The one thing you always have inside is time.

Cell Dreams: The Defeat #3

Things do change for me, after I lose to Michael Stich in 1991. My love for the game has gone. It's disappeared.

I try to work out why I was crying, the night before the final. Okay, I am emotionally vulnerable. Why is this? Maybe it means I don't want to quit yet. But I'm also kind of relieved I didn't win. This is new for me. I think I'm relieved because I escaped the mad deal I made with myself. I didn't win, so I don't have to retire.

So. If I don't love tennis any more but I don't want to quit, what does this mean all together? I think it means I'll have to find a new way. My life has been only about tennis. I have become socially awkward. I've become a hermit – always on my own, no friends, no social life. Just tennis, hotels, practice, rented houses, the same tournaments on an endless annual loop.

So I put a stop to this. I continue to play, but I play with less power, less passion. Probably less commitment. And in the fall of the same year, I meet the girl I will eventually marry, and all of a sudden, I have a new focus. I have a partner. I need to have a home somewhere, a permanent place, somewhere I don't give the keys back when I lose a match.

I will lose matches now, too. Agassi's not going away. He's just settling into grass. This Pete Sampras – he's getting past the semis soon. My era? I can feel it coming to an end. From out of a blue sky, never guessed it, but it's happening, I can sense it the same way I felt it coming to life in 1985.

And I love Borg, but I've seen what happened to him afterwards, and I don't want that to happen to me. I've seen some of the other great athletes that retired too early and went into a downward spiral. So I know the dangers, and I need to find an alibi for me to still sort of play – still good enough to make semi-finals or finals, but nothing will be easy now, nothing will be as it was before.

I need to build up my other life. I need to have a family. I'm an adult now, not a kid.

I was in the servery late one Thursday afternoon in September, coming to the end of another slow week. Playing chess with Alex, the Albanian who lived across the corridor from me. I had remained cautious around him, but all the troubling things I'd found out about him didn't change how good he was at chess, and now the poker was gone, the chess became even more important as a time-burner than it had been before.

INSIDE

We had heard that the Queen was unwell. You saw it on the news in the morning and again at night. Prison is a bad place and men are lost in their own worlds and torments but it was the talk of all the wings. Why wouldn't it be? Her Majesty's pleasure was our own punishment. We were in her house. It was her name above the door.

I'd grown to like *Channel 4 News*. Krishnan Guru-Murthy and Cathy Newman. But this was different. I felt I had to watch on the BBC that week, otherwise I wouldn't believe it and nobody would believe it. So I watched each morning and evening, but as Thursday afternoon drifted on, I was preoccupied with Alex. I was playing too well, and he started losing against me. I didn't want to trigger another headbutt, so I sat in my chair and stretched the next game out a little. I was still going to win; you don't spend your life obsessing over one-on-one battles and ever learn to like losing. But I wasn't going to win too fast. There was no rush. I was enhanced, and I was trusted. We could stay there for a little longer.

The announcement came around 6.30pm. The hum of the public address system. We assumed it was a prison message at first. A disturbance on a wing, an order to return to cells. Maybe a fire drill. We were accustomed to these things. Instead, something none of us had heard before.

– This is an announcement to say that Queen Elizabeth the Second has passed away. To repeat, the Queen has died peacefully this afternoon at Balmoral Castle.

All the time I was looking straight at Alex. Something that made sense but didn't. Something that didn't change where we were but changed everything around us.

– You know what, Alex? We stop now. I want to watch the news.

It can be a madhouse, on the wing in an evening. Boredom and frustration and old scores, wardens off duty or turning blind eyes. People banging, people screaming. As we walked back along Patterson, it was silent. Like the whole prison was on pause. Like they'd emptied the whole place out.

I turned on my little TV and I stayed on the BBC. The black suits and the black ties, the flag at half-mast over Buckingham Palace.

I thought about the times I had met the Queen. In the winter of 1998, when the German president Roman Herzog and his entourage had been invited to Windsor Castle. I wasn't living in London at the time, so we had stayed a night or two at the German embassy in London, me and my first wife, Barbara. I'm not usually a nervous guy. But that night I had to ask ten times. Do I look her in the eye? Do I bow? Do I touch her hand? What do I do? What about her husband, what about the kids?

About 120 people, dining around an enormous table in the St George's Hall. The Queen Mother, the Prince of Wales, the Prime Minister Tony Blair. Even the long, curved driveway up to the castle amazed me, the suits of armour lining the walls inside. Me like a kid from Leimen again. This is like the movies, Barbara, this is like the movies …

I wasn't allowed to look at the Queen or say anything until she spoke to me. That's what I remembered. You bow and she starts talking and then you can lift your head and then you can talk to her, and then you move on. I remembered a long chat in a reception room with Prince Charles and Prince Andrew, because they knew me and they liked tennis. I'm not good at small-talk but you learn. The dining table so big you couldn't see the end. A lot of cutlery. Not knowing where to start because we had five or six courses and silver for every one. Looking at my neighbours, taking note of what they reached for first, and then picking the same knife and the same spoon. Not being placed next to Barbara but with strangers, and finishing my small-talk about God knows what and thinking, what do I say next?

There was another time, when the Queen came to Wimbledon in 2010, and watched Andy Murray on Centre Court, and had an audience with some of the other players, with Roger Federer and Serena Williams, and the older generation of us who were now working in the media. But it was the night in Windsor Castle I thought about that Thursday evening in Huntercombe, as I lay on my thin, uncomfortable bed, and stared at the low ceiling, and the metal toilet without a seat, and the plastic fork and blunt plastic knife. As the cold breeze came in through the narrow vents built into the window, and I pulled open my storage box and took a washed-out hoodie to keep myself a little warmer.

I watched the rolling coverage all of Friday and all weekend. I didn't want to leave my cell. I watched the coffin being taken from Balmoral to Edinburgh, I watched the plane take it from Scotland to RAF Northolt, outside London. I watched it being driven through the streets of the capital to Buckingham Palace and Westminster Hall.

It was a sombre weekend in the prison. Strange conversations breaking out. What happens to Her Majesty's Prison when she is no longer with us? What do they call it now? We answered those questions pretty quickly. Other stories flying around –

we're now prisoners of the King, he owns the prison; yeah, he rents it to the government, the government pays him a couple of hundred pounds per prisoner; okay, multiply that by 80,000 inmates across the country, that's a lot of money the King is now making out of us.

We had, I guess, too much time on our hands. We discussed it all. I kept my connections to myself. I chose not to mention the work I'd done with the Prince's Trust, and so the number of times I'd met the new King. Playing tennis, going to dinners. A strange notion, even for me to get my head around: this man I have known, whose charity I have worked for, and I am detained at his pleasure. He owned me, in a way, if you wanted to put it bluntly.

I couldn't imagine there would be another prisoner in Huntercombe or Wandsworth who had met the new King and the old Queen. But I was sort of glad, too, that this momentous thing had happened while I was inside. I had the time to let it soak in. All the crises that passed through the world during her reign, all the things I had experienced in my own life in the same era. I respected her. I never thought the Royal Family were flawless, and I understood the drama with her family, with her children and grandchildren. Yet she was the one who seemed to keep it all together. In my other busy life, I could never have spent the hours I did now following the processions, the reflections, the state funeral and the committal.

All the way through these discrete moments, a deafening silence at Huntercombe. Never a sense of celebration, even in this place. From these men, who might have been expected to celebrate it all.

* * *

INSIDE

More normal-not-normal. With the work I was now doing in the gym and with the Stoicism classes, I was allowed a visit every fortnight. It had been every three or four weeks before all this. Almost six months in to my incarceration, Lilian was getting used to the strange dance that took place every time she came to see me.

She had become friendly with the guards who greeted her when she arrived outside the visitors' hall. Expecting them to be cruel or at best indifferent, getting to know them and finding more success with her small-talk than I had at Windsor Castle. The guy with the sniffer dog making jokes to relax her, a routine part of her life that she could never have predicted. Understanding the system now, knowing she had to book each visit well in advance or risk finding all the slots filled.

She was coming from Canary Wharf now, thanks to the friend who had come through for us, found her the apartment and moved her in without the tabloids finding out about it. Another good friend lending her his car and driver so she could get the Underground as far as possible and then get a lift deep into the Oxfordshire countryside. It had become her life as much as mine. Strategising what we were going to do next, dealing with the media, dealing with the lawyers and planning my departure, whenever and wherever that might be.

At the same time, I couldn't help but notice the toll it was all taking on her. She had lost weight; her hair was brittle and falling out. She had terrible episodes of joint pain. When the stress was bad she would be so blocked that she struggled to get out of bed.

I felt two contrasting emotions: a guilt about my part in this, and an immense admiration for how she was coping. There were bad times. There had to be. Days where the logjams and inconsistencies in the system drove her crazy, when you couldn't see a way through. When she wasted her days chasing rumours and loose ends. Wasted her energy, wasted her feelings and thoughts.

This is what prison did to you. It made you surprised how much you could endure. That you could expect one thing – an open prison – and then find out about the murderers and people-smugglers and paedophiles, and plans changing all the time, and never a fortnight going by without some disappointment, and always finding a path to thinking, this is not going to be for ever, this is all going to be over at some point.

My two hardest moments, I thought, were those lonely, empty, maddening first four weeks alone in Huntercombe, and then my Covid isolation. But I had never reached my limits. I could sense that now. And that gave me the most powerful thought: maybe I didn't yet know where my limits were. Prison had penned me in, but it had opened me up, too.

I knew she had friends who were telling her she was mad. That she was making the most awful mistake. A suggestion, unspoken or otherwise: you know, Lilian, you're young, what are you doing? You're educated, you can move on, you don't have to do this …

I realised too that she was offended by this sort of advice. There was an inner strength that never seemed to fail, a survival instinct that wouldn't let her give up and wouldn't let her take no for an answer. The only thing that mattered to her was the support of her family. Her father had said to her: I understand you're strong, you're my daughter, you do what you have to do, but you do not leave this man in this situation.

That was enough for her. She was learning that, a lot of the time, you had to run things yourself. She had expected help from certain people close to me and found it not there. She was learning that sometimes it was enough to just know that you were doing the right thing, not be angry about anyone else. That it could be a special thing to know you were there for someone when they needed you most, and they could rely on you, and you could make things ever so slightly better for them.

I loved her for it so much. She didn't have her old life any more. Everything she did, all her energy, every day, was all about me. I didn't want to be in Huntercombe. I hated much of what I saw around me – what this place did to you, its indifference, its callousness. But my God I felt lucky, sometimes. When I spoke to her on the phone, when I saw her walking into the visitors' hall, when we shared a drink we'd bought from the little concession stall run by the little Italian-English lawyer Giovanni.

It was a drink from that stall that brought the next great revelation too. The next exposure of pretence and delusion and scam. Lilian got us both a Diet Coke. She asked about Giovanni. I told her his stories. The stuff about his famous friends, his legal firm outside, the advice he was offering me.

She must have started her research as soon as she got back to London. When we next spoke on the phone, she was full of warnings and barely comprehensible detail.

Giovanni's surname was Di Stefano. He had been convicted nine years ago, sentenced to fourteen years' imprisonment for deception, fraud and money laundering. This wasn't bad luck or a mistake. He had been found guilty of nine counts of obtaining a money transfer by deception and eight counts of fraud. He had pleaded guilty to defrauding a couple of £160,000 and stealing £150,000 from a man who had been in a car accident and lost a limb.

Lawyer? He had never been a lawyer. He had just pretended to be one, year after year, victim after victim. The stuff about some of those bad men? He had been close to former Serbian president Slobodan Milošević. He had been a spokesman and a business partner of the notorious Serbian paramilitary and war criminal Arkan.

The convictions went back and back. Eight and a half years in British prisons in the 1970s and 80s, branded by the judge in one of his trials 'one of nature's fraudsters, a swindler without scruple or conscience'.

The football stuff? He had indeed attempted to become a director of Dundee FC. He was there when the Scottish club signed ageing superstar Fabrizio Ravanelli, at the time the club went into administration. He had been one of the subjects of a BBC documentary series called *Notorious*, with his episode titled *The Devil's Advocate*, where he was quoted saying Adolf Hitler would never have been convicted for killing Jews.

This was the same man who sold us soft drinks in the visitors' hall. Who had told me he could help me with my legal issues. Who was actively helping several other prisoners with their own cases.

It seemed impossible, but it made total sense too. This was prison. Nothing was logical. Very little was the same as on the outside. These things came at you, and you either dealt with them or you didn't, and only the fortunate ones had someone there to help them pick their way through the wreckage.

There was a line Lilian read out to me from the judge's summation of Di Stefano's last conviction. 'You had no regard for your victims nor for their anguish. Your only concern was to line your own pockets. You have shown greed, dishonesty and utter disregard for the sensibilities of others.'

And yet he was carrying on. I stayed away from him, from this point on. I wouldn't even make eye contact with him. Eye contact gives you permission to move it on, to make conversation. I didn't want that with Di Stefano, another bad man in a bad place, another trap waiting to spring on its next victim.

Cell Dreams: The Defeat #4

I change, after I lose that 1991 Wimbledon final to Michael Stich, but some things don't change. We don't get on. That's still the same.

The German media love all this. The contrasts between us, the two superstars that don't like each other. They play with us. They talk up Michael as the smart one again, the northerner who shows you can also win Wimbledon by finishing school, not just by being the wunderkind. For the first time, the media is going at my personality. I'm not the hero any more. And this really bothers me. It hurts my pride. It bothers me for a long time.

It's probably both our fault, but Michael and I are not on speaking terms, after 1991. The locker rooms at tournaments feel small, when we're both in there. There are no more practices with each other. There are no more pep talks. He is the opponent now.

Then come the 1992 Olympics in Barcelona. I arrive a little close to the tournament, and when I get to the athletes' village and the four-bedroom apartment for us, Michael is the new star, and he has decided who is sleeping where, and he gives me the smallest room with no air conditioning.

These are not big rooms anyway, in the athletes' village. We are still not speaking, I see this, and I think I'll sleep one night there, and then find another way. This is 1992, the US basketball Dream Team of Michael Jordan, Magic Johnson, Larry Bird. So I put my antennae out. Okay, where are the superstars sleeping?

There is a great new hotel in the city. US Basketball have booked eighty of the ninety-eight rooms. I take one of the others. I say goodbye to the German team. I say, I'll see you for breakfast or for practice, but I'll be sleeping elsewhere.

The singles I lose to Fabrice Santoro of France, third round. He deserves it, nice player. The doubles comes along. Naturally it's me and Michael, and naturally for the first few rounds we meet half an hour before the match, no warm-up – nothing. We get to the semi-final against Sergio Casal and Emilio Sánchez, but we're not speaking. We're not sharing anything together.

Our coach, Niki Pilić, know tennis and knows tennis players.

'Guys, acting like this you're not going to beat the number one doubles team in the world – the Spanish, on clay, in Barcelona, this year. So I'm going to make you have lunch and dinner. You're going to practise together, the day before. And you have to start speaking, because you need to speak on the court, tactically and technically.'

INSIDE

So we do. We eat food together, and we talk a little. All of a sudden, I think – hey, maybe he's not that bad. I can see he's thinking the same way about me.

We take on Sánchez-Casal, and we probably play our best doubles match ever. We beat them in five sets and we're hugging and high-fiving and everything and all of a sudden, this big love affair starts. We have the Thursday off, and we spend time together and we play cards, and in the final against Wayne Ferreira and Piet Norval from South Africa we beat them in four sets, and everything is beautiful.

I'm organising the celebration dinner for the German team when I find out. Michael has gone straight from the locker room in his tracksuit to the airport. His wife has booked him a flight home.

This is the first gold medal Germany's men have ever won in this event. It's big. It's big like Steffi winning Olympic singles gold in her magic year in 1988. We haven't sat down yet and celebrated what we've done. I know without him I wouldn't have this medal, and I hope he says the same about me. Does this mean more to me than him? Maybe we are so different, after all.

So that's it, for our relationship. When we meet in the quarters at Wimbledon the next summer, it's all about revenge. I win the first set 7–5. He wins the next two on tie-breaks. I take control in the fourth, 6–2. In the fifth, I get into his head. I mess around inside it. He's on a second serve, and I'm ready to receive, and then I stop him in the middle of his service motion, and I turn my back. I speak to people in the crowd.

He double-faults. In today's world, if somebody did that to the other player it would be an outrage. But this is pre-social media, pre-internet. People forget things. So I get away with it, and I'm happy to be under his skin.

Then I lose the semi-final, to Sampras. Straight sets. His serve is bigger, his power is bigger. I'm not really the winner. But this is sport, so you pick the battles you think will help you, and you try to forget the ones that won't.

He's a very good player. That's the whole point. I don't care about the ones who can't beat me. He wins the Davis Cup with a weaker team in 1993, when I'm not there. He gets to number two in the world, he wins the ATP Finals, he makes two other Grand Slam finals. And so we get to the Davis Cup in 1995, and we try talking again.

Okay, we're grown-ups now. We can help each other. We can win this thing again.

It seems to be working. We're doing well, into the semi-finals. We're playing Russia, in Moscow. It's indoor clay, and they're not stupid, up against these two big servers. They water the clay so much it might be the slowest court in the world. It takes me four hours to win my first singles match against Andrei Chesnokov. Michael wins his singles; we are 2–0 up. We play doubles, and we should be unbeatable, but we lose in five sets. My body's in trouble, so our number three, Bernd Karbacher, has to come in, and he loses, so we're 2–2 going into the deciding singles between Michael and Chesnokov.

It would be the USA in the final, with Sampras and Courier and Todd Martin, at home in Germany. Maybe the biggest sporting weekend of the year. Michael is at two sets all. I'm

INSIDE

on the bench trying to support him, but it's difficult, because I feel I've let the team down by not playing on the Sunday morning, even if I couldn't, and Michael playing all three days.

But it's okay, because Michael has match points on his serve. Lots of them. Nine.

He loses in five; 14–12 in the decider. We are gone.

A month later, in his next tournament, he has an awful ankle injury. Everyone who sees it can't forget it. And while he comes back, and makes a French Open final, he retires in 1997, and I retire in 1999, and our relationship fizzles out.

Two men, same country, same sport, same finals. And we don't have any contact. Not a message, not a call, not a hi in the corridors.

Nothing.

Changes came in early October. You feel like you're inside for ever, and so is everyone else, but the machine keeps grinding, even when you no longer notice the noise.

Balak was the first to be released. There wasn't much warning. One weekend we were playing chess, the next there was a new face in his cell.

You always had your date in mind, but dates could come and go and nothing happened, so it was a shock to look around and not see the man you expected. It always took time to get used to a new inmate. To check them out and find out a little about their story. It changes the status quo, when someone none of you know is suddenly there with you in the lunch queue and in the corridors, and it puts you back on your guard, protecting yourself. The wing could also feel a little emptier. You were a friend down. A safe cell was back in live play.

Balak's absence drew me closer still to Ike and Shuggy. We had been going to church together on occasional Sundays, but when Balak left we started going to Mass every week. The three of us would walk in together, read from the books, and return to share lunch in Ike's cell.

You measure trust and camaraderie in different ways in prison. This was the month I started letting Shuggy cut my hair. Until now I had done my beard myself, with the useless blunt razor that had cut my face so badly in the first week at Wandsworth. There was a Palestinian inmate who did my hair. He needed money; deportation was not an option for him, with the situation in his homeland, so he had to stay in the UK, and he had to get the money to make that work. For a while he was fine. We even played chess, occasionally. But then he started asking for more money, and favours to go with the money, and I began to feel vulnerable. Because we were doing it in his cell, and the door would be closed, and he was using scissors and blades that he got from God knows where.

So Shuggy became my barber, both beard and hair. To let another inmate with a sharp knife – don't ask me where he sourced it from, but he had one – put his fingers on your throat and your face, when you are sitting down and there's no one around but you two, takes a lot of faith. But when you have been to church together, and shared food, it feels safer. When I knew Lilian was coming that week, I would ask Shuggy to clip my beard and chop my hair. I would ask him if I could pay him. He would always refuse the offer of money. Instead I would buy his favourite treats from the canteen list, or soft drinks.

INSIDE

And we would share stories, the three of us. The same generation, the same mistakes in our past, the same hopes for a different future. When I was with Ike, when I was with Shuggy, I felt safe. I felt like the bad things and bad people – the poker players, the madmen, the manipulators, the conmen – were at arm's length. We had created a little eddy to the side of the rapids where we could sit and be ourselves, for a few hours every week.

But it always comes for you, inside. At the end of the previous month, England's men's team had played Germany at Wembley in a friendly. It had been as tight as the final of the women's Euros. England had come from 2–0 down to lead 3–2, only for Germany to equalise late on.

Sometime in the hours before that game, maybe after, there had been fights. German fans taking on the English, someone starting it, someone finishing it. Now, two weeks on, the dregs were showing up in Huntercombe. Two young German hooligans, covered in swastika tattoos. Because neither spoke English, they came to the other native German speaker for help.

What do you do? You have a Black ex-wife and two sons who are mixed race, and now you're having to talk to a Nazi who tells you how much he hates Black people. You're having others tell you that there is someone else like you in here, just because you share the same language. Then you're being asked to help them.

One of the two got into trouble in the showers in his first couple of days. His swastika tattoos raised exactly the sort of reaction you might expect from a couple of Black prisoners. The German went back at them. A fight broke out.

He was sent to solitary confinement for a week. And when he came out, it was me who had to talk to him, because he didn't seem to understand what had just happened to him, and how it could keep happening.

– They came at me, I had no choice.

– You're going to have to take the insults.

– I don't take insults.

– Look, there are a lot of African men in here. You clearly hate them. It's written on your body.

– I don't want to be in here with them.

– You'll have to learn. Look at you. There are a lot more people in here who will want to do this to you. If you don't suck it up, next time it will be five of them. Next time, ten.

I guessed he tried to make himself a weapon after that. It was easy enough, if you wanted to. You could stick a plastic knife from the servery in your pants, take it out in your cell and file it down until it became thinner and sharper. You could use a pen. You take a Biro and stick it in someone's neck or chest and it may as well be a knife. Some people boiled water in their kettles and threw it; you could steal a ball from the pool table, put it in a sock and use it like a mace.

The smart ones, the long-termers who knew how the system worked, kept it simple. Big numbers, hard fists. You didn't get penalised as severely if your weapon of choice was your own body. Your sentence didn't get extended, but you made your point.

It was why the gym could feel so dangerous. The free weights were heavy and there to be picked up. There were just two staff members for every sixty inmates in there. The attitude from those guards was always tough as a result, their physiques big and their language clear. You still saw fights, when newbies came in and needed to find their place. When fights happened, the alarms would go and the gym close and the extra officers arrive fast.

All this latent tension, all these sparks firing off in a tinder-box – it was exhausting. I thought about the moment, early in my Stoicism classes, when Andy Small had told me there would come a time when I would be glad to be back in my cell, after all those days when I could not wait to get out of it: 5.15pm, I can get locked up now, and I can relax, I'm safe. I can just do my own things, read a little bit, dream a little bit, watch a bit of TV ...

It had happened. Happy to be locked up. But as you count off the weeks and months, and the day of your supposed departure begins to feel real, you get one overriding feeling: I can't fuck this up.

You're so close to believing you can be free. You don't want to make a single mistake, to say something wrong or find yourself in the wrong place by accident. In October a new female officer arrived at the prison. She was older, apparently very tough. I felt I was known around Huntercombe now. I could walk around pretty freely, at the right times, to the gym for work and to the front office to discuss my deportation order. To be 100 per cent correct, you needed to carry an official letter with you, stating your right to be out of your cell. But no one ever carried one. It was a theory rather than a reality.

Then this new woman stopped me. Fired questions at me – where are you from, where are you going, where are you coming from?

– I was just at the immigration and –
– How do we know? Do you have a letter?

– No, but immigration told me before that I have to go back, and I told the other warden –

– We don't know that. Go back to your cell. Do this one more time we'll be sending you downstairs to solitary.

– Ma'am, honestly you can ask the front office, you can ask the wardens. I asked their permission.

– I don't care, you need a letter, you need a permit.

I was afraid of mistakes like this. I was afraid of being punished for things I should have been thinking about but wasn't. Of being too comfortable, when the end was close enough for me to almost count the days.

I was tired. Of the long, slow days, of the narrow corridors, of the dark green mesh fences and the tight rolls of barbed wire curled along the top of each one.

I would have to be hyper-vigilant. I had come too far. There could be no falling backwards.

Dear Boris

I hope you are good, how's things in Huntercombe? You must be settled now, did you get the gym orderly job?

Wandsworth is going downhill. So much staff have left it's short-staffed here. We keep going into lockdown. The yard's never open. We have one gym session in three weeks. I think it's my time to leave here, I want to go to Highpoint in Suffolk. It's much more better than here. You get to cook your own food, have single cell, gym every day and they have loads of courses to do.

Mo has been shipped out to Brixton, he was happy. Billy went home, he was defo happy. Russell's court date has been pushed to next year, April for sentencing, he's gutted about that.

INSIDE

My appeal is looking good, very positive, but it's all down to the judge at the end of the day. It's a small world at the end of the day because I'm working with a guy called Jonathan Rees and he says he knows Giles, they work together. Do you know him? They are going to put the appeal in any day now.

What is ERSED? Let me know what's happening with your situation.

Take care Boris.

Jake

CHAPTER 11

One morning, a letter arrived. The handwriting was slightly familiar. It was in German. It was from Michael Stich.

I'd never thought he might write. It had been so long. I'm a logical man, but when I saw his name, and his signature, I could feel fate tugging at the sleeve of my grey hoodie. As if he had sensed me thinking about him, as if he were in the same passage of his life, somewhere far away.

I took my time reading it. When I had finished, I read it again, and then again.

There was so much in there that showed he had been thinking about me, and all we had done together. That probably would have been enough for me. But there was more. As I read on, I could feel the frayed threads connecting us tightening and pulling us back together.

I knew I was in Lilian's mind. I knew my sons thought of me. But you forget, inside, of the other lives you have been part of. You forget that you too would be thinking these same things of old friends and old foes and those who floated in the uncomfortable places in between.

Of all the things he talked about there was one thing above all the others that would stay with me, in the following days: I realised I had almost half my life ahead of me. How I used this time was in my hands.

I was so moved that I couldn't let go of the letter. All of it felt so powerful: that he was thinking of me, that we had been thinking the same way about our experiences. I didn't write back, not in that moment. I needed time to let it all seep in. I wanted to speak to him in person. I wanted to thank him; I wanted to suggest we get together and celebrate our Olympic gold medal together for the first time. I wanted to start again.

Winter was coming to Huntercombe. To the trees out there in the distance, stripped of leaves, dark and bare against the grey sky. To the corridors, colder than they had been before, to our cells, with their pallid walls and damp corners.

In the hot days of summer it had been stifling in my cell. With the solitary window permanently closed and buttressed by another thick pane of glass just beyond, there was never enough air circulating once your door was shut. The ventilation panel at the side was narrow and did almost nothing. That was why I had jammed it open. Breaking it allowed just enough of a breeze inside to keep you from climbing those walls.

Now the frosts had come and November was biting hard, the cold kept chasing in through the same broken grate. There was no heating and no heater. I couldn't get it to shut again, but I didn't want to complain. I didn't want the risk of being moved to another cell. This was my space. It was my home. I had my neighbours, Ike and Shuggy. So I said nothing, and I wrapped myself up any way I could. I slept in two tracksuit tops, in two pairs of socks. I wrapped a towel around my head. But I was still cold. I was so, so cold.

Dark mornings, fresh arrivals. Further down the corridor, a new prisoner took over a recently vacated cell. He was young, slight, with long dreadlocks. Word spread in the forest fire way it always did: this guy is another paedophile. He's raped a little girl.

That was enough for Baby Hulk. One Saturday afternoon, he went to the man's cell, started a conversation and provoked him. The guy had no idea who Baby Hulk was, no clue about his personal hatreds and his anger and strength. So he started hitting first, which is what Baby Hulk wanted, and then Baby Hulk beat the living shit out of him.

He borderline killed him. The guards came very slowly, because they always did, and when they arrived, they just couldn't stop Baby Hulk. So he was put in solitary confinement. He was in there for three weeks. He lost his job as a gym orderly. Snakes and ladders, back to the start.

But you would never have known. When he walked back onto the wing, his solitary time served, the inmates gave him a standing ovation. He had beaten up a paedophile. He was a hero. He had proved his character as well as his strength. Baby Hulk had been a name in Huntercombe before, because of his size and unusual look. Now he was an even bigger star. It was like he was a celebrity.

I wanted to protect him. I understood why he had done what he had. So I tried talking to him. About all that anger, again. About the consequences of it all.

– Thomas, you have to control your temper, okay? You're hurting yourself.

– Boris, I couldn't help it.

– I know. But now you've lost your job.

– I have to go to the gym.

– Sure. But you've been in solitary. It's going to take a long time to get you back.

I talked to Andy Small. I begged him, pretty much. Told him how much Baby Hulk needed an outlet, and how only the gym and its heavy weights could do that for him, and what the repercussions might be for the whole prison if he was just locked up all day with nowhere to put all that energy and rage.

Within a month he had his job back. I'd never seen it happen so quickly. And even as I hated what his victim had done, and wished I could help Baby Hulk change, I profited from his demons and his celebrity. Hulk was the guy who walked with me to the showers, to the servery. To the gym, when he had been allowed back. That was our little gang: Thomas, Ike, Shuggy and me. He was my protection. The twisted respect he received came my way – in diluted form, but there all the same. No one was ever going to touch Thomas. No one was going to touch Thomas's friends.

This is how it worked. You tried to win respect for yourself through your actions and character, but what really mattered was the way prison decided to see you. I wasn't Boris Becker now. I was the ground floor of Patterson. I was Ike, and I was Baby Hulk. I was all of the gym orderlies.

Another new arrival, as winter stamped out the last bright colours of autumn. His name was Zac. A strange guy, wearing a weird rubber cap over his head. More rumours flying around: this guy's got mental health problems, watch him.

I was coming back from lunch one day with my tray of food. Our cell doors were open so we could eat inside. It felt normal. Just another bad meal on a grey day.

We all knew the rules: you don't go into anyone else's cell unless you've been invited. Certainly when they're not there. That's a huge no-no. If they are, you don't look in, you don't stop. When someone has cried in front of you, the rules are different. With Ike and Shuggy, we were tight. Eating together, listening to music together. So as I walked past Ike's cell, I looked in.

No Ike. Just this Zac.

He had his back to me. Like he was looking around. Taking something, planting something. So I spoke up.

– Hey, hey. This is Ike's cell. What are you doing in here?

He came straight at me.

– Who the fuck are you?

– My name is Boris. This is Ike's cell. You're not Ike. So what are you doing in here?

I had my tray of food in my hand. That didn't feel like much to have between us. He was bigger than me, maybe mid-thirties. His hands were clenched and coming up fast.

I stepped backwards out of the cell. He followed me. Fingers in my face now. Spitting words at me.

– I'm going to fuck you up. I'm going to break your head.

Shouting it now.

– I'm going to slit your throat. I'm going to kill you –

Suddenly, two men were in front of me. Shuggy and someone else. Six men coming out of their cells across the corridor. Bodies and chests between us, both of us pushed back. Noise and yelling, more inmates coming in as back-up. Someone saying to me: okay, Boris, you just turn around and go in your cell. We'll take care of it.

As I walked away, I could hear the change. This guy's voice muffled now. Him shouting through the bodies: it's a misunderstanding, it's a mistake.

Ten minutes later, Ike came running into my cell. Angrier than I had even seen him but calm, too. Apologising to me.

I tried to brush it off.

– Ike, it's not your fault.

Ike in total control.

– Boris, Zac is going to come and apologise to you.

I was still afraid. The adrenaline still in my chest and fingertips.

– Ike, it's not necessary.

So Ike told me. He knew Zac from Belmarsh. This was the backstory: Zac had killed another man at the age of eighteen. He had been inside for seventeen years already, and his head was gone.

– Prison's got to him. It's got to him.

That was the line Ike kept saying. And suddenly I almost felt sorry for Zac. Not for his crimes, but for his inability to cope. For being another of the lost and out of control.

– Ike, it's okay. Who am I to tell him where to go or not to go?

But Ike was firm. Boris, he will be talked to. He will come to you and apologise. He must.

Three days later, Ike walked me to the laundry. His place of work, the room with all those big noisy machines. A place you could talk in private.

Zac was there. It was the first time I'd seen him since the confrontation. I felt fear again. Something quite visceral, like a memory magnified and feeding on itself. Yet when he saw me, he fell to the floor. He knelt at my feet. He started kissing my hand.

I was embarrassed. For him, for me.

– No no. Get up. Get up. Listen, you've been prison before … I mean, who am I to –

But he kept going. Bowing, apologising. Asking for forgiveness.

I pulled him to his feet. I gave him a long hug. I could feel the muscles in his chest and back wound up tight and tense.

– Zac, no hard feelings. I'm sorry I disrespected you.

– No, you didn't disrespect me or anything. I disrespected you.

I got it. He wasn't just apologising to me. He was apologising to my whole group. To Ike, and his influence, and his soft power.

That's who he couldn't disrespect. That's what he was scared of. There is an order in prison, and everybody has to respect that order. An institution run not by wardens but the prisoners. On Patterson, Ike was the boss. Whoever did something wrong had to make it right with Ike.

Zac knew it too. He wanted to be part of it. To have the same protections and alliances. Before he left, he told me he played chess. He said he'd heard I played. He asked if I would maybe have a game with him at the weekend.

Of course I didn't want to. I also didn't want to say no. I understood the invisible laws now as well as he did. No one in here could save you from yourself. But they could protect you from the others.

INSIDE

Cell Dreams: The Match #1

I'm not scared, before the Wimbledon final in 1985.

I'm determined, and I'm excited, but I'm not nervous. It's the people around me who look scared. Who are different than they were before I won my semi-final.

My coach, my manager. They're doing things they didn't do before. They're talking too much about the final – what I have to do, what I should eat, the tactics. It's like they want to change my whole routine.

I'm relaxed. I can see my picture in all the newspapers, and all these headlines with my name in. I can see all these articles about an unseeded teenager being in the men's singles final. But my English is limited, so I don't read any of it, and I don't take in any of this hype about me, or the fact that I'm about to do what I'm not supposed to do at seventeen years old.

We're staying in the centre of London. The Londonderry House Hotel, on a little side street near the Hilton on Park Lane. My semi-final has taken two days, because of the rain on Centre Court. I've started against Anders Järryd on the Friday evening and I've lost the first set badly and I'm a break down in the second. He is so much better than me.

I get lucky. They call a halt to it. And I carry myself into the darkness, and that night I sleep on it, on the match and his strategy, and I have time to work it out. I come back out on the Saturday, and suddenly he's really nervous, and I beat him fairly easily in four sets.

Now the others start changing. My coach Bosch, my manager Tiriac. They want to talk about the final now, before we even do the long drive back from Wimbledon to Park Lane. I tell them to relax. I tell them we stick to our routine.

– Let's talk about the final Sunday morning, really …

I'm pretty sure about myself. I have my routines and my patterns and I must know what I'm doing, otherwise I wouldn't be here. I'm the calm one.

I know Kevin Curren is the favourite. Makes sense. He beat Mac in the quarters and I saw him destroy Connors in his semi. I'll have to be on my A-game on Sunday. So Saturday evening, let's not waste too much energy. I like my chances; I've won Queen's, and I'm in the final here.

Maybe that's why I dream the way I do, this Saturday night at the Londonderry.

I dream I'm holding the trophy. I can feel it in my hands. I can see it as I lift it in front of my face.

I had someone new come to visit me, in this period. I had invited two journalists from a German television channel. A reporter and an editor, thinking about how I might tell the truth about all this when I left.

I was thinking more and more not just of my release date but the weeks and months after it. At some point I would want to tell my story as it was, not how it had been represented in my absence. So I booked them in, and they looked shocked when they arrived, and scared shitless when they left.

The reports back home were of an open prison. There had been tabloid stories about me getting cushy jobs. The reality – those high green fences and rolls of barbed wire, the noise, the guards, the murderers and rapists and paedophiles – was not what the journalists had been expecting. It was good to see

INSIDE

them, and good to see their reaction. I was glad they had witnessed it for themselves. The story could not be told without an honest understanding of its location and characters.

Back on Patterson, the slow churn continued. Alex, my Albanian neighbour who I had been playing chess with when the Queen died, was dangling on a long string. His release date was supposed to be the last week of September. That came and went and nothing happened, and then early October was given to him, and that drifted past without any movement too.

You could see him getting itchy. Wondering whether it would be November now, or suddenly Christmas. Frustrated at the slow grind of the system, at the way it caught your loose threads and dragged you down into it. For all his latent violence, even the matter-of-fact way he had told me of his intention to return to the old ways of making money as soon as he was out, I didn't want to lose another neighbour I trusted more than many others. My birthday was coming up on 22 November, and I had half an idea about gathering the inner circle around me at some point on that Tuesday – maybe saving up to buy some soft drinks and chocolates from the canteen menu, seeing if I could be allowed a few more in my cell if I asked in advance and left the door wide open. Arguably that was selfish. But the prospect of Alex leaving made me sad in a way I hadn't anticipated. Even though he was crazy, and dangerous, we had formed a relationship that worked for both of us. A game of chess, right opposite my cell, whenever lock-up made it possible. A protection, by proxy, from the other Albanians inside. And you want Albanians on your side, not up against you, trust me.

That rage was always there with Alex, sometimes just below the surface, sometimes on top. There was also another side of him, one which should have made no sense with the way he'd chosen to live his life and how quickly the storms could blow in, but one which seemed to coexist in some strange ethical equilibrium.

He made desserts. Outstanding desserts – a small cake, or a tray of biscuits, always something sweet that tasted richer and sharper than the bland bulk of most prison food. There was no oven to access, no microwave I knew about. You didn't ask. You were just appreciative when he shared something with you during a game of chess, when we played in the canteen. It didn't mean he was going to be anything except a drug dealer again when he left. It was just part of his complex self. No one is 100 per cent bad.

Then there was the time, late in this wintry month, when he asked me inside his cell. That was an honour or a red flag in itself; you don't let anyone in your cell unless you trust them or want to hurt them. Alex wanted my help. He had a German wife, and a teenage son. He wanted someone they had heard of to talk positively about him, and the man he could be inside, and the man he might be when he was released. So I spoke to them, from the phone in his cell, and afterwards I crossed the corridor back to my own cell opposite and I thought about what it meant for him and what it meant for me.

You don't show your private life and your secret fears to anyone, as a long-term prisoner. If anything, you build a high wall around them. You don't want anyone knowing something they could use to hurt you, during your time inside or when you thought you were free. I would never have allowed anyone to speak to Lilian, or to Noah or Elias. But this was the other side of Alex. He was crazy and dangerous. He had killed two men.

INSIDE

He was a convicted murderer. But when he spoke about his family, he was soft-spoken and emotional. Then he was the husband and the father.

How did it make me feel? Most people you meet in your life, there isn't that separation. If someone is a loving father and partner, they don't carry demons who make them headbutt strangers. Ike only had one side, and that was good and beautiful. Shuggy as well. But Alex was all violence and unapologetic criminality and then, in his cell when nobody was watching him, vulnerability and love and pride in where he came from. He would tell me how wonderful Albania was in summertime, how he would host me for a long weekend and it would be much better than anywhere else I'd been, anywhere in the world. So I had to let him into my world, a little. One foot inside the door, one outside.

Sometimes a departure could bring joy. A happiness that someone you liked was free, a reflection on the pleasures your relationship had brought. The Somalian lad from my football team in the summer, the prolific striker who had scored the goals to win us the tournament, the one I had given my red shirt to as a thanks for all he had done – we had continued to talk, and get on, and enjoy any time we spent together.

We mainly talked about football. But that was fine, for it was our shared language. In respecting each other's opinions on the Premier League we were respecting each other as men. We shared news of scores and who had played well and who might move where.

He told me, in between the stories of Mo Salah and Erling Haaland and Kylian Mbappé, that this was his third stint inside. He was a young guy. So I kept talking to him.

– Man, it's your third time in here. You're only thirty-two years old. That's crazy

– I know. I know. But ... I don't know. Selling drugs, it's so easy.

– But obviously they catch you every time so it's not that easy. Don't you ... you seem like a bright guy, and you have a good charisma and you can talk about everything.

– Yeah, but nothing is easy money like this ...

So I sort of thought I knew what would happen, when he left. But the night before he did, when prisoners would often give away anything they didn't need to those who might appreciate them, he wandered up from his cell further down the corridor and gave me something I have kept ever since: his comb. Now an Afro comb for a Black man is an important thing. I appreciated what it meant, when he shook me by the hand, and held it out for me.

Arrivals and departures, old friends and fresh challenges. I did end up playing Zac at chess the weekend after his attack on me. He turned out to be surprisingly good – harder to beat than I thought. But whereas Alex had demonstrated over the months that you could beat him at chess and it wouldn't been seen as some kind of challenge or insult, I couldn't yet be sure with Zac. I had already seen his temper in action. So I let him beat me, that weekend, although I made it close, and when he started coming to the chess club held each Tuesday evening on another wing, I put on a good show but let him beat me again.

Always thinking of the hidden currents, always assessing the secret alliances and deals and connections everyone was making all the time. When I had first arrived in Huntercombe, that Polish guy Robert had helped me, and they had become my first allies, the Polish. When he left, it had all changed. I started having problems with the Poles. Yet for all the turnover of old prisoners and arrival of the new, there were some things that stayed the same with every passing season. Ike was in for twelve years, the Romanians upstairs for ever. You could see the reassurance these long-term patterns of control gave the wardens. The wings and the landings within them would have to be run by someone. Better it was a gang you knew was staying in power. The Romanians upstairs on Patterson, Ike down below. The Albanians in the wing over there, even when Alex eventually came to leave.

Maybe I was the same. I was no longer resisting. Inadvertently or not, I was part of it. I had become one of its cogs.

I liked the certainty of knowing the Romanians ruled upstairs. I didn't like the idea of someone new in Alex's cell opposite mine. Every unfamiliar face in prison is unsettling. You don't know who they are, you don't know what they've done, you don't know what their alliances are. If you get two or three in a single week, you can feel the tension spreading across the wing.

You never knew for sure. That was the thing. The paedophile that Baby Hulk had battered, the one who had raped a young girl? Someone came into the gym one day and said their wife had googled him. Now the story was different. He had molested four boys, apparently. Was that better or worse? Nobody asked. He just got put in a different box.

People like certainty, inside. Sometimes something is true, sometimes it's not true. That matters less than knowing which box they're in.

I kept seeing him around. Of course I did. He was in this prison. He had to shower, and he had to eat, and he had to exercise. And while I hated both the two rumours about him, and for weeks refused to even acknowledge him, and when I did was very defensive around him, just as we all were, as November crawled past, I began to come to a different conclusion.

I wasn't God. I wasn't even a fallen angel. Every one of us in this place was here for a reason. I wasn't the one who made the decisions about our sentences and when we would be let out. These men were going through shit, I was going through shit. We stayed in line and we took it and we had no choice about any of it.

Except our attitude towards ourselves. Who was I to judge that my crime was any better or worse than anyone else? So I told myself, one night, like a twisted prayer before bedtime: I'm going to shake everyone's hand. I'm going to say hello to this guy.

I won't be his friend, but I won't be his enemy. I can't be. There are too many wars in here already.

Cell Dreams: The Match #2

I sleep late, this Sunday morning. I get up hungry and eat some food and we get in the car with Tiriac and Bosch and we drive along the Brompton Road and through Chelsea and Wandsworth onto Church Road and the All England Lawn Tennis and Croquet Club.

I walk to the practice courts and warm up with Pavel Složil. Nice guy, good doubles player. Twelve years older than me and experienced, which is good, because you don't want your hitting partner being the nervous one. I want him hitting the ball well and keeping it together.

INSIDE

I'm looking for rhythm. Ten minutes of warming up, fifteen minutes of groundstrokes and volleys and not many breaks and not many misses either. Tiriac's more the coach, now. Bosch organises the balls, the towels, the water. Tiriac's looking at my game, at my ball toss and if I'm low enough on the returns, if the volley is early enough. Five minutes of serving and then the last five minutes we play points.

I have a ham and cheese sandwich. I stretch. I take a shower. I read a magazine.

It's quiet now, in the locker room. It's been busy all week. Mac being loud, dominating the place, trash-talking. Connors doing the same. It's always the Americans who are the loud ones. The Americans and the Australians.

It's quite small in here. Pegs on the walls, your own locker, given to you at the start of the fortnight. I'm number seven, right in the middle, which isn't great because you want to be on either side. You want a corner so you can have your back to the wall and look out at the rest of them.

But this afternoon it's only me and Kevin Curren. No one's speaking to anyone. He's not making eye contact. So I stare at him.

I stare at his face. I stare at his back, when he turns away. Then I stare at him in the mirror.

I stare at him like a boxer before a world title fight. Eyes open. Expression neutral. Never blinking or glancing away.

He knows I'm looking. He walks away. When he comes back I'm staring at him again.

He turns his head away once more.

15–0 to me.

It's 1.15pm now. I get my left ankle taped, the one I broke last year. I do a little skipping, just enough to feel a stretch. I sit down and read my book and all is calm and all is bright.

Something Tiriac says to me, before I put my racket bag over my shoulder and walk out for the match. Boris, you take the first chair. When you walk on court, you take the one on this side of the umpire's chair. Don't let him take it.

So I push myself into the hallway so I can walk out first. I go out from the cool and the shade into the noise and bright sunlight. I stay ahead of Kevin Curren and I sit on that first chair, and he stops in front of me and looks like he wants to tell me to fuck off, but I ignore him, and start taking rackets from my bag, and after a moment he turns and walks past the umpire to the other chair.

30–0.

I can see the Royal Box to my right. I can see the players' box on its left, Tiriac and Bosch taking their seats. I can see my parents on the row behind.

I win the toss. I elect to serve.

Seventeen years, seven months and fifteen days old. I am already so much in my world.

Quiet please, ladies and gentlemen. Mr Becker to serve.

So to the night before my birthday. What a strange thought that would have been, in all the years gone, to think I would be celebrating my fifty-fifth year in prison.

Something had always happened for me on 22 November. I became world champion on my twenty-fifth birthday; 1992 I won the ATP Finals in Frankfurt. Most years as a player it meant the ATP Finals. When I turned thirty-five I was playing the Seniors event in Frankfurt, and we had a huge party inside a sort of circus tent called the Witzigmann Palazzo, a stage with performers and comedians and pretty girls. There must have been a couple of hundred people there.

That was the way it was, back then. I wasn't bothered about my birthday most of the time, but every five years I would do it properly. My fortieth I celebrated in London and rented out an Italian restaurant and bar with three floors called Carpaccio, and I had friends coming from all over the world and we had a whole weekend of it. My forty-fifth I was married to my second wife Sharlely, and all seemed blissful in the world. My fiftieth I had about a hundred people at a famous hotel in Munich – rented the whole place, the restaurant, the bar, the nightclub. All sorts of loud craziness. So that was my reputation: every five years, Boris throws a big party.

How far away and foreign those days seemed now. How distant that man. I knew what prison was like now. It didn't care about you as a person. It wasn't designed to. I had no expectation whatsoever that tomorrow would be a special day inside. None. I had seen Lilian and Noah the day before; the visiting times did not coincide with the 22nd. They hadn't been able to give me a gift. They weren't allowed to bring anything in. Lilian was able to send me some new photos for my cell walls a few days before. That was it.

We didn't look back. We looked forward, hoping that in three weeks' time, touch wood, we were going to be together again, and holding back on that emotion, because nobody else was supposed to know. It wasn't necessary any more for her to send me gifts and be gentle and caress me. She was busy on the outside, thinking about the practicalities of where we might go and where we could stay. Enough of the emotions – we've done the emotion enough before. This is now about practicalities.

The first shock came when the cell doors were unlocked in the morning. Ike was standing there. Nothing unusual in that. It was that he was carrying a chocolate cake – a big one, five inches across, covered in icing.

How he had baked it I had no idea. He didn't have an oven or a grill. I didn't think he had a mixing bowl or whisk. You could buy chocolate from the canteen, you could buy sugar, you could buy biscuits. But this was a proper cake. It had candles on it, and I could blow them out.

That was first thing in the morning, and we cut a slice and he ate a piece and I ate a piece. We hugged and I smiled. I phoned Lilian and I told her and she sang me 'Happy Birthday'. The next person to come round was Shuggy. He'd made a lemon cake.

I had been blown away by Ike's visit. I couldn't believe what Shuggy had done now. So we cut slices and he ate a piece and I ate a piece. And then, at one in the afternoon, Alex came over from his cell opposite. With a carrot cake.

There were more of them, this time. Alex and Shuggy and Ike and so many others from our wing. They gave me a handmade card. It was cut from yellow card and had the words HAPPY BIRTHDAY in multi-coloured letters stuck on the front. Underneath, in coloured felt-tip pen, was written 'Time to CELEBRATE: 55th'

Everyone had signed it. Everyone I cared about.

To Boris, thanks for your help with the Stoic course. Stay Stoic! Happy birthday, Andy Small

INSIDE

Hello Boris! I hope you enjoy the day as best you can. Happy happy b-day. All the best, pure love all the time. Sugan, Cell 23

Bro. You are still the Becker they know and love. hxB. IKE

Hey Boris!! I wish you a very happy B-day. Have a wonderful day. I wish you all the health in the world. God bless you. From Alex, Cell 29

So we showed the cakes to everyone, and I shared them with whoever wanted to have a bit from my landing. Never in my life, on the outside, had I ever received three birthday cakes on the same day. Not in Frankfurt at the ATP Finals, not in the circus tent with performers and comedians and pretty girls. Not across three floors in London or a hotel and restaurant and bar and nightclub in Munich.

And I thought again about my fiftieth birthday, and how I had really felt on that wild night with the noise and hundreds of guests and every drink you could ever order right there for you. I was probably at the worst point of my life. I was separated from my second wife. I was five months on from being declared bankrupt. I was rock bottom. Even though nobody there that night knew, I felt it.

I'd said something to myself, that night. Boris, you have to change your life on all levels, because you're not going anywhere. You're unhappy, you're in bankruptcy and your wife has a boyfriend. I knew I had to start again from zero and just begin building again.

This night, when the doors slammed shut in Huntercombe and men all around shouted and screamed in their sleep and the stars shone bright in a cold sky, I thought something else. I'm fifty-five now. Most of these changes have already worked. Even though I'm in prison and I haven't seen my partner – and I knew it now, my wife to be – all this will happen. I've made the decision to go from the wrong side of the tracks to the right.

I lay there on my sagging cot and I smiled my biggest smile for weeks and long months and years. I knew I was leaving, if everything went well. And now the miracle of the cakes, and the handmade card, and how they represented the friendships we had formed.

I lay there and I felt the love from these men – lost, dangerous, recovering and unrepentant. I lay there and I smiled and I felt good. So good.

Cell Dreams: The Match #3

I've taken the first set 6–3. I've lost the second in a tie-breaker and then won the third in a tie-break – even though Curren had been 4–3 up with a break. Then I've broken him in the first service game of the fourth set, and it's 5–4 and I'm serving for the match. For the championship.

There's something weird happening now that hasn't happened before. There's a different sound coming from the crowd. Almost like a humming. I'm on my chair with my towel over my head, just trying to stay in the moment, but now this noise is getting through and I'm not thinking about what I have to do, I'm wondering what this noise is.

It's their excitement coming back at me. That's what it is. Suddenly, for the first time, I feel the nerves. I feel what Tiriac and Bosch were feeling. And it's like your vision can't settle on what you want it to. It's like you've had too much coffee, or your muscles are in spasm. It's a loss of control.

INSIDE

I walk to the baseline and my legs feel like they're made from wood. I double-fault.

Now my left arm feels tight and my right arm feels heavy.

Something strange is going on with my right hand. When I try to throw the ball in the air for my serve, it's like it gets stuck in my fingers. It's either coming out too low or too high.

I try to breathe. You've done this before, Boris. You've done it 200 times a day.

I go wide to his backhand side. 15–15. I come to the net and punch a volley into his backhand corner, and he goes into the tramlines. 30–15. Another serve wide to his backhand. 40–15.

Match point.

Now the humming is even louder. It's all I can hear. It's all I can think about.

The ball is glued to my hand. I can't let go of it.

Horrible first serve. Second serve halfway down the net.

I look up, now, at the bright blue London sky. I start praying.

– God, I owe you. Give me a first serve somehow. Give me that first serve! Because I don't know what I'm going to do with the second serve. I have no control anymore. It's completely loose …

Looking up and saying these words.

– God, I'll do anything for you. Just give me a first serve!

It's an instinct serve. Out to the backhand side corner. My favourite corner throughout my whole career.

I know from the feeling of the ball on the racket. From the timing of it. The sound.

BORIS BECKER

Suddenly it's pure emotion and you're not aware any more. My legs have become very light, like I'm on a trampoline. It's really easy to jump. And it is so loud. Everybody is screaming. It's uncomfortable on my ears. It actually hurts.

I look at my box. At Tiriac. I look for my parents. My father has a pocket camera out. No matter there's maybe eighty photographers courtside, and they all have long lenses and incredible cameras. He wants to take a picture of his son winning Wimbledon.

I'm holding the trophy again. I can feel it in my hands. I can see it as I lift it in front of my face.

This time it's not a dream.

They take the trophy from you, before you go back into the locker room. My parents are there. I hug them. There's the German president, Richard von Weizsäcker. He wants to shake my hand. Then there's Tiriac and Bosch. Curren is somewhere in the corner, but he doesn't matter any more.

That's when I notice it. They're looking at me in a new way. Like I'm not the son they've known all these years. Like I'm not the kid who walked out of this room two hours ago.

This is how they're looking at me: you're from planet Mars. What you've just done, it's impossible ...

We fly to Nice the next day and take a big car to Monte Carlo, but we don't go back to my flat. Tiriac rents two rooms in the Beach Hotel. And all week long he tells me what just happened and how my life is changed for ever.

He won't leave me alone. We have lunch and dinner, lunch and dinner. He tells me how I'm supposed to dress now. Boris, with brown shoes, you don't have a black belt, you

INSIDE

have a brown belt. At lunch, you wear jeans and a jacket and shirt. At dinner it's trousers not jeans.

We fly to Indianapolis for a tournament on clay. There are thousands of people even at my practice sessions. We play again in Cincinnati and he flies us to LA on a private jet to appear on Johnny Carson's Tonight Show.

I don't quite believe what Tiriac is telling me. I don't quite believe it because I don't think I have changed.

But already I'm living in a box. I don't like it. It's too restricted. There's too many rules: people telling me what to say, what to think, what to eat. He starts making commercial deals for me that will make a lot of money. I don't like it because it takes away my freedom off the court, and I need my freedom off the court to have some creativity and freedom on the court. I need to enjoy what I do. I need to feel free. And I'm not allowed.

I have completely lost my privacy. Now, whether I like it or not, the whole world knows who Boris Becker is – where he is from, the parents, the sister, the girlfriends.

I know what's right and what's wrong. That's not the danger. People are the danger. They're the sharks.

You don't know. How could you? These people don't look like sharks. They don't look like bad people, bad women, bad men, but eventually they catch you and you don't know how to defend yourself. And they bite and they bite and they bite.

I'm open, I'm friendly, I'm talkative. I don't want to be shut away in my hotel room all week. I mean, how boring is that?

So I talk, I meet people and then, if you're very good at pretending to be someone alluring, I fall for you. Of course I do. Women ... of course I want to meet women. Who doesn't? So I fall for that too.

The question becomes: when are you going to make the mistakes? Not if, when. You just want to make sure the mistakes are not too bad. But you have no choice. You cannot survive without getting hurt.

Everything has changed. For ever.

It seemed set now, 14 December. So I asked the three women who worked in the front office, the ones who liked tennis, who were always friendly. They talked me through the practicalities. The day of your deportation, you would be taken by the police to the airport. You would be kept in handcuffs. Maybe it would be on the exact date agreed, maybe it would come a few days later. It depended how many others were being deported to the same country as you; it was cheaper and easier to do you in batches.

On the plane, the officers would sit next to you. You would remain in handcuffs while you were in British airspace. When you landed in Germany, you would be handed over to immigration officials there. Your passport would be returned.

I kept thinking about the paparazzi and the TV news crews. The reporters and the cameramen standing on stepladders for a clearer shot. Southwark Crown Court felt like forever ago, but there were many parts to the experience I had not forgotten. The media scrum as I arrived every morning, the clatter of cameras as I left for Wandsworth in the white Serco van.

Was there a way I could escape them all this time – the blurry shots of me in cuffs and faded tracksuit bottoms, someone's smartphone photo of a police escort along the aisle of a plane to the toilet, the moment I saw Lilian again when I could embrace her as a free man? I had a friend back in Germany who had always been there for me. A man whose life had worked out well. He had his own private jet. So I called him.

– I know you're crazy and I know you love me. I need your help. Could you lend me your plane to fly me home to Germany?

These are the conversations you never think you'll have. They're the ones you don't forget, when the person on the other end of the line says, Boris, of course, no problem. Just tell me when.

The three ladies in the front office enjoyed this part, when I asked them about it. No one had ever left Huntercombe on a private plane, for obvious reasons. They had a lot of questions they wanted answering. Who owns the plane? Which airport will you leave from? Which airport will you be going to, because we can't have you taking off from Britain and landing somewhere else in Britain and carrying on as if deportation wasn't a thing.

Word came down from above too. Mr Becker, nobody should know about this. The plan stays among us in this office. You can't tell Ike, you can't tell Shuggy. Not the date, not the plane. If they find out, it's not going to happen. Understand?

So I turned my attention to the sweet distraction of sport, once again. Just as Wimbledon had seen me through late June and early July, so the men's football World Cup turned up at a time I needed to be taken elsewhere.

You always watch the World Cup, as a kid growing up outside, as a kid who wants to hit balls and kick balls and fight other kids for them. I was six years old when West Germany hosted it in 1974, the Kaiser Franz Beckenbauer strolling around at the back, Gerd Müller scoring goals, Paul Breitner the militant boss of the defence. Like all Germans my age I watched the final against the Netherlands, when Uli Hoeneß gave a penalty away in the first minute and then Breitner equalised the same way before Muller won it. Sepp Maier in goal with his pale blue jersey and black shorts and huge gloves, Helmut Schön managing this team of wild talents and disciplined workers.

The World Cup stayed important for me after that. West Germany went on to lose other finals: 3–1 to Italy in 1982, when I was fourteen, 3–2 to Argentina in 1986, when I was eighteen and Diego Maradona did what he wanted and no one could stop him.

This World Cup in Qatar filled our days and took over our discussions. Three matches a day in the group stages, and if Germany were poor, losing to Japan and never getting going, I watched it all, and so did almost every one of us.

During the day the matches were on the television in the gym. In the late afternoon and evening we could return to our cells and know the man in the cell next to you was watching and the guy next to him too. Poles hollering for the Polish team, the West Africans for Ghana and Cameroon. Most of the Muslims very happy for Saudi Arabia when they somehow beat Leo Messi's Argentina. Any conversation was only about Germany and England and France and Spain and Brazil. It was maybe the best time in prison, because we were all so preoccupied, and time passed more surreptitiously than in any other month.

INSIDE

I stayed a diehard supporter of Germany, but I was pissed off with how we played. Not the style, more the lack of effort. But no one else was talking about Hansi Flick's team. England were the least popular team inside, but I had a soft spot for them; I always did, having lived in London for so long. I always liked Harry Kane, even in these pre-Bayern Munich days, and I appreciated the abilities of some of his teammates like Bukayo Saka and this kid Jude Bellingham. I understood too why I was in the minority. When Olivier Giroud scored the winner in their quarter-final against France you could hear the banging on the cell doors on every floor of every wing.

All the while, the slow crawl of the prison system. The idea of a private plane back to Germany was now logged. That didn't mean it was stamped and good to go. The questions kept coming, some of them practical, some of them arcane. How do you check in? How much earlier do you have to be at the airport? What size luggage are you allowed?

I didn't have much to take. The clothes I had in my cell, the letters I'd received and saved. I had thought about what I might do with some of the other things, and I liked the approach of my Somalian striker; I'd give away everything I didn't need to inmates who might. Luggage was not going to hold me up.

The airport where my friend's plane could land, the place I could leave from – that was taking longer. The closest one was at Kidlington, just north of Oxford. They didn't like that one. I suggested Northolt, on the M40 in the north-western suburbs of London. That also got a thumbs down. They suggested Biggin Hill, south of London but inside the ring of the M25. It was two hours away by car, much further than the other two options. Since it was their choice, Biggin Hill got the nod.

BORIS BECKER

At least, I hoped it had. Nothing was certain in this world. I thought we were set. I leave Huntercombe in a white van. I get taken to Biggin Hill. They watch me climb on a plane, and they see it take off. I land in Germany. Cue end credits. Instead, this was when the negotiations really kicked in.

– Okay now, Mr Becker. Biggin Hill. Let's find the exact date when you leave.

– What do you mean? It's December the 14th. I've got the paperwork.

– No, Mr Becker, that's your last day in prison. That doesn't mean you leave the next day.

– What? I'm finished with prison, but I have to stay in prison?

– Hardly anybody leaves the next day. Usually the week after, two weeks after.

– But it's Christmas. I want to be with my family at Christmas. Could you please make it happen before Christmas?

And that's when the silence started.

Mr Boris Becker
Date of Birth: 22.11.1967
HMP Huntercombe Prison
United Kingdom
From: Lucan, Co. Dublin

Dear Mr Boris Becker
I am writing again as we enter the autumn season and we start putting on our winter woollies! If I hear from you soon I will include you in my 200m Euro lottery syndicate for the lark! We won 10 euros last week and I feel our luck will improve with your help!

INSIDE

It's tough on the circuit, but you were amazing with your new power serve in Wimbledon back in the good old days. I also followed Steffi Graf from Germany who had a very powerful serve as well.

You might be interested to know that Nasa is going back to the moon this week. After 50 years we are returning to the moon with a new rocket. Do you plan to buy real estate on the Moon? Ha ha!

Please write or email me if you feel interested in an Idaho expression, shooting the breeze! I spend a lot of time studying French and Russian during each day and write letters to people who wouldn't receive much.

Regards

CHAPTER 12

Hey Boris

Paul Annacone here. I wanted to reach out to you to see how you were doing? I'm sure challenging times, but I wanted you to know you have a lot of people who keep you in their thoughts. I for one know that when this chapter is over for you there will be plenty more good to come! Family, kids and the rest of life's joys will be ready for you to fully embrace soon - sending you good thoughts my friend.

   Best,

   Paul Annacone

December 1st. Thirteen days to go. Don't fuck it up. Don't fuck it up. Don't fuck it up.

Twelve days to go. Don't fuck it up. Don't fuck it up.

Eleven days to go. Don't fuck it up.

Don't fuck it up, but make this release date happen. The only other Germans in Huntercombe were the two football hooligans. They weren't getting out in December. Was this good news for me, because I wouldn't have to hold on until their departure, or bad news for me because I might have to wait six or seven weeks?

INSIDE

More questions from the front office, rather than answers. Now they wanted to speak to my friend in Germany. They wanted to make sure he existed. They wanted the number of the airplane and its projected route. They wanted to speak to someone in Brussels who controlled European airspace, so they could be sure this flight with this number on the wing was going to leave Biggin Hill at 11 o'clock and land in Stuttgart at midday.

Nine days to go. Don't fuck it up.

Eight days to go. They told me my deportation date was changing. It was now Thursday, 15 December.

Nine days to go. I know time slows here, but I never thought it would start going backwards.

Eight days to go. Make it happen.

I called Lilian. Lilian called a lot of people. She managed to arrange a conference call between my friend in Germany and the office in Huntercombe. The machine creaked and groaned, but it kept moving.

Seven days to go. No one fuck it up. Okay?

Six days to go. My friend connected Huntercombe to the right person in Brussels.

Five days to go. That's when a snowstorm hit the south of England.

I slept badly from the intense cold and howling wind. When I woke up, the view from my cell window was like something from a Victorian Christmas card, if Victorian artists liked snow-covered barbed wire as well as snow-covered woodland and fields. I turned on the BBC news. Flights were cancelled from Heathrow and Gatwick.

Of course I felt the strain. I looked out at the low sky and the whiteout below and I listened to the forecast on the TV and felt the freezing air whistling round my cell, and I prayed.

Please God. You've punished me enough now. Please don't have it snow again. Don't let it be too icy. I've got to leave on Thursday. I've got to leave.

Four days to go. Monday, 12 December. A call to go to the front office.

– Mr Becker, we're finalised. You're going on Thursday.

I went back to the chill in my cell and I walked around that tiny space and tears came. I looked at the walls and listened to the noise, and I thought about Lilian and what it would be like to see her and hold her with no one else watching. I couldn't think about the flight yet. I couldn't think about Germany, or the bed I might sleep in. That all felt too implausible for now.

I called Lilian at the flat in east London. She had settled the rent, tidied it up. She had packed her clothes and what was left of my stuff, which wasn't much after the bankruptcy. An old TV, a few suits and shoes. No furniture. All that had gone.

She almost didn't want to believe the finality of the news. She didn't, because of how it might be if it failed to happen, but at the same time she did, much more, because of what could happen if it did. So she kept it practical. Settled the bills. Put the things she couldn't take into storage, arranged a van to take them to wherever we might end up in Germany, whenever that might be.

Tuesday I did my gym orderly job. I tidied my cell. I ate my food. I went to the showers with Ike and Shuggy and Baby Hulk.

You spend time anywhere as a human being and you get accustomed to it pretty fast. It's one of our more useful attributes, in some ways. You come up hard against the rules at the start and then you are shaped by them and after a while you don't even think about them any more. They just are. But as I began to realise that I really was leaving Huntercombe, I felt no gravitational pull to the place. I had never become attached to it. I felt instead for my friends. They were the draw. They were the bond.

I was emotional around Ike and Shuggy, on those final few afternoons and evenings. I couldn't tell them how I was getting away, and I couldn't tell them exactly when. I was pretty sure Andy Small knew, but he said nothing. He knew those regulations. To Shuggy and Ike I spoke in hints and codes. I told them I would hopefully be away before Christmas. We embraced each other before our cell doors were locked, and we wrote our phone numbers down, and we made promises for the stuff we couldn't say.

– Shuggy, maybe I'll be gone first, but you'll come hopefully in a week or two. And then you're going to be in Sri Lanka and the sun's going to be shining and you're going to be eating food that's hot and spicy and kicks like nothing does here.

– Ike, you're going to come as soon as you can. You're going to be in Hamburg, and I'm going to be somewhere else in Germany and we're going to stay in touch and come visit each other.

Something else happened on that Tuesday night, before lock-up. It was chess club. Zac wanted to play me again. And maybe I shouldn't have done this, but the old tennis player in me kicked in, the kid who had been number one in the world. We played; I beat him quickly. We played again and pretty soon he was losing again. He closed his fingers around his pieces and the temper started slipping and then he was shouting.

There was a guard present. That was the end of the game, thankfully. I played it sensible, just about in time.

– Zac, listen, you're better than me. I got lucky tonight.

Knowing I was leaving in two days' time. Wanting to remember I beat him the last time we played. This daft maniac thing I have inside me, having to make sure the last two times I come up against him, I'm able to get to him.

I watched the first World Cup semi-final that night. Argentina thumped Croatia. Messi was getting closer. Almost like it was preordained. Like happy endings could happen, even when you thought the moment had gone.

Wednesday morning. Going through the clothes I was leaving behind. I took a small pile to a friend of Ike's who had eaten fufu with us on a few Sundays, a guy the same size as me. When he saw me doing it, Ike knew. It's close. Shuggy knew. We looked at each other and we said nothing but our eyes told it all. I had a woolly hat for the winter that someone had left for me. One of the German hooligans didn't have one of his own. I walked to his cell and threw it in his bed and turned away.

– Don't ask. I don't need it any more. I'm giving it to you.

That was maybe my main mistake. Now he knew I was leaving for sure, and he could tell those who wanted to know. There had been leaks to the German media from Huntercombe in the past month or so. Rumours about when I was going. Stuff about the set-up in my cell, about what I liked to eat and do. I had wondered where they came from. What I didn't know yet was that someone was working things out from the way I was behaving now. Someone would tell a contact in Germany that I was leaving in a day or two. The TV stations and newspapers were poised. Reporters in place, stories ready to go.

INSIDE

Wednesday afternoon. One night to go. Last-minute sums being done by the front office. Would it be better for them if I left before the other prisoners woke up, or when they were at work? They decided on 6am, but they couldn't even tell me that. Just that they had calculated the drive from Huntercombe to Biggin Hill could take three hours, and that I should expect a warden to arrive in the early morning. One final line, after all those weeks of dialogue:

– Pack your bag and be ready whenever we come.

I lay on my bed and I turned on the TV and I watched France play Morocco in the second semi-final. I wanted the underdogs to win. They didn't.

Boris, don't fuck it up ...

Cell Dreams: The Love #5

There was a way it used to be, with me and women. A lot of the time, I could see it on their faces, read it in the way they were.

I want to be with you because you're famous. I want to be with you because you're rich.

Now I am no longer rich. Sure, I'm still famous, but not always for the same reasons as before. I'm bankrupt, I'm a convicted criminal, I'm serving time in prison. It's not a great hand to play.

But Lilian still wants to be with me. She wants no money, she wants no gifts, she wants no publicity.

She wants me as a person. She wants me for what I have left, when everything else is stripped away.

This is new to me. It's actually a shock to realise it. It makes me think again about my other relationships, makes me re-evaluate them.

Was Barbara in love with the Wimbledon champion and everything that came with it? Then I would have to ask the same question about Sharlely. Or was it ever just the boy from Leimen?

It's almost too difficult for me to handle. Was I wrong, all along? Was it me, Boris Becker, who failed to ask the right questions?

All these thoughts in my brain, strange and new and unsettling but also kind of good. Like the shock of cold water on a hot day, like coming out of a bad dream with a sudden start and you look around and it's daytime and the danger that was chasing you has blown away.

This wasn't supposed to happen. I was divorcing when I met Lilian. I was divorcing for the second time. I was fed up with relationships; I was never going to be in another one. My story was going to continue without a woman. I was done, after what I'd been through. I was done with serious relationships. I was done with marriage.

I've never had something like this. She didn't want to come to London. She didn't give me her number for almost a year. She kept her distance.

It's all so different. So I re-evaluate it all too, because this can't be right, but I keep searching and I can't see any downsides.

It feels more real. It feels more honest. When we are with each other, it's like we are two loners living together. That's how I was, when I had my best years. I was alone a lot and I liked it.

Lilian and me? We don't need each other. We don't take things from each other. We are together because we choose to be. I have to look after this.

And I think, maybe that's what I got wrong. Maybe I was with the wrong people for fifteen, twenty years. Maybe I have to change that.

Who else has stuck with me? Not so many. There's people who promised us things. To look after Lilian, to help out when I asked. But from 29 April to now, they have shown their true colours. I'd say 90 per cent of my old friendships have gone.

I think I'll have a completely new circle of friends, when I get out. They have stayed with me and I will stay with them. The others? They won't be part of our equation. Whoever has supported us – and it has been a small group, a very small group – whoever helped with something is part of our group now; whoever didn't show up is gone. It's like the Lil' Kim song 'Slippin'. An old-school hip-hop track that has stayed in my head. Plain and simple.

It's going to be different when I get out. There's only going to be a handful of people I let back in. I am going to protect this unexpected fragile thing that I have found with Lilian. I'm going to be very careful who we spend dinners with, who we drink with. Very careful.

This is not the way it used to be. I am not the man I was. Something has changed, and I don't want to go back.

I didn't sleep a single hour. I sat there on my bed, fully dressed, with my plastic bag by my side, and I waited.

The knock came at 5.30am. The hatch in the door sliding open.

– Are you ready? Are you ready?

– I'm ready.

– Okay. We'll be back at six.

They were. I was standing now. The key turning in the lock, the door opening. Stern words in a low voice.

– Stay quiet. Follow us. Don't say anything.

So strange, to be back in the reception area, with another plastic bag with my Wimbledon tie there waiting for me, and all those clothes I'd packed in April in our little flat and never got to use. Books and magazines and toiletries that never made it in. Medicines. More surprising still to be asked to remove my clothes and prepare for the same internal search as when I was processed all those months ago. Why would you smuggle things out? Because you had nowhere to go, maybe, and you needed money for the streets. You needed things to sell for food and a place to stay. Some prisoners want to get caught. Better to be inside being fed and staying dry than out there in the snow and ice and no locked door between you and the world any more.

You find your gallows humour again, in these surreal dawn moments.

– Guys, I have nothing hidden up my ass. Trust me, I want to leave. I want to leave.

They could have taken everything off me at that point, if it meant walking through those gates a minute earlier. All except one thing. I wanted to keep my prison badge. The one with the photo of my tired face and bags under the eyes. The one with A2923EV printed on it. I had kept my last ever player's pass

INSIDE

from Wimbledon, from my final tournament in 1999. I had my last BBC pass as a commentator. These were the things you kept, these badges, because badges are the only thing left after the tournaments have gone. But as I got ready to leave, and the doors were being opened, and the winter morning wind blew in, one of the wardens walking with me put his hand on my arm.

– Mr Becker. Please do me a favour. Can I keep your badge, for my memory?

I would have given him anything. So I gave him even that, even though it's something I would miss in all the years to come. Something I wanted to have, to look at and think again, to show my children. As much a part of my story as Wimbledon and the BBC.

– Sure. Anything you want, as long as you let me out.

The van was waiting outside. A people carrier. So too, beyond the fence, were the paparazzi. So one of the police officers had a look and told me that normally I would be sitting next to him on the back seat, but this time please would I put my head down by the floor and keep my head down until we were clear.

Doors slamming. The engine starting. The van moving forward, slowing as the gates opened, revving past the crowd and into the snowy countryside. I had a glance back, then. I looked around. It appeared so different to my memories of when we had arrived. It looked different to the way I'd pictured it when I was inside – smaller, somehow, or maybe the world was bigger than I remembered, and Huntercombe just diminished in comparison.

I noticed the trees, still heavy with snow. I noticed the bright lights on the perimeter, the small windows reflecting that perpetual glare. It even looked cold from the outside. When I had left Wandsworth and its Victorian towers and grey stone, there had been an aura about it. A personality, even if it had been a sick, dysfunctional one. Huntercombe had ... nothing. Just the low-rise two storey blocks, the mesh fence and the lights.

The whole car ride I was nervous. Thoughts and loose fears clattering round my head.

– The road's icy. We could slide and crash. We could burst a tyre. Or the driver makes a mistake ...

Breathing slowly in and out, like I used to in the locker room before matches, as I did in my chair on Centre Court before the first game in 1985. Not talking to the policemen. Trying to pull the disparate thoughts back to one tight line: we've got to get there. We've got to get there. We've got to get there.

I saw it was sunny that morning. It was beautiful, a winter wonderland. Everything was white and the sun was shining. A land from your dreams. An England remade for an alien day.

I had told Lilian we would be at Biggin Hill for 11am. But we were early. We were so early. Who would be out driving in this frozen morning of ice and snow? There was nothing on the motorways and only a few going to work. We walked into a small departure room, the three policemen and me, and I thought about phoning Lilian but then realised I had no mobile and no money and nothing to do but wait, and wait, and wait.

I heard her footsteps first. Coming down the corridor behind me, steady to begin with, then running. I began to turn and as I did she jumped onto my back and I span round and lifted her and of course we cried. We held each other and we cried.

The policemen were nice enough to give us some privacy. No more cuffs. They knew where I wanted to be, and it wasn't here.

INSIDE

I held Lilian, and she held me, and in the background I could hear the TV and the midday news, telling me that German tennis player Boris Becker was this morning released from prison, and was being deported to Munich, in Germany.

The plane was there, suddenly. When we walked across the apron, arms around each other's waists, the policemen covered our faces with opened umbrellas. The paparazzi had made good time. They got some good shots of our legs and the backs of three considerate policemen.

The last thing they said to us, before we walked up the steps? Mr Becker, here is your passport.

We were inside the little plane and I was nervous. More of those untethered paranoias – what if the pilot has a bad day, if an engine blows, if there's more snow coming in. I was still nervous as we took off, and I was still nervous as the English countryside opened up below. I was nervous when I saw the coast and the blue beyond, and I was nervous when we were over the sea and I couldn't make out anything beyond. Then the electronic flight map on the panel above our seats showed a tiny airplane icon and a country below called France, and I thought, if something happens now, we can land in Europe. We can land in Europe.

I would find out later that there were hundreds of news crew and paparazzi at Munich airport and almost the same in Frankfurt. No one had guessed we were landing in Stuttgart. The plane bounced down and came to a halt and the doors opened, and there were just two officers from the German border police, no more.

And they nodded, and they said, welcome home, Mr Becker.

BORIS BECKER

Email a Prisoner
Prison Message: 254216
Message sent: 22-11-2022
Message with reply to: Boris Becker A2923EV Huntercombe
Message from: Win Blodgett

Hello, I'm a long-term fan from West Palm Beach, Florida. I had wondered if there was a way to contact you and enquired through a Facebook group to no avail. But I figured it out. I'm fifty-nine and back in 1997 I had a series of calamities. My wife got very ill, my business suffered, I auctioned off my business assets, and then my house burned down and the only possession left was a pair of gym shorts. All these losses were very humbling and transformational because it put me in a place of seeking. I can imagine after all the incredible highs that you have experienced that this period has been very difficult but I hope it will be transformational and a catalyst for you to become something even greater. Wishing you inner peace and support from all your fans all over the world.

Best wishes and happy Thanksgiving from USA.

CHAPTER 13

It was a day of lots of tears. When the two men from German border control said those words, I cried again. They took me to a van, and through the airport a back way; we saw no media and no one gave me a second look. The officers didn't even ask to look at my passport.

We drove to the flat of a friend. He had a place with a tiny one-bedroom guest apartment attached. That's when I opened my first bottle of beer in eight months. I drank that and I was already dizzy and half gone. Start slow, Boris, start slow. Give yourself a moment.

Lilian brought out some of the things she had sent ahead. Clothes, a couple of books, a few personal keepsakes that really mattered to me. She ordered some pizzas and we had a few more beers and we listened to the TV news telling us that Boris Becker had been deported to Munich.

For now, on this afternoon, I didn't want to speak to anyone but Lilian. I was still in a state of shock. I wanted to call my children and my mother, my sister, but I needed to eat and sleep and recover first. I would see Noah in a few days, Elias when he could fly to Europe.

The pizzas seemed enormous. You could eat one slice and

pick up another straight away. It was warm and the cheese was melting and the crust soft and chewy. No one stopped you opening the next box. We went through some messages on Lilian's phone, and my eyes were so heavy that I could barely sit up straight.

The apartment was small but clean. There was a little balcony where we could sit out and listen to the traffic and breathe in the fresh air. An ashtray on a table, when I was ready for a cigarillo. Inside there were pictures on the wall. Two suitcases, the TV from the old flat. All of it driven over by a man from São Tomé that Lilian had met, a friend of her aunt. He was the one who had helped her move from Ennismore Gardens to Canary Wharf at the start of all this, when the paparazzi were waiting outside every time she left the flat and absolutely certain they could track her to her new place. A man she knew she could trust, who would not decide to make himself £10,000 by telling the newspapers where we were, but who could equally carry boxes and bags up 100 stairs from the street down below to this little place with no elevator at the very top of the building.

My friend had come through for us. Not asking for a formal rental contract, just a token amount while we tried to adjust, while we worked out the next steps. He didn't even know when we were coming. All this secrecy around the deportation date, the doubt and the late delays. The first time he knew we were there was as he walked home after work and saw lights in the very top window, bright in the December gloom.

I felt I was moving slowly through a thick soup, that evening. Free of the walls and fences and doors but half my head in England and half my head here in my homeland. Maybe a fair amount of it floating in between. When the longest journey you've done in six months is a walk along a corridor from a bed to a shower, from a locked door to a gym changing room – well, a drive and a flight and a drive is the most exciting thing in the world. But also confusing and strange and so intense, all at the same time.

Friday morning. A world around me made soft and forgiving. So quiet, in this bedroom, in the little kitchen. A coffee that tasted of coffee and sat in my belly and warmed me and began to fire the engine. I should have made breakfast, but I hadn't done so for so long, and I was so full of pizza still I couldn't imagine eating for days.

My body was wrecked. I could feel it in every mundane movement. All those nights on a narrow, bowed bed, the cold and the damp, joints and tendons battered by long ago sliding and diving and serving and falling. My shoulder didn't really function; I couldn't lift my arm at all. My lower back was locked up, my knee was hurting, my ankle bad. I could stand up but I could no longer walk in a straight line.

I called up an osteopath I knew in Munich. Borrowed my friend's car, had the unfamiliar yet familiar experience of driving fast along the autobahn once again. The osteopath couldn't compute the sight of me with the headlines he had seen on the news the night before.

– This is really you, and you came out of prison in England yesterday, and now you're here and you want me to work on you?

It must have been like trying to manipulate a mannequin. Nothing in my spine moved. My muscles were closed and fractious. I was one body made up of a hundred tangled ropes, frayed and knotted and pulling on each other. He was nervous.

Boris, you're in a bad way. This will take a long time. I can't do too much. I might break you. You could snap.

We went back the next day. To move forward you have to be capable of movement. Each day I ate food that I chose and went to bed when Lilian and I wanted and still couldn't sleep without the bedroom door being firmly shut.

We watched the World Cup final together on Sunday evening. I had started watching the tournament as a prisoner at Huntercombe. The second semi-final had fallen on my final night there. I needed to close this chapter out, and I wanted Argentina to win. Or rather, I wanted Leo Messi to win, as the greatest footballer of his generation. It was nothing against France; I just wanted to see him lifting the trophy, like I'd seen Beckenbauer lift it in 1974 and Maradona in 1986. Like Lothar Matthäus in 1990. It was an amazing final, the best I'd ever seen, better than the 3–2 of 1986. When Gonzalo Montiel buried the winning penalty I jumped up and celebrated and everything hurt and I didn't care.

All of it was unreal and all of it came at you fast. People looked at me like a holy ghost, when I shuffled through the streets. An apparition from another time, a refugee from a place they didn't understand.

It wasn't true I had no money. I had less than that. Even though I had lost my 10 million-euro finca in Majorca, my 2 million-euro house in Leimen, my £2.5 million flat in London and £1 million in the bank, I still owed my bankruptcy trustee £500,000. Imagine that – to serve eight months and five days in prison and when you come out you still have to give more.

I needed money, and I wanted to tell my side of the story. Which is why on Monday I recorded a long and detailed interview with a German television station, the same presenter and producer who had come to Huntercombe the previous month and been so shocked by what they'd seen.

When I talked about Patterson and Huntercombe and Wandsworth, they could make a little sense of it now. What confused them was how I was. I think they expected a broken man. A fallen hero, in the worst moment of his life.

– But you're totally normal, still.

– Yeah I'm okay. I'm out.

– But what you went through, I mean, it's impossible to be like that.

– Maybe. Maybe not. You have a choice, in how you react. Do you know about the Stoics?

We talked through it all. The host Steven Gätjen kept mentioning newspaper stories, and I had to keep disappointing him.

– Sorry, that didn't happen.

– But *Bild* said …

– Yeah, it wasn't true.

We recorded it on Monday afternoon and Tuesday afternoon. I wore a black suit jacket over a black T-shirt. They did my hair – combed it, cut it, styled it. I didn't tell them the last person to do it was a Sri Lankan man in prison for gang-related murder.

The interview went out that evening at 8.15pm. It went on for an hour and threequarters, until 10pm. We sat in a hotel room in Munich and I sweated and watched it all. Did I care what people thought? Still yes – maybe more than I let myself believe. Did I want my fellow Germans to know the truth? I wanted as many of them to watch as possible. I wanted to tell how it was. I wanted to tell them about Lilian, and all she had done for us. This is the woman who saved my life. This is the woman I hope to be with for ever.

Some people were different to me, now I was out. They told me they had wanted to call but didn't know how. That they had intended to write but assumed nothing would get through. They told me how much they had always liked Lilian. We listened to it all and argued with no one.

Four days outside now. I wanted to see my mother. Never before had I been so long without seeing her. And after ten months away, considering her age, she looked pretty good, on the surface. But I knew, from the months before my trial and the few times I had been able to speak to her on the phone from prison, that dementia was taking a firmer hold. I wasn't quite sure what to expect. I was a little afraid.

She was less emotional than I thought she might be, in the first minutes. Some of this was her, the child who survived the Second World War and a refugee camp. It was always my father who was more open and instinctively warmer. She was surprised to see me, and she was surprised how composed I was. The criminal she had been reading about in her newspapers and the man she saw in front of her were not the same person.

She wanted to take Lilian and me out for lunch. She kept saying the same thing – don't worry, I can pay, I can pay. I didn't want her to worry. I didn't want her to believe the gossip magazines more than her own son, and I felt a filial disappointment if she did, but then I felt sorry for her too. I knew the media had been harassing her. I was pretty sure a neighbour of hers was taking money from one of the tabloids to alert them to my arrival, so they could take the first photo of the disgraced son and his ashamed mother.

INSIDE

I could see that, to my mother, even now, I was still her boy. Always the boy who doesn't really know what he's doing and needs protection. And so conversation was difficult. You can't really talk about your experiences in prison with your mother. You can't really talk about the hardship you went through. I didn't want to talk about my future. I didn't want to talk about my plans because I was afraid that maybe, in an afternoon or two, she would spill the beans to someone who might be a reporter or might get paid by a reporter. Not meaning me any harm, but just for the sake of talking. Not understanding this mercenary world around her.

What then are you going to talk about? Dementia makes you repeat yourself. Every half an hour you start again with the same thing that you said before. As a listener you can find yourself getting impatient and frustrated. I'd never dealt with anybody suffering with dementia, let alone my own mother. So now I was thinking like a boy again – she doesn't understand me any more. Doesn't she want to understand, or is it she can't understand?

Her past was alive in a way her present was not. She could tell me things about the Davis Cup when I took her and my father to Mexico in 1986; she could tell me where we stayed and where we played and which of us West Germans lost. But she couldn't tell me what she had done yesterday. When Lilian and I drove back to our borrowed flat that afternoon, I was subdued. I realised something had maybe passed me by in the closed world of Huntercombe: I was losing my mother. Maybe not physically, but emotionally. I couldn't be sure how much longer I would have her. And, all the time, she wouldn't know any more what she was missing. This is the reality of dementia. You live in your own impenetrable bubble.

There was something else that made me uncomfortable. It had always been a difficult thing for me to accept, as an adult, that I had lost all my privacy. Like I didn't own myself any more, or my relationship with my loved ones, with my immediate family. It made me uncomfortable because I had changed my life. I wasn't the person my mother may have read about. I wasn't the man she last remembered, whether that was losing on the red clay of Mexico City or raising my arms on the flawless grass of Wimbledon. I couldn't blame my mother. It wasn't her fault. It was the symbiosis in the system around me: the ones who thought they owned me, the ones who could sell me. How much I had given away, and the price I had paid for it.

I had to start making my own decisions. Who I allowed back in, who I didn't. There had been a time when I had given up and let it all happen. When I thought – that's the way it is, I can't control it, I can't change it.

Prison had given me the time to think about things. It had brought me to a new point. I'm not giving up on this. I'm not going back.

All this was with me as we flew to São Tomé to spend Christmas and New Year with Lilian's family. As we ate fresh fish for lunch on the twenty-fifth and went to the beach on Principe for New Year's Eve. As we sat around a bonfire late into the night.

There were parties around us on the sand, and drinks. Lilian's father and stepmother and sister were alongside us. Music was playing and the waves breaking. And the emotions came in with them, and picked me up, and carried me away.

– Ike's inside. Shuggy's inside. All the other guys are inside.

I was happy and I was sad in the same compressed moment. I was sorry for my inmates, for the few friends that I had and for all the people that had to go for another five years. I felt lucky. Lucky I had been deported, not spending this Christmas and the start of a new year in Huntercombe. Lucky to be sitting on this beach having wine and fish and my partner next to me and enjoying freedom and harmony. Lucky to have come through it all.

The tears came out quite naturally. At first as I sat there at the table with my bare feet in the cool sand, then getting up and walking on my own. Lilian coming to find me, under the big equatorial moon, with the parties in the distance and the music playing. I held her and we talked – about us and Ike and Shuggy and Alex, and where we might go and what we might do.

I'm not ashamed to cry. We walked back to the others and I spoke about it at the table. All of it was open now. All of it on the outside. I looked around and I held it close. The moment, the friendship, the stars and the sea.

I wanted to be real again. Like the kid I had been in Leimen, riding the trams, chasing returns, hitting a white tennis ball against a wall until it frayed and tore. To be authentic to the person I was now, because not being authentic had got me into trouble. I wanted to be surrounded by people I could trust. By those who had stayed with me when I was in the shit. Not the others. Never to be the lost man, ever again.

My hair had grown longer in prison. I couldn't dye it blond in there, and there were no mirrors, and who gives a shit in that moment, anyway? Now I was out the idea of bleaching it again, of going back to the old look, wasn't sitting right with me. I didn't want to go back to being the man I had been after tennis.

I liked the idea of my hair being its natural strawberry blond colour, with grey around the edges

I took a trip, a few days later, to the local street barber. He took out his clippers and shaved my scalp to a buzz cut. I felt free. It felt like I had shed the last part of the old me. Like: this is who I am. No disguise, no cover-up, no role-playing. Take it or leave it. I'm going to be me for the rest of my life.

Prison lives on inside you. I could sleep on a big king-size mattress now. When we were in São Tomé, in the little flat at the top of the stairs in Stuttgart. I could roll into the middle of the bed, if I wanted. I could have five or six pillows, big deep ones all around me.

But I wouldn't. Wherever I was, I would sleep right on the very edge, close enough to almost fall off. As if I were taking this huge mattress and reducing it to a thin cot. I would take one small pillow and put it between my shoulder and my neck.

We didn't go out for food often. We stayed in the flat, just the two of us, and we cooked and had a glass of wine. When we did go to a café or restaurant, I took none of it for granted. There had been a time when I never bothered looking at the price on a menu. I never looked at the total on a bill. I just put my credit card down.

I no longer had a credit card. When we went out, I looked at every cost. There were these new questions for me – Can I afford it? Is it too expensive for what it is? – and fresh answers to go with them. Then I will say no. Then we won't come back.

I became a good sleeper. I knew when I was tired. I wasn't afraid to go to sleep, and I didn't need to take sleeping pills or drink a couple of whiskies. I stopped having nightmares.

INSIDE

It was quiet inside my head now. That's why I could sleep. For years my brain was going head over heels. Like a tumbler in the circus, like a ball spinning from the taut strings of a racket.

Now I was still. I had come to rest.

I couldn't stay in Germany. That much had gradually become apparent. The media intrusion, the lack of privacy. The old ghosts and dangerous ways of living.

A new life meant a new home. A place to be that we hadn't been before. We thought about Spain, for the quiet and the weather. We thought about Austria. Easy for the language. But always we kept coming back to Italy.

I had always loved the culture, the people, the food. Rome is the most beautiful city in the world and it was Lilian's birthplace. But then there was Milan, too. A working city. More organised, a place to live rather than holiday. Lilian said – Boris, you're not good in Rome, you're much better in Milano. Rome is you ten years ago. It's the opposite of who you are now.

So we drove across the Alps from Germany, and we booked a hotel for three days and we explored. We looked for a new home. It took us two and a half months. And then we walked into one apartment, and saw its old stairs and big windows and heard the trams down below, and we felt it and we knew.

We shook hands with the landlady and signed a lease. We drove back to Stuttgart and went out to a local Italian that night to celebrate, spaghetti and Pinot Grigio, and woke up to find the restaurant owner had sold our bill to the tabloids. Okay, that seals it.

I had always bought my houses before – I always could. It didn't feel weird renting this one. There was no choice; I didn't have the money to buy anything. And this place was us. It was our lease, Lilian Monteiro and Boris Becker. Both of us named as tenants. Another commitment together, another landmark in our relationship.

We moved in during the first week of April. A year on from Southwark Crown Court and all that it brought. We had nothing except a TV, a blow-up sofa and a blow-up mattress. Nothing else. Each morning the mattress would be deflated because it was cheap and I was heavy. The blow-up sofa was worse. All of it was wonderful.

Each month we could add a little more. A small table and two chairs. Picking some cutlery together. Getting some clothes sent over from Stuttgart. None of it familiar. All of it a thrill.

I knew sometimes Lilian found it hard. Not where we were, but the ties holding us to the old world. Wanting to be free of bankruptcy and lawyers and old relationships. Understanding there is no perfect life and no perfect solution.

Almost by stealth, we settled into it. There were no paparazzi outside the apartment building. No putting on hats and dark glasses to go for a walk. There was nothing to hide, any more.

I found a new routine. Each morning I would go for a long walk, feeling my body coming back towards balance, exploring the streets and arcades around the Duomo and La Scala. Lilian managed to rescue a few mementoes from my tennis career and put a photo of the teenage me winning Wimbledon on the hall wall. From the roof terrace we could look down at the streets and the trams, and I could think back to the sound of the tram line that ran past my childhood house in Leimen, all those years ago.

INSIDE

It wasn't that I had my life back. I'd been given a second chance, the opportunity to build a new one. Living better than I'd lived for a long, long time.

Part of the old Boris was returning. I had been a disciplinarian, when I played my best. I was disciplined almost to the point of crazy. It was my way of focusing on the match at night and the final on Sunday and then the next week. What I ate, what I drank, my daily routines.

I had lost it, in the wild years, in the twenty years since I played my last match at Wimbledon. You can call it the comfort zone, you can call it getting fat and lazy, being sidetracked. It means you can't concentrate for longer than ten minutes. It means you're tired too early and you sleep too long.

Now the old discipline was coming back, and I welcomed it first like a mirage and then like a favourite song. Back in the lost days I would drink to make people and places more interesting. I would drink until the party became fun and then talk about nothing, stupid things, until three in the morning. And then I would fall asleep and the next morning I couldn't actually remember what we talked about.

It feels good, for a while. Even though it's fake – and after the second beer, you don't know any more if it's fake or not – you like to be celebrated, cherished. You like the feeling that you know everybody, even if they are just pretending to have a good time with you. But there's a laziness there. It's being bored with your life and not really caring about yourself.

That wasn't happening any more. I would walk away if I felt it happening. We would go for dinner with some acquaintances, and the chat would start about what everyone had done in the 1990s, and an hour and a half in I would have nothing to say to these people. It would become exhausting. I would find a polite way to say I was tired or something, and Lilian and I would leave and go home and balance on the inflatable sofa and feel much better.

It wasn't always easy. I had to say no to a lot of people. And if they didn't understand a polite no, you had to be a bit firmer. Sometimes they were pissed off. Then it was, accept my no. I don't want to go on holiday with you, I don't want to play golf with you. I don't want to go to a party tonight. I was still a friendly guy. But there was an invisible wall around us, now.

I wasn't sure if this was a good quality in me. But sometimes, when I looked at myself in the mirror, at this man in his late fifties with a buzz cut and lines around his eyes that weren't there before, I would think: I can be your best friend and your worst enemy. If you're close to my heart and somebody is attacking you, I will hunt that motherfucker down.

Did I like this? Deep down in my core, this was who I am. A man in touch once more with the fearless boy he had been.

Every morning I woke up with Lilian I felt a calmness. A gratitude. I had got to know her properly in 2019. As a man, in that moment, I was tired – a second divorce, four kids. I had thought maybe this is me now. Maybe I can't or don't want to start another relationship. When you're tired as a man, then you cut corners. You don't look after yourself any more, you eat too much, you drink too much.

Meeting women was never the issue for me. But to start a relationship? I couldn't see that again.

It had taken my insolvency, the embarrassment of it, my imprisonment, the global humiliation – it had taken all of that to realise that this was me. To understand I had to change

INSIDE

completely. When I met Lilian for the first time, I saw a light I didn't believe existed any more. That's why I was so determined to find out. What is this? What can we be?

Inside, I had seen things that most people don't see. That you shouldn't be seeing. I had been forced to confront deep truths about myself, some of which were painful. It had simultaneously made me a more serious person – because I would think, why am I worrying about these little things? – and, precisely because I had experienced such darkness, capable of delighting in all the small positive things. The spring sunshine on my skin, the sight of Lilian's hair worn natural. An espresso on the terrace, a WhatsApp message from my sons.

I lost the ability to handle bullshit. When your time has been taken away from you, you have no more time to waste. If I tell you a joke, it better be good. If there's a story, it's because it's important. It goes somewhere. It tells you something.

As a tennis player, you live in the now. You can't think about the backhand that's just gone in the net, or the passing shot you might play in two points' time. You can't think about what might happen if you win this trophy or what they're going to say if you crash out. It's just you and the ball and the pure moment and what you do with it.

This was me again. Just really being aware of the moment. Trying to live as long as I could in the now. Of course we planned for the future and we learned from the past. But I wanted to be in the present. Not anywhere else.

Spring became a heavy Milanese summer, which became a warm winter. Rumours came in from Huntercombe, sometimes texts, too. You could get what you wanted, inside, if you wanted it enough. I would receive emails from other inmates who had been released or deported. Sometimes people wanted things from me. Andy Small had warned me about it and advised me to stay clear, when I was gone. But you still cared about those men, and when news came through you thought about them again and you wondered.

The first bad rumour was about Baby Hulk. He had taken my advice and agreed to deportation back to Lithuania in April, but a story did the rounds that he had been killed in a car crash. It took a voicemail from Andy to reassure me he was okay. He was apparently training to be a UFC fighter, which made me smile and wince at the same time. He needed something to do with all his strength and his aggression, but I still worried about him. He was only twenty-five, still young enough to find a new path. Had he learned to control his emotions or care about the consequences? I hoped so. It's harder to change at that age. He was still young and wild and crazy.

Paulo made it back to Naples. I don't know if he ever opened his restaurant. Alex got to Albania and he invited me over for the summer; I was grateful, but I didn't want to go. Jake kept writing from Wandsworth and I was glad he did. Shuggy left Huntercombe not long after me, and I spoke to him over the phone a few times in Sri Lanka. Every time I did it made me smile.

Some of the Romanians got in contact on social media. I didn't respond because I was told it wasn't safe. It bothered me because I feel like I'm a man of my word, and I said we'd stay in touch, but Andy kept reminding me.

– Boris, don't do it. Don't do it.

So of course I keep speaking to Andy. I did another Stoicism conference with him, this time not at His Majesty's Pleasure. He told me of a plan he had to get the Stoicism course into German prisons; I promised him all the help I could give. I called Michael Stich, soon after I got out, and I thanked him for his letter. I said we should celebrate our gold medal again. I want to speak to him more often.

I knew Ike had been released. We texted. He was in Hamburg. He seemed okay.

November 2023, and my birthday came around. One year on from the three cakes, from the handmade card. I didn't want to do anything special. Maybe a meal out with Lilian.

She took me out in the afternoon, and we stayed out until about 7.30pm. We went back to the flat and I pushed open the door, and there was a cheer and laughter and twenty of my closest friends were there, from London, from Germany, from Africa.

I was in shock. I'd spoken to some of them that morning, and none of them had given anything away. We had cocktails, and all was cool. Then, at 9pm, the doorbell rang again, and I excused myself and went over and opened the door.

It was Ike. Ike dressed in a suit and a tie and proper shoes.

I cried like a baby; it took me a while to speak.

– Damn!

– Hey, Boris …

Ike with a whole new neck tattoo, a bouquet of roses. Up until that moment I was the star of the night, and then Ike and our story took over. I told him, in front of this room full of the people I cared about most: thank you for saving my life.

Lilian had organised it all. Sorted his flight and a taxi from the airport, his first trip on a plane since deportation. He'd got a little lost at the airport and was late, but this was always

Lilian's plan: hide him upstairs, wait for me to settle, produce the *pièce de résistance.*

It took me a while to calm down because I wanted to tell everyone what a strong and cool guy he was, that he was also my saviour, in a way. And then we were sitting outside after midnight. He hadn't touched alcohol in probably twelve years and then, in my honour, he had a glass of red. One moment he was sitting there, the next he was asleep. He fell asleep with his head on my shoulder.

At two or three in the morning, we walked him to the hotel Lilian had booked for him. The next day he came by at lunchtime and we spoke all afternoon. We let all the emotions come out. I drove him to the airport that night, and I stayed with him as close to the gate as I was allowed, and we hugged.

That was the last time I've seen him. We speak sometimes. He couldn't handle things in Hamburg. He said that the world had changed too much; he had gone inside when there were no iPhones. He couldn't cope with the speed of life now. He couldn't cope with the coldness of the people.

He went back to Nigeria. He told me: I don't belong in Germany any more. I have to go back to my home. He sends me videos on WhatsApp of him working out. He looks happy. He talks about a wife, but the wife seems to change every month.

And I think about him a lot. About his prayers and talking to God, about his love of the gym and the fufu he made. About the time he saved me from Zac, and the mornings I heard him singing to his radio. About the sense of security in a time when all could have collapsed in on me.

I think about him, and I hope he has found his peace.

AFTERWORD

It is a warm September afternoon on the Italian Riviera. I am, I think, looking good: white tux, black bow tie, short hair.

The woman standing next to me is looking better. White strapless dress, hair pulled back, eyes on mine.

I look around. My sons Noah and Elias by my side. Sitting around the walls of this courtyard, under its arches, are our closest friends and family. The buildings on the hillsides are all pale pinks and yellows and greens. Out beyond the terrace is the deep blue of the Mediterranean.

All is quiet. Just the wind in the leaves of the lemon trees and Aleppo pines.

I speak first.

– Amore. From the moment we met, I knew that my life would change for ever. You brought love, light and peace into my world in a way I would never have imagined. You showed me the real meaning of partnership, and together we built a love that is strong and impregnable.

– Today, I stand in front of you, and I promise you that I love you unconditionally. In everything that you do, I will support you. With all the joy and challenges that life will bring, I will stand by your side.

– I promise you I will keep my heart open. I will always listen and always appreciate every moment we spend together. I promise to be your partner in every part of your life, to smile with you when you're happy and to console you and comfort you when you're sad. I'll be your biggest supporter in everything you do. I'll be your confidant and your best friend.

– Amore, you're my love, you're my anchor and you're my biggest inspiration. Because of your love, I can become a better man every day. Today, I choose you – now and for ever – to be my wife, my partner and my eternal love.

I look at her, and I smile. At my boys, at our friends. And then Lilian steps forward, and it is her turn.

– Amore. The moment I met you, I didn't know yet that my life by your side would change me for ever. But I have learned to love myself more because I see how you love me unconditionally. You give me the sensation of being unique. You give me confidence and you teach me every day how to use my power.

– Together, our love was tested with all the challenges we had to go through. But every time, we got stronger together when we went through them. You brought luck, joy and a fresh meaning to my life. Today, I stand in front of you surrounded by loved ones and I give you these promises, these vows.

– I promise to support you in your dreams and support you when we build our future together. I promise to listen to you with an open heart and with honesty and respect to speak to you. I promise to appreciate and cherish what we're building together and to never take it for granted. I promise to be your partner, confidant and your best friend in good and in bad days … and hopefully more good days now – we've done the bad …

INSIDE

– I will celebrate you in moments of laughter, and I will hold your hand in moments of despair. You're my love, my rock and my safe haven. With you, I have found a love that is deep, that is real, and is for ever.

– Today, I choose you – for now and for ever – as my husband, my partner and my biggest love.

We put rings on each other's fingers. We kiss. I cry a little.

And we look out over the Mediterranean, and the small boats and yachts, the waves down below and the sparkling trail of the sun, and we feel the future reaching out to us and welcoming us in.

ACKNOWLEDGEMENTS

First of all, I'd like to thank my wonderful wife, Lilian. Amore, you're my love, my anchor and inspiration. Thank you to my four children, Noah, Elias, Anna and Amadeus. I love you all, and that will never change. To my sister Sabine and her children Carla and Vincent: you stayed by my side.

There are people who made all the difference to me inside. Andy Small, Ike, Shuggy, Jake, Mo and others. Prison changed me, and you helped make sure it changed me for the better.

To my fantastic publishers, Katya Shipster and Daniel Oertel, and to their hard-working teams: Daisy Ward, Sarah Hammond, Clare Sayer; Claire Ward, Alex Layt, Orlando Mowbray and Kate Neilan, Tom Dunstan and Dom Brendon. To the brilliant team at Curtis Brown: Jonny Geller, Ciara Finan, Natalie Beckett, Sophie Baker, Katie Harrison. To my agents at IAM Entertainment: Sonal Vara-Palmer and Ash Palmer. To David Luxton, and to Archie O'Reilly. Thank you to all of you.

Finally, to my writer and friend, Tom Fordyce. We have spent more time with each other talking, understanding, preparing and writing this book than with our families. It takes a village! Our first call together was in December 2023 (I was on holidays in Sao Tome), and we finished it in March 2025. I couldn't have

BORIS BECKER

put my thoughts on paper without your help and inspiration. Proud to call you my friend.

Boris Franz Becker

PICTURE CREDITS

All images courtesy of the author with the following exceptions:

Page 2, top left: Bob Thomas Sports Photography via Getty Images
Page 2, top right: © Paul Zimmer
Page 2, bottom: © Paul Zimmer
Page 3, top: Leo Mason/Popperfoto via Getty Images
Page 3, bottom left: Leo Mason/Popperfoto via Getty Images
Page 3, bottom right: Bongarts/Getty Images
Page 4, top right: Associated Press/Keystone/Sigi Tischler/Alamy Stock Photo
Page 4, bottom: Wiktor Szymanowicz/Anadolu Agency via Getty Images
Page 5, top: PA Images/Alamy Stock Photo
Page 5, bottom: Karwai Tang/WireImage/Getty Images
Page 6, top left: Associated Press/Andrew Medichini/Alamy Stock Photo
Page 8: Tom Oldham